# Questions God Asks in the Bible

# Questions God Asks in the Bible

## 100 Meditations to Instruct and Inspire

by
Frank R. Shivers

Copyright 2025 by
Frank Shivers Evangelistic Association
All rights reserved
Printed in the United States of America


Unless otherwise noted, Scripture quotations are from
The Holy Bible *King James Version*


Library of Congress Cataloging-in-Publication Data

Shivers, Frank R., 1949-
Questions God Asks in the Bible / Frank Shivers
ISBN 978-1-878127-55-6


Library of Congress Control Number:
2024901919


Cover design by
Tim King


For Information:
Frank Shivers Evangelistic Association
2005 Congress Road
Hopkins, South Carolina 29061
www.frankshivers.com

Because
I have found Jesus to be everything He promised to be—
my Savior, Friend, Guide, Comforter, Helper, Teacher,
Shepherd, Sustainer, and much, much more—

I am excited to present this book to

_____

Date

_____

From

_____

with the prayer that reading its pages will enhance your walk with Jesus and be used by Him to minister to the needs and cares of your life.

# Publications by Frank R. Shivers

"We are not writing upon water but carving upon imperishable material."[1]

– C. H. Spurgeon

The Preacher's Struggle and Stamina (Vol. 1)

The Preacher's Struggle and Stamina (Vol. 2)

Morning by Morning

Questions God Asks in the Bible

Questions People Ask in the Bible

The Widow's Comfort

When Things Just Don't Make Sense

When the Rain Comes

The Treasure of Grace

Persecuted for Christ's Sake

Basics of Biblical Praying

Christian Basics 101

Grief Beyond Measure, but Not Beyond Grace

Grief Beyond Measure, but Not Beyond Grace (Funeral Home Edition)

Growing Old, Honorably and Happily

The Wounded Spirit

The Wounded Spirit: Companion Workbook

Growing in Knowledge, Living by Faith

Marriage and Parenting Boosters

Caught Up to Heaven

Expositions of the Psalms (Three Volumes)

Life Principles from Proverbs

The Evangelism Apologetic Study Bible

Hot Buttons on Apologetics

Hot Buttons on Morality

Hot Buttons on Discipleship

The Pornography Trap

The Poison of Porn

Heavy Stuff

Heavy Stuff (Companion Workbook)

Clear Talk to Students

Nuggets of Truth (Three Volumes)

Soulwinning 101

Spurs to Soulwinning

Evangelistic Preaching 101

Evangelistic Praying

The Evangelistic Invitation 101

The Minister and the Funeral

Revivals 101

Children's Sermons that Connect

Be Careful Little Eyes

How to Preach Without Evangelistic Results (Pamphlet)

False Hopes of Heaven (Tract)

First Steps for New Believers (Tract)

The Goal Line Stand (Tract)

The Death Clock (Tract)

Scripture quotations taken from the Bible that are unmarked are from the King James Version.

Scriptures taken from the Holy Bible, New International Version®, NIV®. Copyright © 1973, 1978, 1984, 2011 by Biblica, Inc.™ Used by permission of Zondervan. All rights reserved worldwide. www.zondervan.com. The "NIV" and "New International Version" are trademarks registered in the United States Patent and Trademark Office by Biblica, Inc.™

Scripture quotations marked (NLT) are taken from the Holy Bible, New Living Translation, copyright ©1996, 2004, 2015 by Tyndale House Foundation. Used by permission of Tyndale House Publishers, Carol Stream, Illinois 60188. All rights reserved.

Scripture quotations marked (TLB) are taken from The Living Bible copyright © 1971. Used by permission of Tyndale House Publishers, Carol Stream, Illinois 60188. All rights reserved.

Scripture taken from the New Century Version®. Copyright © 2005 by Thomas Nelson. Used by permission. All rights reserved.

Scripture quotations taken from the Amplified® Bible (AMPC), Copyright © 1954, 1958, 1962, 1964, 1965, 1987 by The Lockman Foundation. Used by permission. www.lockman.org.

Scripture quotations taken from the Amplified® Bible (AMP), Copyright © 2015 by The Lockman Foundation. Used by permission. www.lockman.org.

Quotations marked ESV are taken from the ESV, (The Holy Bible, English Standard Version), copyright 2001 by Crossway, a publishing ministry of Good News Publishers. Used by permission.

"And it came to pass, that after three days they found him in the temple, sitting in the midst of the doctors, both hearing them, and asking them questions."
– Luke 2:46

# To

### Dr. Terry Frala and Tim King

No published book is the sole work of its author. A skilled team has to take the PDF from his/her hand and walk it through the various publication stages. Terry Frala and Tim King, outside of the actual publisher and pressman, make up that team for me. Without the expertise and work of these men, most of my 47 books would not have been published. Without a doubt, God orchestrated their ministry partnership.

Dr. Terry Frala joined the team sixteen years ago as editor. In a quest (or search) to find a book editor, Marie Frala, who worked for a Christian publication, suggested her husband, Terry. The rest is history. Terry's expertise in English, congeniality, patience, experience, knowledge of the Scriptures, and devotion to Christ immediately made him an excellent fit. In addition to editing, Terry makes sure the PDFs to the publisher meet their strict standards for submission.

Tim King joined the team nineteen years ago as a graphic designer. In search of a book-cover artist, I contacted a shirt company in Florida that provided graphically designed Christian-themed shirts. Tim was recommended, and upon contact, he graciously consented to help. Tim's love for our Lord, spirit, experience, belief, and skill made him a perfect fit out of the gate. Not only does Tim design the jackets for the books, but he also submits the final PDF for publication (which sometimes has its obstacles).

Thank you, Terry and Tim, for helping me to extend the Gospel through the printed page. No better team members could be wanted or found.

"Putting questions is Jehovah's frequent method of instruction. [They] are very often the strongest affirmations."²
— C. H. Spurgeon.

Contents

Preface

## Part 1: Questions Asked by God in the Old Testament

1. "Where Art Thou
2. "Is Not My Word Like as a Fire?"
3. "Is Anything Too Hard for the LORD?"
4. "Who Will Go for Us?"
5. "Can I Not Do with You As This Potter?"
6. "What Is That in Thine Hand?"
7. "Can These Bones Live?"
8. "How Shall I Give Thee Up?" (Unbelievers)
9. "How Shall I Give Thee Up?" (Believers)
10. "What Aileth Thee?"
11. "What Doest Thou Here?"
12. "Doest Thou Well to Be Angry?"
13. "Wherefore Do Ye Spend Money for That Which Is Not Bread?"
14. "Wherefore Do Ye Spend Money for That Which Is Not Bread?"
15. "How Shall I Pardon Thee for This?"
16. "Shall He That Contendeth with the Almighty Instruct Him?"
17. "How Long Will It Be Ere They Believe Me?"
18. "Why Have They Provoked Me to Anger?"
19. "Can Any Hide Himself…That I Shall Not See Him?"
20. "Who Is Blind, But My Servant?"
21. "Wherefore Criest Thou Unto Me?"
22. "Get Thee Up; Wherefore Liest Thou Thus upon Thy Face?"
23. "To Whom Then Will Ye Liken Me?"
24. "Where Did You Come From and Where Are You Going?"
25. "Who Put Wisdom in the Heart or Gave the Mind Understanding?"

26. "What Is This That Thou Hast Done?"
27. "Why Are You Angry?"
28. "To What Purpose Is the Multitude of Your Sacrifices unto Me?"
29. "How Long Wilt Thou Refuse to Humble Thyself Before Me?"
30. "Is It a Time for You Yourselves to Live in Your Paneled Houses, While This House Lies in Ruins?"
31. "Why Do You Complain?"
32. "Have You Eaten from the Tree of Which I Told You Not to Eat?"
33. "How Shall I Put Thee Among the Children?"
34. "Wilt Thou Not from This Time Cry unto Me, My Father, Thou Art the Guide of My Youth?"
35. "Who Would Set the Briers and Thorns Against Me in Battle?"
36. "Why Then Is This People…Slidden Back by a Perpetual Backsliding?"
37. "No Man Repented Him of His Wickedness, Saying, What Have I Done?"
38. "What Is Your Name?"
39. "In What Way Have You Loved Us?"
40. "How Wilt Thou Do in the Swelling of Jordan?"
41. "Where Were You When I Laid the Earth's Foundations?"
42. "Where Is…Thy Brother?"
43. "Who Told You That You Were Naked?"
44. "Can the Ethiopian Change His Skin, or the Leopard His Spots?"
45. "Why Have You Done This?"
46. "Have I Not Commanded You?"
47. "Will a Man Rob God?"
48. "What Seest Thou?"
49. "Hast Thou an Arm Like God?"
50. "Who Hath Made Man's Mouth?"
51. "Is the LORD's Hand Waxed Short?"

52. "Who Put Wisdom in the Heart or Gave Understanding to the Mind?"
53. "Have the Gates of Death Been Opened unto Thee?"
54. "What Have We Gained by Obeying His Commands?"
55. "What Seest Thou?"
56. "And the LORD Said to Satan, Whence Comest Thou?"
57. "Did Ye at All Fast unto Me, Even to Me?"
58. "Have I Been a Wilderness unto Israel?"
59. "Why Did Sarah Laugh?"
60. "How Long Will You Mourn?"
61. "Who Makes the Mute or the Deaf, or the Seeing or the Blind?"
62. "What Seest Thou?"
63. "How Shall We Know the Word Which the LORD Hath Not Spoken?"
64. "Can a Woman Forget Her Nursing Child?"
65. "Can a Woman Forget Her Nursing Child?"
66. "Have I Any Pleasure at All That the Wicked Should Die?"
67. "Are Ye Not as Children of the Ethiopians unto Me, O Children of Israel?"
68. "Do Not My Words Do Good to Him That Walketh Uprightly?"
69. "Is the Spirit of the Lord Straitened?"
70. "Is Not This a Brand Plucked out of the Fire?"
71. "Where Is Mine Honor?"
72. "And Ye Say, Wherein Have We Despised Thy Name?"
73. "What Seest Thou?"
74. "Is There a God Beside Me?"
75. "Who Hath Begotten the Drops of Dew?"
76. "Should I Not Have Compassion on Nineveh?'
77. "Will You Say That I Have Done Wrong, That You May Be Made Right?"
78. "Who Is This That Darkeneth Counsel by Words Without Knowledge?"

79. "What Men Are These with Thee?"
80. "Who Then Is Able to Stand Before Me?"

**Part 2: Questions Asked by Jesus in the New Testament**

81. "If the Salt Has Lost His Savor, Wherewith Shall It Be Salted?"
82. "Will Ye Also Go Away?"
83. "Lovest Thou Me More Than These?"
84. "What Do You Want Me to Do for You?"
85. "But Whom Say Ye That I Am?"
86. "What Think Ye of Christ?"
87. "What Think Ye of Christ?"
88. "Are Ye Able to Drink of the Cup That I Shall Drink Of?"
89. "Can Any of You Live a Bit Longer by Worrying About It?"
90. "What Shall a Man Give in Exchange for His Soul?"
91. "What Man of You, Having a Hundred Sheep?"
92. "My God, My God, Why Hast Thou Forsaken Me?"
93. "Why Go Ye About to Kill Me?"
94. "Why Are You So Afraid?"
95. "How Much More Shall Your Heavenly Father Give the Holy Spirit to Them That Ask Him?"
96. "Is a Candle Brought to Be Put Under a Bushel, or Under a Bed? and Not to Be Set on a Candlestick?"
97. "Judas, Betrayest Thou the Son of Man with a Kiss?"
98. "Where Are the Nine?"
99. "What Will a Woman Do if She Has Ten Silver Coins and Loses One of Them?"
100. "Why Do You See the Speck That Is in Your Brother's Eye but Do Not Notice the Log That Is in Your Own Eye but Do Not Notice the Log That Is in Your Own Eye?"

# Preface

The Bible contains 3,298 questions—1,024 in the New Testament and 2,274 in the Old Testament.[3]

*Questions asked by God* in the Bible were to enhance understanding; generate thinking; reveal and clarify the truth about Himself (nature and attributes), man, salvation, and the Holy Scripture; summon decisions; compel action; prompt conviction; expose hypocrisy; provide instruction; constrain examination; and divulge sin. Though often specifically addressed to a person or nation, the questions bear poignant challenges and insight to all people of all times, either directly or by inference. (Making God's questions and answers adaptable to all is the work of the Holy Spirit).

Spurgeon asserts, "No Scripture is of private interpretation: no text has spent itself upon the person who first received it. God's comforts are like wells which no one man or set of men can drain dry, however mighty may be their thirst. A well may be opened for Hagar, but that well is never closed, and any other wanderer may drink at it."[4] With that in mind, put yourself in the shoes of a question's original recipient and claim it and its answer personally for the enrichment and edification of your soul.

*Questions God Asks in the Bible,* and its companion *Questions People Ask in the Bible,* contain 100 questions and answers, ideal for devotionals, small group study, and sermons.

# PART 1
# Questions Asked by God in the Old Testament

## 1
### "Where Art Thou?"

The Bible's first recorded question of God is what Adam was asked in the garden after his sin: "Where art thou?" (Genesis 3:9). The divine interrogation takes place with every man personally about his spiritual condition and standing with God.

1. Its Inquirer.

1) The God against whom you sinned asks the question. The inquiry is not by the church, preacher, or evangelist. It is from Him who is seated upon the throne in Heaven in majesty, holiness, and righteousness.

2) The God from whom you hide asks the question. Though you hide from God in the thickness of the forest and its foliage, as Adam and Eve did, God will find you.

3) The God by whom you are relentlessly pursued asks the question. He will go to the furthest extent to seek you out. "For thus saith the Lord GOD; Behold, I, even I, will both search my sheep, and seek them out" (Ezekiel 34:11). God says, "Where art thou?" "I am come to find thee, wherever thou mayest be. I will look for thee, till the eyes of My pity see thee. I will follow thee till the hand of My mercy reaches thee, and I will still hold thee till I bring thee back to Myself, and reconcile thee to My heart."[5] God is the good and compassionate Shepherd who leaves the ninety-nine in the fold to find and rescue the one wandering in the wilderness of sin (Matthew 18:12).

4) The God to whom you must give account asks the question. "It is in the plan that all men die once. After that, they will stand before God and be judged" (Hebrews 9:27 NLV). Judgment cannot be averted. Clement said, "Since then all things are seen and heard [by God], let us fear Him, and forsake those wicked works which proceed from evil desires; so that, through His mercy, we may be protected from the judgments to come. For whither can any of us

flee from His mighty hand? Or what world will receive any of those who run away from Him?"

5) The God from whom you cannot escape asks the question. "Ye have sinned against the LORD: and be sure your sin will find you out" (Numbers 32:23). Your effort to escape God is futile. Hide in a cave like Elijah, in the bow of a ship like Jonah, amidst the trees in a garden like Adam, in the far country like the prodigal, and yet God will find you. Distance will not prevent (Psalm 139:7), the lapse of time will not deter (Numbers 32:23), secrecy will not stop (Hebrews 4:13), nor will material defenses protect (Amos 9:2–3) the arrest of the sinner.[6] There is no hiding place from God (Psalm 139:8–10; Proverbs 15:3). William Secker states, "A man may hide God from himself, and yet he cannot hide himself from God."[7]

2. Its inquiry.

The personal and pointed query of God is everyman's.

1) The Lord asks the unsaved: Where art thou? What is your spiritual state? Is it well with thy soul? Are you saved or lost? Have you, by faith, repented of sin and embraced Christ as Lord and Savior? Have you been washed in the soul-cleansing power of the blood of Jesus? Are you in God's family or not? At death, will you spend eternity in Heaven or Hell?

2) The Lord asks the Christian: Have you pushed Me into a secondary place in life? Are you adrift from your first love and allegiance to Me? Are you entangled in a sinful indulgence? Have you neglected the prayer closet, Bible study, witnessing, giving, and faithfulness to church? Are you a spiritual man or a carnal one? Are you living by My divine plan and calling?

3. Its intention.

The question is asked to awaken you to your sin and prompt you to acknowledge it and repent (Psalm 143:9). The quickest path to mercy, forgiveness, and restoration is through confession and repentance of the wrong done (1 John 1:9).

"Questions from the Lord are very often the strongest affirmations."[8]—C. H. Spurgeon

2

"Is Not My Word Like as a Fire?"

"Is not my Word like as a fire?" (Jeremiah 23:29). The false prophets in Israel led the people astray into idolatry through their lies, deceit, and "dream theology." Asking rhetorically, "Is not my Word like as a fire?" God states that His Word would prevail over the heretical teaching (Jeremiah 23:28). There are eight ways that God's Word may be likened to a fire.

1. Fire has melting power. Under anointed preaching of the Word, hardened hearts melt and become responsive to the will of God.

> Thy word, almighty Lord,
>     Where'er it enters in,
> Is sharper than a two-edged sword,
>     To slay the man of sin.
> – James Montgomery (1771–1854)

2. Fire has consuming power. Ignite a small stick in a brush pile and watch the fire spread to the whole. The Word of God is unbound and, once sounded, spreads as wildfire, impacting all in its path (man and evil).

3. Fire has purifying power. Jesus prayed, "Sanctify them through thy truth: thy word is truth" (John 17:17). David attests that man's life maintains purity and holiness "by taking heed thereto according to thy word" (Psalm 119:9). As fire purges impurities from gold, the Word cleanses the dross from the soul. It refines life into a vessel pleasing unto the Lord.

4. Fire has illuminating power. It sheds light. "Thy word is a lamp unto my feet, and a light unto my path" (Psalm 119:105). It is not within man to know how to traverse the dangerous landscape

of life; therefore, a lamp (Holy Scripture) is provided to show the way (Jeremiah 10:23; Proverbs 14:12).

5. Fire has warming power. Nothing consoles, comforts, and uplifts the weary and brokenhearted like the Word of God. David said, "When I am hurting, I find comfort in your promise that leads to life" (Psalm 119:50 CEV); "I am weary from grief; strengthen me through Your word" (Psalm 119:28 HCSB).

6. Fire has stinging power. To insert the hand into a blazing fire brings horrendous pain and discomfort. The Word applied to man's conscience causes it to burn with guilt over the sin done, prompting repentance and confession. Verily, it is "mighty through God to the pulling down of strongholds" of sin and Satan, and to the bringing of even the very thoughts of men into captivity to the obedience of Christ (2 Corinthians 10:4–5).

7. Fire has uniting power. The blacksmith forges separate objects into one using the anvil and the fire. Through the anvil of the Word, believers are fused into a close-knit fellowship called the Body of Christ (2 Chronicles 30:12; Acts 2:42–47).

8. Fire has non-replicating power. As fire cannot be counterfeited, neither may the Word of God. The inevitable results of the true message of God distinguish it from all aberrations of it.

God's Word, says Spurgeon, not as skilled and polished orators proclaim it, "but the Word of God itself, the truths which are revealed in this wonderful Book…[t]hese [God says,] are 'like as a fire.'"[9] Therefore, let us proclaim it with the ability of which God has given, and do so with the fullest confidence that it possesses the power of the Holy Spirit to accomplish the purpose to which it is sent (Isaiah 55:11).

"The exhibition of false doctrines saves no man and benefits no man, but a simple preaching of Christ crucified is the power of God unto salvation to millions of the human race."—Charles Simeon

## "Is Anything Too Hard for the LORD?"

"Is anything too hard for the LORD?" (Genesis 18:14). God posed this question when Abraham and Sarah laughed at the idea of having a child in their old age (Genesis 17:17; 18:12). But it is likewise a question from God to every believer that strikes at the heart of belief in His ability to do anything, even that which is considered impossible. Man's response to it reveals the depth of his faith in God's ability and power.

Nothing is too hard for the Lord. The assertion is well-founded.

1. The nature of God proves it. To ponder God's mighty work in creation, making something out of nothing, ruling the heavens and earth with precision management (like keeping the oceans in bounds, the Sun the exact required distance from the earth, and the right speed of the earth in its rotation cycle), and His ability to sustain and preserve all of life is to realize nothing is too hard for Him to accomplish.

2. The name of God assures it. "I am Jehovah." Because He is God, He is omnipotent and limitless in what He can do. Spurgeon asserts, "The name of Jehovah reminds us that He has within Himself sufficiency for all His will. He hath adequate power of performance for all His purposes and decrees. Jehovah wills, and it is done."[10]

3. Experience substantiates it. The testimony of billions through the ages is that God can do whatever He wills. There is no sin that He cannot pardon, no problem that He cannot solve, no pain that He cannot relieve, no promise that He cannot keep, no person that He cannot save, no provision that He cannot provide, and no prayer that He cannot answer. "For with God nothing shall be impossible" (Luke 1:37). The bottom line is: "We ought to give God strong faith because there is no evidence which could justify mistrust."[11]

When asked the question (Jeremiah 32:26–27), Jeremiah declared, "Ah, Sovereign Lord, you have made the heavens and the earth by your great power and outstretched arm. Nothing is too hard for you" (Jeremiah 32:17 NIV).

Spurgeon suggests the believer use the text in five ways.

1. Use it as a preventive measure against unbelieving sin.

2. Use it for consolation in times of trouble. Jehovah hath delivered those who trust in Him, and He will yet deliver us.

3. Use it as a window through which you look expectantly.

4. Use it as a stimulus to launch out into the deep. Fall back upon God's omnipotence and then go forward in that strength.

5. Let the text be a reason for adoration.[12]

Nothing too hard for Jesus!
   And so I am trusting in Him!
I lean on His strength almighty,
   There is nothing too hard for Him!

– Birdie Bell (1917)

"With him, nothing is impossible, no difficulty insuperable."[13]—Matthew Henry

## 4
## "Who Will Go for Us?"

"Who will go for us?" (Isaiah 6:8). At King Uzziah's death, hope for Judah's spiritual restoration was dashed. Corruption within the nation and Church was immense, and flagrant hypocrisy and immorality were widespread among the people. In this decadent climate, the Lord called for workers, saying (my paraphrase): Who will rise against the wicked leaders with stern reproof? Who will bear divine reproof, warnings, and instruction to the hypocrite? Who will expose the fallacy and sin of the priests? Who will gladly forsake home and comfort to experience difficulty, trial, and hardship, perhaps even death, for MY namesake? Who will call MY people to repentance and the lost to salvation? "Whom shall I send, and who will go for Us?" As a teenager hearing that call, Isaiah promptly answered, "Here am I; send me!"

That same call and challenge are sounded loudly and urgently from the throne of God today. "Who will go for Me?" Who will sacrifice family, friends, and earthly comfort to tell the untold in distant lands the Good News of God's saving grace? Who will stand in the gap between Holy God and sinful man with the call to repentance, renewal, and regeneration? Who will boldly declare the whole counsel of God, whether welcomed or not, to a perverse and wicked generation at home and abroad?

David Brainerd heard that call and wrote in his journal, "Here am I, Lord; send me. Send me to the ends of the earth; send me to the rough and savage pagans of the wilderness; send me from all that is called comfort in the earth; send me even to death itself, if it be but, in Thy service, and to promote Thy kingdom." Over a hundred years after Brainerd received that call, David Livingstone said, "In Christ's service, I wish to live; in it, I wish to die." J. Hudson Taylor wrote Amelia, his sister, about the call to serve as a missionary in China, saying, "If I had a thousand pounds, China should have it. If I had a thousand lives, China should have them. No, not China, but Christ. Can we do too much for Him?" These, and the many others before and after them who heard the call, paid a costly price to bear the news at home or abroad that Jesus saves.

All the redeemed are to go in a general sense. However, some are explicitly called, as Isaiah and those mentioned above, to serve God vocationally as missionaries, pastors, evangelists, and musicians. Listen for the call. Be ready to respond to the call. Surrender to the call once it is heard with the unconditional response of Isaiah: "Here am I; send me."

Spurgeon says, "May the Lord push men out, thrust them out, drive them out, and compel them to preach the Gospel."[14] If you are called to go and don't go, you are still called to go. The call is irrevocable. "For the gifts and the call of God are irrevocable" (Romans 11:29 RSV). Nothing can substitute for obeying. "Woe is unto me if I preach not the Gospel" (1 Corinthians 9:16 KJ21).

Note seven keys to understanding the call of God.

1. An open and submissive heart to do what He says and go where He sends without question.

2. Communion and devotion. Lucado says, "We learn God's will by spending time in His presence. The key to knowing God's heart is having a relationship with Him—a personal relationship. His heart is not seen in an occasional chat or weekly visit."[15]

3. Prayer. By prayer, a request is made for wisdom to discern God's plan and will for one's life (James 1:5; Jeremiah 33:3).

4. Meditation upon the Holy Scripture. Henry Blackaby says, "When God gets ready to do something in your life, the Spirit of God uses the Word to make that known to you."[16]

5. Counsel from the godly. Consult with those who are deeply spiritual, possess great spiritual discernment, and will be candid in their advisement. "Considerable weight," asserts Spurgeon, "is to be given to the judgment of men and women who live near to God, and in most instances, their verdict will not be a mistaken one." Remember Samuel's experience as a child? He was asleep and heard a voice saying, "Samuel, Samuel," but he understood it not to be that of God. Eli, a mature believer, helped him to know that God's voice was calling out to him (1 Samuel 3:10). Many identify with Samuel. They need help in recognizing God's call.

6. Spiritual markers. Spiritual markers (life-altering events spiritually) are places and reference points identifying a transition, decision, or direction when God gave guidance. If past markers align with a new marker (for example, a call to ministry), you are likely moving in the right direction. Blackaby says, "When God is ready for you to take a new step or direction in His activity, it will always be in sequence with what He has already been doing in your life. He does not go off on tangents or make meaningless detours. He builds your character in an orderly fashion with a divine purpose in mind."[17]

7. Sensitivity to the inner voice of the Holy Spirit. The Quakers call the impression of the Holy Spirit in one's heart the

"inner light" that makes known the good and perfect will of God. The Scripture states, "For as many as are led by the Spirit of God, they are the sons of God" (Romans 8:14). The impression of the Holy Spirit clarifies and confirms God's call.

> God calling yet! I cannot stay.
> My heart I yield without delay.
> Vain world, farewell! From thee I part.
> The voice of God hath reached my heart!
> – Gerhard Tersteegen (1697–1769)

How will you respond to God's question, 'Who will go for Me?' The clock is ticking. A time will come when it will be too late to "go." Laborers are few. The work is plenteous. The fields are white unto harvest. Go NOW if chosen for vocational ministry.

"Should you be one of the chosen to carry His message vocationally, then count it all joy and the highest of honors, refusing to turn back or give up regardless of cost or consequence. Nothing is more important than expending your life doing what God designed. The will of God—nothing less, nothing more, nothing else."—F. E. Marsh

## 5
### "Can I Not Do with You As This Potter?"

"Can I not do with you as this potter?" (Jeremiah 18:6 ESV). God, the master potter, in shaping Israel into the nation of His design, found her unwieldy and resistant to His molding touch, resulting in a distorted vessel fit only for destruction. The clay must be broken up and remolded into the potter's masterful design. The process was repeated often in the history of Israel.

By asking this question, God compares Himself to a skilled potter who fashions flawed and broken vessels into something beautiful and valuable. Four lessons are gleaned from the story of the potter and the clay.

1. God has a plan for every man. "O Lord, Thou art our Father; we are the clay, and Thou our potter; and we all are the work of Thy hand" (Isaiah 64:8). There is an architectural blueprint fashioned by the Potter (God) that covers every facet of a man's life. ("The steps of a good man are ordered by the LORD"—Psalm 37:23.) Most of the blueprint is revealed in the Bible. It says it is God's plan that you become a Christian (2 Peter 3:9). It's God's plan that you grow spiritually (2 Peter 3:18). It's God's plan that you live a separated life (2 Corinthians 6:17). It's God's plan that you yoke with godly companions (2 Corinthians 6:14). It's God's plan that you engage in fellowship with the saints (Hebrews 10:25). It's God's plan that you seek to win others to Christ (Acts 1:8). It's God's plan that you serve Him with and according to the abilities with which you have been gifted (1 Peter 4:11). It's God's plan that you put Him first in allegiance and honor (Mark 12:30). Note, God's plan may involve Christian ministry.

2. Man cannot tell the Maker how to make or design his life. In Romans, Paul argues for God's sovereign authority and right to design man as He chooses: "Who do you think you are to question God? Does the clay have the right to ask the potter why he shaped it the way he did? Doesn't a potter have the right to make a fancy bowl and a plain bowl out of the same lump of clay?" (Romans 9:20–21 CEV). The argument plainly states that God possesses the right to do whatever He wants with a man because He is His Maker and knows what's best. It is the height of impertinent presumption and unreasonableness for a sinful and ignorant person to question or find fault with the administration of Sovereign God. Benson says, "Nothing can more strongly represent the absolute dominion God has over us than this image of the potter fashioning his clay into what form or vessel he pleased."[18]

3. The plan may become marred and spoiled. A flaw in the clay (man) mars it, spoiling the Potter's (God's) design.

a. The flaw might be a sin. Sin is powerful enough to thwart God's wondrous plan. One sin dethroned King Saul. Moses was God's choice to lead the Israelites into Canaan, but a sin thwarted it. Lysimachus' ravaging thirst led him to trade his kingdom for a supply of water. Afterward, he cried, "O wretched man, who for a little joy has lost so great a kingdom." Throughout history, many have echoed the same after sinning.

    b. The flaw might be a stubborn protest of the plan. Resistance to and disinterest in God's plan prevent His best intentions from being experienced. Clovis Chappell said, "No man ever flees from duty without incalculable hurt, not only to himself but to others as well." Saith Spurgeon, "How ridiculous does man appear when he attempts to argue with his God! Our safest and happiest place is under His all-wise and gracious hand (1 Peter 5:6). If it cannot be changed through prayer and wise action, believe that God has a larger purpose and a higher way to something even better."[19]

    c. The flaw might be a slothfulness in devotion and duty. Ryle asserts, "Many, I fear, would like glory, who have no wish for grace. They would have the wages but not the work, the harvest but not the labor, the reaping but not the sowing, the reward but not the battle. But it may not be."

    d. The flaw might be a wrong companion. The Potter's plan is unfilled because of another's wanton influence. Of Ahaziah, the Bible states that he "also followed the evil example of King Ahab's family, for his mother encouraged him in doing wrong" (2 Chronicles 22:3 NLT).

    4. Broken lives and plans can be mended or remade. Herein lies the chief lesson of the story. God specializes in putting broken and damaged lives back together. Peter marred his life, and God mended him. He found Jonah marred and mended him. He found David marred and mended him. Despite our failures, sins, and mistakes, the Potter will remake us into a vessel of honor upon our request and repentance. God is the gracious giver of second chances (and third, etc.).

> Thou art the potter, I am the clay.
> Mold me and make me after thy will,
> While I am waiting, yielded and still.
>                          – Adelaide A. Pollard (1906)

"A potter can only mold the clay when it lies completely in his hand. It requires complete surrender."—Corrie Ten Boom.

## 6
### "What Is That in Thine Hand?"

God rebuffed Moses' hesitation to speak to Pharoah, asking, "What is that in thine hand?" (Exodus 4:2). Moses replied that he had a staff, not knowing it was an instrument of divine power and an ensign of his holy authority by which the assigned task could be accomplished.

What's the divine gift in your hand? Whether staff, slingshot, or sword, God will use it to do great things for His namesake. Note that God asked Moses, "What is that in thine hand?"—not, "What doest thou prefer to be in thy hands?" but, 'What hast thou got in thy hands?'[20] God does not require that we fetch stronger slings, taller staffs, or bigger swords to do His work. He is pleased to use the simplest of instruments in our hands. Note the simple rod of Moses became a mighty instrument that wrought miracles. "Little is much when God is in it." F. B. Meyer states, "The weakest man who knows God is strong enough to do exploits."[21]

"What is that in thy hand?" (Exodus 4:2). For David, it was a sling; Moses, a mere shepherd's rod; Shamgar, an ox-goad; Samson, a jaw-bone of an ass; and Dorcas, a needle and thread. What is in your hand? Take it and use it to do exploits for God.

Carey said, "Expect great things from God. Attempt great things for God." The doing always will follow the believing, provided the belief (faith) is sure and steadfast in the Lord. Nevin says, "God takes the weakest instruments to accomplish His mightiest ends."[22] Use the gift(s) God chose to bestow and watch Him turn it into a powerful rod to accomplish incredible feats. "If there be degrees in glory," says Spurgeon, "they will not be distributed according to our talents, but according to our faithfulness in using them."[23]

"God, in doing His great works, does not need any instruments, but uses them simply of His own sovereign will; and this appears in their obvious inadequacy in themselves to the results which they, nevertheless, produce."[24]—R. A. Hallam.

## 7
### "Can These Bones Live?"

"Can these bones live?" (Ezekiel 37:3). Divinely assigned to preach the message of restoration to a congregation of dry bones (Ezekiel 37:1–4), the prophet Ezekiel was asked, "Son of man, can these bones live?" Can dead bones live? Can the dead in trespasses and sin be quickened to life? Can the morally shipwrecked be restored? Can the hardest of hearts be transformed? Should the answer hinge on logic, religion, and the ability and power of man, the answer is that they cannot. But if it hinges on the Holy Spirit, the answer changes to a resounding yes: "The things which are impossible with men are possible with God" (Luke 18:27).

Note six lessons from the Valley of Dry Bones narrative for the Christian worker.

1. Christian workers are divinely placed. Note the Spirit "carried" Ezekiel to the First Church of the Valley of Dry Bones, a post where he remained until the assignment was done. Like Ezekiel, a worker is to go where directed and stay where placed until "carried" by the Spirit elsewhere. Kyle Yates said, "The highest form of obedience is to remain at our post of duty when we cannot see why we are kept there."[25]

2. Despite an assigned task's seeming impossibility or grave difficulty, the worker must undertake it by faith. "We must discharge our trust," says Matthew Henry, "must prophesy as we are commanded, in the name of Him who raises the dead and is the fountain of life."[26]

3. Dead bones cannot resurrect themselves (procure salvation). No hope for the dead exists in the world—not in religion, reformation, philosophy, the church, good deeds, or morality—

only in the Spirit's power to raise them. The Bible says, "The Spirit is the one who gives life. The flesh doesn't help at all" (John 6:63 CSB).

4. The worker's words are powerless (tinkling cymbals and sounding brass) until made powerful and productive by the Spirit (Luke 4:18). Ezekiel had no confidence in his prowess (eloquence of speech, expertise, or seminary degrees) to make the bones live. But He did in God's ability. A Paul may plant and an Apollos water, but God giveth the increase (1 Corinthians 3:6). Paul testified, "My speech and my preaching was not with enticing words of man's wisdom, but in demonstration of the Spirit and of power" (1 Corinthians 2:4).

5. It takes the ministry of the Word enveloped with prayer (empowered by the Spirit) to raise the dead. Matthew Henry says, "See [in the narrative] the efficacy of the Word and prayer, and the necessity of both, for the raising of dead souls."[27]

6. The truth that the Holy Spirit miraculously brings life to those "dead in trespasses and sins" instills hope for salvation, even for the vilest of sinners and the deadest of churches. Write no sinner or dead church off. The same power that smote a blaspheming Paul with conviction, bringing him to conversion, is at work today. The seemingly irrational and impossible in ministry happen with God in the equation. Under the preaching and praying of Ezekiel, "the breath came into them, and they lived, and stood up upon their feet, an exceeding great army" (Ezekiel 37:10). Spurgeon asserts, "Yet the dry bones can live! Under the preaching of the Word the vilest sinners can be reclaimed, the most stubborn wills can be subdued, the most unholy lives can be sanctified! When the holy 'breath' comes from the four winds, when the divine Spirit descends to own the Word, then multitudes of sinners as on Pentecost, hallowed day, stand up upon their feet—an exceeding great army—to praise the Lord their God."[28]

Be encouraged, Christian worker. Whatever the assignment, however challenging, the same power that changed the corpses in the world's largest cemetery in a silent valley into mighty roaring soldiers is at your disposal. Go and minister confidently in that power. "Not by might, nor by power, but by My Spirit, saith the Lord of hosts" (Zechariah 4:6).

"What we need is not more learning, not more eloquence, not more persuasion, not more organization, but more power from the Holy Spirit."—John Stott.

## 8
### "How Shall I Give Thee Up?" (Unbelievers)

"How shall I give thee up?" (Hosea 11:8). In Israel's evil and rebellion against God, worship of Baal in the high places and Astarte in the groves, God yet tenderly and compassionately says to them, "How shall I give thee up?" Their sin deserved severe punishment, but God's tender heart "struggled" with the thought of it. That's the compassionate nature of God. "The Lord is long-suffering and slow to anger, and abundant in mercy and lovingkindness, forgiving iniquity and transgression" (Numbers 14:18 AMPC). See Psalm 78:38.

"How shall I give thee up?" How far is God willing to go to rescue man from the plight and peril of sin? As far as it takes short of manipulation and coercion.

How far? All the way to an old Rugged Cross, where He gave His only Son to atone for man's sin. "He that spared not His own Son, but delivered Him up for us all" (Romans 8:32).

How far? To the deepest pit of depravity, as He did with Manasseh, and to the far country of wantonness and emptiness, as He did with the prodigal.

How far? To the extent of sending missionaries, evangelists, and soulwinners to him, orchestrating circumstances to awaken him spiritually.

Only after going this far, without avail, will God give man up to the wanton and carnal desires of the flesh (Romans 1:24). Mercy and justice co-exist in God. Where mercy is scorned, the justice of God is manifested. Simeon says, "Soon God will not deliberate, but decide; not relent, but laugh at their calamity; not resolve to pardon, but swear they shall not enter into his rest."[29]

Solomon warned, "He, that being often reproved hardeneth his neck, shall suddenly be destroyed, and that without remedy" (Proverbs 29:1). Ironside states, "Hardening the neck is a figure taken from the manner in which a refractory bullock turns away from and avoids the yoke. In this way, men, in their stubbornness, persistently refuse to heed reproof and set their wills stubbornly against what would be for their own best interests, thus ensuring their destruction. God is gracious and long-suffering, slow to anger. Yet even *His* patience with the unrepentant comes to an end at last. He will plead and strive and warn till it is manifest the heart is fully set upon having its own way. Then He leaves the hardened soul to its doom, giving it up to sudden destruction. Many are the scriptural examples of this, but I only remind the reader of Korah, Dathan, and Abiram; of Belshazzar; and of Jezebel."[30]

Man's stubborn resistance to repentance and salvation is to blame for estrangement from God and condemnation to Hell. "Ye will not come to me, that ye might have [eternal] life" (John 5:40).

"When God was to give up his Son to be a sacrifice for sin and a Savior for sinners, He did not say, 'How shall I give Him up?' No, He spared not His own Son; it pleased the Lord to bruise Him; and therefore, God spared not Him, that He might spare us."[31]—Matthew Henry.

## 9

## "How Shall I Give Thee Up?" (Believers)

Rhetorically, God asks, "How shall I give thee up?" (Hosea 11:8). How shall God give up believers and let them become spiritual castaways? The answer is self-evident and unmistakable.

1. He will not give them up, for He loves the redeemed with everlasting love (Jeremiah 31:3).

O Love that will not let me go,
I rest my weary soul in thee.

— George Matheson (1882)

2. He will not give them up, for He promised (and God cannot lie) everlasting life to all who believe in Him. It is not everlasting life if it is temporary or can be forfeited.

3. He will not give them up, for the penalty of sin (eternal damnation) paid in full at Calvary by Christ for all who believe in Him cannot be invalidated. The author of Hebrews says, "Our sins are washed away and we are made clean because Christ gave His own body as a gift to God. He did this once for all time" (Hebrews 10:10 NLV).

4. He will not give them up, for He decreed that conversion would be irreversible. The born-again can never be unborn. The gift of salvation is irrevocable (Romans 11:29).

5. He will not give them up, for nothing can break His hold upon the redeemed soul. Jesus says, "And I give them eternal life, and they will never, ever [by any means] perish; and no one will ever snatch them out of My hand" (John 10:28 AMP). Absolutely nothing can snatch a born-again person from God's hand.

"We are in Christ, who is God," says A. T. Robertson, "and no burglar, not even Satan himself, can separate us from the love of God in Christ Jesus (Romans 8:31–39)."[32] And I add, not even man himself can break the bond ("They will never...perish"). Comforts, health, and a thousand other things may perish, but not the redeemed soul. The promise is not that the house will not be burned but that those in it will escape.[33] Spurgeon states, "The man himself shall never perish. He may think he shall, the Devil may tell him he shall, his comforts may be withdrawn, he may go to his death-bed full of doubts and fears about himself, but he shall never perish."[34] God can keep safe and secure that which is His (2 Timothy 1:12; 2 Timothy 4:18).

6. He will not give them up, for God guarantees that He will see to completion the work of salvation wrought in those He saves.

Paul said, "He will enable you to hold out until the end and thus be blameless on the Day of our Lord Yeshua the Messiah" (1 Corinthians 1:8 CJB), and "And I am sure that God who began the good work within you will keep right on helping you grow in his grace until his task within you is finally finished on that day when Jesus Christ returns" (Philippians 1:6 TLB). See Ephesians 5:25–27.

7. He will not give them up, for He willed from the beginning eternal salvation to all who believe. Jesus said, "This is the will of him who sent me, that I should lose nothing of all that he has given me, but raise it up at the last day" (John 6:39 RSV).

There is no reason for Christians to fear or be anxious that, at the last, they will perish. A man crossing the Mississippi, on foot, on the ice, fearing that it would crack and give way, began to crawl on all fours in terror. When he reached the shore, exhausted, another person rode by him happily, seated upon a sled loaded with pig iron. Sadly, too many Christians, like the crawling, terrorized man, travel to Canaan's fair land with trembling, fearing that at any moment, the promises of everlasting life will break under their feet and they will plunge into Hell when, in reality, they are secure enough to hold them up and incite jubilant song.[35]

"Whatever happens, whatever mistakes we may make, we shall come safely home. Slippings and strayings there will be, no doubt, but the everlasting arms are beneath us; we shall be caught, rescued, and restored. This is God's promise; this is how good He is."[36]—J. I. Packer

## 10

### "What Aileth Thee?"

"What aileth thee?" (Genesis 21:17). The question was asked by God to Hagar in the wilderness as her son, and she was about to die due to lack of water. The need was supplied, and both survived. The question is presented to all who are afflicted with adversity or infirmity.

*What aileth thee?* Is it horrendous sorrow over the death of a loved one?

*What aileth thee?* Is it the shackles of some besetting habit that hold you prisoner?

*What aileth thee?* Is it anxious concern about the unknown?

*What aileth thee?* Is it the weight of sin borne?

*What aileth thee?* Is it the uncertainty of salvation?

*What aileth thee?* Is it the fear of death?

*What aileth thee?* Is it spiritual coldness, a departure from your first love for God?

*What aileth thee?* Is it the dark night of the soul when plagued with despair and depression?

Whatever the ailment, God provides a well springing up with hope and healing waters to grant rescue and recovery. Says Spurgeon, "He [Christ] is the only universal doctor, and the medicine He gives is the only true catholicon [a cure-all], healing in every instance. Whatever our spiritual malady, we should immediately apply to this Divine Physician. There is no brokenness of heart that Jesus cannot bind up. We have but to think of the myriads who have been delivered from all sorts of diseases through the power and virtue of His touch, and we shall joyfully put ourselves in His hands. We trust Him, and sin dies; we love Him, and grace lives; we wait for Him, and grace is strengthened; we see Him as He is, and grace is perfected forever."[37] But, alas, the gushing well of healing and help is often unseen, as with Hagar, until God opens the eyes to it (Genesis 21:19; Psalm 146:8; 2 Kings 6:17).

> Open my eyes that I may see
> Glimpses of truth thou hast for me.
> Place in my hands the wonderful key
> That shall unclasp and set me free.
>
> – Clara H. Scott (1895)

*"He gives sight to those that have been long deprived of it; the Lord can open the eyes of the blind, and has often given to His afflicted people to see that comfort which before they were not aware of."*[38]—Matthew Henry.

## 11

### "What Doest Thou Here?"

Elijah's courage and tenacity before King Ahab and the priests of Baal at Carmel dissipate to dismay, weariness, and despair at a cave in Horeb. God meets him there with the interrogative question, "What doest thou here?" (1 Kings 19:9).

None are exempt from hopelessness and despair, not even Elijah, Paul, or Spurgeon. The strongest of saints are, at best, weak. What prompts despondency?

1. Bodily affliction. Elijah became overwrought and worn out (1 Kings 19:4–8). The state of the body impacts the elation or depression of the spirit. God's servants require "a breathing space in a life of toil."[39] Spurgeon says, "The bow cannot always be bent without the fear of breaking. Repose is as needful to the mind as sleep to the body. While we are in this tabernacle, we must every now and then cry halt and serve the Lord by holy inaction and consecrated leisure."[40] Come apart or fall apart.

2. Loneliness. Elijah said, "I, even I only, am left." Loneliness often casts the soul into the pit of gloom and despair. "Loneliness…is a fertile source of depression."[41]

3. Fruitlessness. Elijah felt the work performed was all in vain. He said, "The children of Israel have forsaken thy covenant, thrown down thine altars, and slain thy prophets with the sword" (1 Kings 19:10). Spurgeon states, "Non-success is a trial of faith that has been endured by many a trusty servant. Did not the disciples toil all night and catch nothing? Do not, then, grudge the time or the strength you lay out in the service of our great Lord because you do not see your efforts thrive, for better men than you have wept over failure. Remember, too, that if you really do serve the

Lord thoroughly and heartily, he will accept you and acknowledge your service, even though no good should come of it."[42]

4. Slothfulness. Elijah's idleness (desertion from the work) fueled despair of the heart. "An idle brain is the devil's plaything." When experiencing the deep darkness of the soul, it's best to stay at your post of duty.

5. Doubt and unbelief. Elijah's wavering faith (unbelief), prompted by fear of Jezebel, led to his flight to Horeb to escape responsibility and duty. "The noblest of mankind are nothing when once the fire of trust is quenched in the soul. 'The just shall live by faith'; when faith dies, every good and noble thing dies with it."[43]

Distrust in God saps joy, hope, and peace. Jeremy Taylor states, "It is impossible for that man to despair who remembers that his Helper is omnipotent." When Peter took his focus off Jesus, he began to sink into the raging waters.

6. Sin. Elijah's sins (disobedience, lack of trust in God, cowardice) contributed to the dark state of mind he experienced. Recall David's sin produced the same in his heart and was only resolved upon his confession and repentance (Psalm 32; Psalm 51).

In the presence of God and hearing His "still small voice," Elijah's despair was lifted as his body and soul were refreshed, confusion about what God was doing and would do was rectified, and a new task was assigned. The distraught who spends time alone in God's presence (quiet waiting and prayer), aligns with His will and ways and leans heavily upon His Word (precious promises) will find deliverance. "Unto the upright there ariseth light in the darkness: he is gracious, and full of compassion, and righteous" (Psalm 112:4).

"What doest thou here?" Perhaps only a flickering of light is seen in the dark cave where you now dwell, but rest assured that that mere flicker is the promise of God of greater light to come. Don't lose hope. "Weeping may endure for a night, but joy cometh in the morning" (Psalm 30:5).

"The greatest faith is born in the hour of despair. When we can see no hope and no way out, then faith rises and brings the victory."—Lee Roberson.

## 12
### "Doest Thou Well to Be Angry?"

"Doest thou well to be angry?" (Jonah 4:4). Ninevah's being spared from judgment angered Jonah, who wished for their destruction more than their salvation. This unjustifiable and indefensible attitude met with God's incisive condemnation. The question may be asked of all who exhibit uncontrolled anger.

Its answer may be "Yes." Spurgeon states, "We do well when we are angry with sin, because of the wrong that it commits against our good and gracious God; or with ourselves because we remain so foolish after so much divine instruction; or with others when the sole cause of anger is the evil that they do."[44]

But often, its answer must be "No" because of its poisonous impact.

1. Anger poisons life. Anger is included among the seven deadly sins because of its disruptive and destructive nature to a person's life (Proverbs 6:16–19). Twain said, "Anger is an acid that can do more harm to the vessel in which it is stored than to anything on which it is poured."[45]

2. Anger poisons relationships. "Hot tempers cause arguments" (Proverbs 15:18 GNT). Anger alienates children from parents, marriage partners from one another, and friends from friends. Anger can silence communication with others.

3. Anger poisons respect and testimony. Adrian Rogers said, "There is nothing more debilitating to your Christian testimony than for you to fly off the handle."[46] "People with understanding control their anger; a hot temper shows great foolishness" (Proverbs 14:29 NLT). Ambrose Bierce said, "Speak when you are angry, and you will make the best speech you will ever regret."

4. Anger poisons others. Explosive attitudes of rage that demean, ridicule, and berate others are contagious. The Bible warns, "Don't make friends with people who have hot, violent tempers. You might learn their habits and not be able to change" (Proverbs 22:24–25 GNT).

5. Anger poisons health and well-being. Anger can exacerbate anxiety, shorten life, cause heart attacks, and damage the lungs.[47] Charles Stanley says, "One of the most harmful consequences of uncontrolled anger is depression. Over time, inner turmoil and unresolved conflicts will take their toll on a person's mental health."[48]

6. Anger poisons happiness. Ralph Waldo Emerson wrote, "For every minute you are angry, you lose sixty seconds of happiness."

7. Anger poisons the soul. A fit of temper or rage is a sin, for it is "giving place to the Devil; grieving the Holy Spirit, contrary to the mind and example of Christ; inconsistent with the profession of the Gospel; degrading human nature; a work of the flesh."[49]

Daily die to the rule and rage of anger (1 Corinthians 15:31). Ask God to keep it in check. The Bible teaches that a man who controls his temper is a greater warrior than he who conquers armies (Proverbs 16:32). A philosopher advised Caesar to say nothing when he was angry until he first repeated all the letters of the Greek alphabet. When provoked to anger, do likewise or something similar until coolness prevails.

Spurgeon says, "Do not say, 'I cannot help having a bad temper.' Friend, you must help it. Pray to God to help you overcome it at once, for either you must kill it, or it will kill you. You cannot carry a bad temper into Heaven. Let in the light of Christ's love on it, and the vile thing will be made to die."[50]

**"The greatest remedy for anger is delay."**—Seneca.

## 13

## "Wherefore Do Ye Spend Money for That Which Is Not Bread?"

"Wherefore do ye spend money for that which is not bread?" (Isaiah 55:2). The question to the spiritually deficient Israelites (and all like them) may be paraphrased: Why do you waste time and resources feeding at the table of materialism and religion when it cannot satisfy, only intensify, the hunger of the soul?

To seek "bread" in pleasures, friendships, possessions, wealth, and religion, which are "no bread," is not only foolish but also futile. Lord Byron, the poet, discovered the emptiness of a life that feeds on worldly stuff for peace and satisfaction. In his poem "On My Thirty-Sixth Year," he wrote, "The worm, the canker, and the grief are mine alone."

Solomon testified similarly: "So life came to mean nothing to me, because everything in it had brought me nothing but trouble. It had all been useless; I had been chasing the wind" (Ecclesiastes 2:17 GNT). What was thought to be bread to Byron and Solomon turned out to be chaff (John 4:13). Bread that is not bread can never satisfy the hungry soul or sustain it in life's journey. The authentic Bread is Christ, who said, "I am the Bread of life: he that cometh to me shall never hunger; and he that believeth on me shall never thirst" (John 6:35).

Christ, the Bread, fills longings deep in the soul. "He [the Lord] satisfieth the longing soul, and filleth the hungry soul with goodness" (Psalm 107:9). What He affords means needing or wanting nothing more.

He mends broken hearts. "He healeth the broken in heart, and bindeth up their wounds" (Psalm 147:3). He sustains in times of affliction and adversity. "God is our refuge and strength, a very present help in trouble" (Psalm 46:1). He graciously forgives sin and grants a fresh start. "But you, Lord our God, are compassionate and forgiving, although we have rebelled against you" (Daniel 9:9 GW). He provides peace in the face of death. "Even when walking through the dark valley of death, I will not be afraid, for you are close beside me, guarding, guiding all the way" (Psalm 23:4 TLB).

Says Spurgeon, "Some have tried to stay their hunger by the narcotics of skepticism…; and others have endeavored to get ease through the drugs of fatalism. Many stave off hunger by indifference, like the bears in winter, who are not hungry because they are asleep….But depend upon it, the only way to meet hunger is to get bread, and the only way to meet your soul's want is to get Christ, in whom there is enough and to spare, but nowhere else."[51]

1. Who may come? Everyone thirsty for the eternal things that God affords. "Ho, everyone that thirsteth, come ye to the waters" (Isaiah 55:1a).

2. How to come? "Without money and without price" (Isaiah 55:1b). Come empty-handed, in simple child-like faith, relying upon Him to save. Salvation cannot be purchased with humanitarian deeds, religious ceremonies, work and gold, church membership, baptism, the Lord's Supper, and moral goodness (Ephesians 2:8–9; Romans 11:6). Say with Toplady, "Nothing in my hands I bring; simply to Thy cross I cling."

3. When to come? Seek the Lord now. "Seek ye the LORD while he may be found, call ye upon him while he is near" (Isaiah 55:6). Note Paul said, "Behold, now is the accepted time; behold, now is the day of salvation" (2 Corinthians 6:2). A person can never seek God too soon, but he can too late.

"Let a man truly know the grace of our Lord Jesus Christ, and he will be a happy man, and the deeper he drinks into the spirit of Christ, the more happy will he become."[52]—C. H. Spurgeon.

## 14

### "Wherefore Do Ye Spend Money for That Which Is Not Bread?"

"Wherefore do ye spend money for that which is not bread? And your labor for that which satisfieth not?" (Isaiah 55:2). Why continue to trust in a religion that fails to bring peace to the heart, hope for the future, and life-satisfaction?

To base salvation upon duty, merit, deeds, and observances, or in anything other than the shed blood of Jesus Christ, is to spend money (waste time and energy) for that which is not bread (that which cannot save or satisfy). Christ is the true bread of life who alone remedies the problem of sin, satisfies the deep thirst and hunger of the soul, provides comfort and consolation in times of storm, grants meaning and happiness to life, and gives hope for Heaven at death (Jeremiah 2:13; John 6:35–51). "For he satisfies the longing soul, and the hungry soul he fills with good things" (Psalm 107:9 ESV). Nothing else can do for man that which Christ, "the bread of life," does (John 6:35).

Why continue to labor to earn righteousness sufficient for God's approval and acceptance when the best you can attain is "like a menstrual rag" (Isaiah 64:6 CEB)? Why keep using every means available, except Christ, to fill the emptiness in the soul that only He can satisfy?

The want of bread prompted the prodigal son's reconciliation with the father. Let its want bring you to Christ, who awaits with open arms to forgive, save, and satisfy.

Stop spending money on that which, in truth, is not bread (entertainment, religion, pleasure, fame) but its opposite, something that not only fails to alleviate your hunger and thirst but exasperates it.[53] The psalmist challenges the hungry soul, saying, "Taste and see that the Lord is good. Oh, the joys of those who take refuge in him!" (Psalm 34:8 NLT).

"True life is impossible where the bread of life is not eaten."[54]—J. Higgins.

## 15

### "How Shall I Pardon Thee for This?"

"How shall I pardon thee for this?" (Jeremiah 5:7). God asked Israel, "Is the enormity of your sins within the scope of My mercy to forgive?" It is a question all ask and may be answered by response to four questions.

1. Is God willing to pardon all sin? History and the Scripture attest to God's willingness and ableness to forgive the most hideous sin and vilest sinner. No wrongdoing (sin) is exempt from pardon (Romans 5:20). Your sin may be big, but God's lovingkindness and mercy to forgive stand bigger. He says, "Come, let's talk this over, says the Lord; no matter how deep the stain of your sins, I can take it out and make you as clean as freshly fallen snow" (Isaiah 1:18 TLB). The psalmist declares, "Our guilt overwhelms us, but you forgive our sins" (Psalm 65:3 NCV). The only unforgivable sin is the one unconfessed.

2. Is there a condition of pardon? God says, "Return unto me" (Isaiah 44:22). Forgiveness is based upon a repentant return to God. Isaiah says, "Let the wicked forsake his way, and the unrighteous man his thoughts: and let him return unto the LORD, and he will have mercy upon him; and to our God, for he will abundantly pardon" (Isaiah 55:7). John says, "If we confess our sins, he is faithful and just to forgive us our sins, and to cleanse us from all unrighteousness" (1 John 1:9).

3. What happens when a person is pardoned? Upon repentance, sin is blotted out (cast into the sea of forgetfulness), purity fills the heart (Ezekiel 36:25–26), peace rules the mind (Philippians 4:7), and power governs life (Ezekiel 36:27; Micah 7:19). The forgiven exclaims with David, "Happy is the person whose sins are forgiven, whose wrongs are pardoned" (Psalm 32:1 NCV).

4. Why does a Holy God choose to pardon? Micah answers, saying, "Because he delighteth in mercy" (Micah 7:18). God finds joy and pleasure in forgiving sin; that's His nature (Ephesians 2:4; Isaiah 43:25). The jubilation and celebration of the Father (Luke 15:22–24) at the return of the wayward son picture God's heart toward all who repentantly come home from the far country of rebellion and wantonness.

> Thy sins, though like scarlet or crimson,
>   His love as a river doth flow;
> Oh, plunge in this fountain of cleansing,
>   And thou shalt be whiter than snow.
>
> — A. Pratt (1907)

Don't bear the weight of sin a moment longer when forgiveness and cleansing await at the foot of the Cross. Says Spurgeon, "Kiss the pierced hand of Jesus which is now held out to you, and this very moment you shall be forgiven, and you shall go your way a pardoned man, to begin a new life, and to bear witness that 'where sin abounded, grace did much more abound.'"[55]

**"The power of pardon is permanently resident with God: He has forgiveness ready in His hand at this instant."**[56] —C. H. Spurgeon

## 16
### "Shall He That Contendeth with the Almighty Instruct Him?"

"Shall he that contendeth with the Almighty instruct Him?" (Job 40:2). The reprimanding question to Job may be paraphrased: 'Shall a man argue with God, telling Him what to do? Shall God receive instruction from every peevish complainer, changing His plans accordingly to suit him?'[57]

Lessons the question suggests:

1. It is an appalling presumption for a frail and vile man to think he is wiser than Almighty God. To judge and criticize the works of God and to seek to give Him counsel is the height of pompous conceit. Why? Scripture answers: "This foolish plan of God [that which seems foolish in the eyes of man] is wiser than the wisest of human plans, and God's weakness is stronger than the greatest of human strength" (1 Corinthians 1:25 NLT). Paul asks, "Who has known the mind of the Lord? Who has been able to teach him?" (1 Corinthians 2:16 NCV). The emphatic answer is no

one (1 Chronicles 29:14). God is God and needs no man to give Him instruction or counsel.

2. Some things God does are not within man's comprehension (Isaiah 55:8–9). "His judgments, and His ways [are] past finding out" (Romans 11:33). "Past finding out" means "that which cannot be traced out" or "that which cannot be tracked out."[58] "The word could be used of a bloodhound who found it impossible to follow the scent of a criminal, or of a guide who could not trace out or follow a poorly marked path in the woods."[59] Despite the bountiful, all-sufficient truth about God's dealing with man and the world in the Scriptures, and man's intense study of them, he must confess with David, "Such knowledge is too wonderful for me; it is high, I cannot attain unto it" (Psalm 139:6).[60]

3. Don't try to figure out the *why* of happenings that God has chosen to keep secret. Divine secrets are not to be sought out (Deuteronomy 29:29). God deems that the *why* of some things is best to be revealed and explained later. "Be not curious to search into the secrets of God; pick not the lock where He hath allowed no key."[61] Matthew Henry asserts, "The judgments of His mouth, and the way of our duty, blessed be God, are plain and easy. It is a highway; but the judgments of His hands, and the ways of His providence, are dark and mysterious, which therefore we must not pry into, but silently adore and acquiesce in."[62]

4. The proper response to the inexplicable and abstruse ways of God is trust. "The better God is known," states Matthew Henry, "the more He is trusted. Those who know Him to be a God of infinite wisdom will trust Him further than they can see Him (Job 35:14); those who know Him to be a God of almighty power will trust Him when creature confidences fail, and they have nothing else to trust to (2 Chronicles 20:12); and those who know Him to be a God of infinite grace and goodness will trust Him though He slay them (Job 13:15)."[63] Trust God where you cannot trace Him.[64] "For we walk by faith, not by sight" (2 Corinthians 5:7).

**"If we saw through the whole administration of God, if there were no mystery or perplexity in His dealings, we should be living by reason and not by faith."[65]—R. M. Edgar.**

## 17
## "How Long Will It Be Ere They Believe Me?"

"How long will it be before they believe me?" (Numbers 14:11 ICB). Only Joshua and Caleb, of the twelve spies, reported that Caanan could be possessed as God promised. The others' dismal report caused murmuring in the camp, prompting this question of God.

When will sinful man trust God for salvation, the redemption of his soul?

1. Not until errant religious belief is seen as false. As long as a man counts his belief true, though untrue, he will not believe in God or trust in His means of salvation.

2. Not until there is a search for spiritual truth. Not looking for the truth about God, judgment, eternity, and salvation is choosing to remain blind to it. Billy Graham said, "It is far better to know God's Truth than to be ignorant of it."[66] Quest for the truth ultimately brings man to the truth. Jesus said, "Ye shall know the truth, and the truth shall make you free" (John 8:32). See 1 Timothy 2:4 and Proverbs 8:17.

3. Not until there is an openness to the gospel message. The close-minded keep the light from streaming into their darkened mind by refusing to consider the Gospel's truth. Spurgeon asserts, "The battle of grace is with man's unwillingness to see those truths against which he is naturally at enmity. When a man does not want to see, he cannot see; when he is determined not to learn, when the truth is unpalatable to him, when he designedly twists it from its meaning, then his eye is diseased, and the light is hindered from its due effect."[67]

4. Not until sin is loathed. A love for sin keeps man from seeking God and His salvation (John 3:19; 2 Timothy 3:4).

5. Not until the blindness of the mind is penetrated. "The god of this world hath blinded the minds of them which believe not" (2 Corinthians 4:4). Spurgeon said, "If a man wills to see the honest truth and submits himself to the enlightenment of the Holy Ghost,

he will not be left in darkness."[68] The preaching or presentation of the Gospel is the one thing that can open blind eyes to the truth of the gospel (2 Corinthians 4:3–4). Calvin asserts, "The blindness of unbelievers in no way detracts from the clarity of the Gospel; the sun is no less bright because blind men do not perceive its light."

6. Not until man sees himself as a depraved and damned sinner. As long as a person counts himself morally righteous, alive when he is dead, "in need of nothing" from God, there will be no movement toward repentance and faith. To come to God, a man must humble himself as a little child (Matthew 18:2–4), saying, "I am poor and needy" (Psalm 40:17), "in me...dwelleth no good thing" (Romans 7:18), AND "Father, I have sinned against heaven and against you" (Luke 15:21 NIV).

7. Not until man wills to come to God on His terms. The Lord said, "If any man will come after me, let him deny himself, and take up his cross daily, and follow me" (Luke 9:23). Many walk away from God, saying, "This is tough teaching, too tough to swallow" (John 6:60 MSG). Someone said, "If the truth makes you uncomfortable, don't blame the truth....blame the lie that made you comfortable."

8. Not until man chooses to be found. Picture being hopelessly lost deep in a forest at midnight when a light appears. Its source is discovered to be the burning headlamps of a jeep. Upon the hood of the jeep, in plain view, is a detailed map showing the way out of the forest. Immediately, you tear the map into small pieces and demolish the headlamps of the jeep. If this happened, who would be responsible for your remaining lost? The jeep? The headlamps? The map? The person responsible for the jeep, headlamps, and map? None of them. You alone would be guilty.[69]

God has provided the LIGHT and the MAP to show man the way out of lostness in sin. Man, not God, not the LIGHT or MAP or the JEEP (the preacher, missionary, evangelist, soulwinner) is responsible for failing to use them to find eternal life. Sorrow of sorrows is to hear Jesus say, "And ye will not come to me, that ye might have life" (John 5:40).

"There's none so blind as they that won't see."—Jonathan Swift.

## 18
### "Why Have They Provoked Me to Anger?"

"Why have they provoked Me to anger with their graven images and with strange vanities?" (Jeremiah 8:19 KJ21). Israel provoked God's anger and judgment by idolatrous worship.

The question reveals four insights about the wrath of God.

1. The wrath of God is inseparable from His love. Adrian Rogers said, "And when you say that God is a God of love, that is truth, but it's not all of the truth; it is part of the truth. And when you try to take part of the truth and make part of the truth all of the truth, that part of the truth becomes an untruth."[70] God is a God of love, "but also a God of wrath and a God of judgment."[71]

2. The wrath of God is provoked by sin. Eight times we are told in the Old Testament that God is "slow to anger." He prefers to deal with man in lovingkindness and tender mercy. But a time arrives when His anger is ignited against a nation or person who refuses to turn from their wretched and despicable conduct. No transgressor is immune to God's judgment (Hebrews 12:5–11).

3. The wrath of God brings judgment. Punishment is dispensed in retribution for sin. "It is a fearful thing to fall into the hands of the living God" (Hebrews 10:31). As Jonathan Edwards preached this subject, the terror of God's wrath fell upon the people, so much so that out of fear that they may plunge downward to Hell, they gripped tightly to the pew. In the sermon, Edwards said, "The wicked must not think, simply because they are not physically in Hell, that God (in whose hand the wicked now reside) is not, at this very moment, as angry with them as He is with those He is now tormenting in Hell; and who, at this very moment, feel and bear the fierceness of His wrath." The message awakened many to salvation and catalyzed the First Great Awakening. Solomon said, "The fear of the LORD is the beginning of wisdom"

(Proverbs 9:10). To think one may trample upon the sacredness of holy things and show disdain for God without punishment is the height of folly and foolishness (2 Kings 24:20).

4. The wrath of God is momentary. "His anger lasts for only a moment [for the repentant]. But his favor lasts for a person's whole life. Weeping can stay for the night. But joy comes in the morning" (Psalm 30:5 NIRV). Judgment for sin lasts for the night, but joy is promised to come to the truly repentant afterward. Says Spurgeon, "God puts up his rod with great readiness as soon as its work is done; He is slow to anger and swift to end it."[72] Matthew Henry states, "The return of His favor to an afflicted soul is as life from the dead; nothing can be more reviving. Our happiness is bound up in God's favor; if we have that, we have enough, whatever else we want. It is the life of the soul; it is spiritual life, the earnest of life eternal."[73]

The wrath of God (the judgment of eternal punishment in Hell) rests upon the unrepentant (John 3:36). The only escape from it is in Jesus Christ (John 3:16).

"It is amazing that we hesitate to talk about the wrath of God for fear of making sinners feel fearful. The fear they feel this side of the grave will be nothing compared to the fear they feel when they stand before Almighty God."—Ray Comfort

## 19

### "Can Any Hide Himself…That I Shall Not See Him?"

"Can any hide himself in secret places that I shall not see him?" (Jeremiah 23:24). The false prophets preached that God was distant and unaware of what was happening among men (Job 22:13–14). The rhetorical question countered that false teaching, affirming God's omnipresence and omniscience.

Is it possible for a man to hide from God?

*Not so, says God.* "For mine eyes are upon all their ways: they are not hid from my face, neither is their iniquity hid from mine eyes" (Jeremiah 16:17).

*Not so, says Paul.* "Knowing that God is watching us" (2 Corinthians 2:17 NLT).

*Not so, says Solomon.* "The eyes of the Lord are in every place, beholding the evil and the good" (Proverbs 15:3). The "eyes of the Lord are in every place" (that is, there is nothing hid from Him; nothing of which He is not aware both with man personally and the world at large), beholding the "evil and the good" (He sees man's "private" and public sin as well as his good, moral deeds). The Proverb "underscores God's unrestricted presence in space and His unrestricted moral assessment of every individual."[74]

*Not so, says Job.* "He watches every step we take" (Job 34:21 GNT).

*Not so, says the Psalmist.* "You know when I sit down and when I get up. You know my thoughts before I think them" (Psalm 139:2 ICB).

*Not so, says Matthew Henry*, "Secret sins, services, and sorrows are under his eye."[75] He says further, "No arts of concealment can hide men from the eye of God, nor deceive His judgment of them."[76]

*Not so, says D. Martyn Lloyd-Jones.* "This is the fundamental thing, the most serious thing of all, that we are always in the presence of God."

*Not so, says Spurgeon.* "Thou dost surround me even as the air continually surrounds all creatures that live. I am shut up within the wall of Thy being; I am encircled within the bounds of Thy knowledge. Waking or sleeping, I am still observed of Thee."[77]

*Not so, says Simeon.* "He is everywhere present to protect His people and to defeat the plots of their adversaries."[78]

Knowledge of the omnipresence of God serves as a deterrent to sin (Habakkuk 1:13), encouragement in service (Deuteronomy 20:4), comfort in sorrow and suffering (Psalm 23:4), and incentive for hope in crisis and the hour of death (Isaiah 43:5).

"GOD is everywhere. HIS circumference is nowhere, but HIS center is everywhere."[79]—C. H. Spurgeon

## 20
## "Who Is Blind, But My Servant?"

"Who is blind, but my servant?" (Isaiah 42:19). Israel ("my servant") and the priests ("my messenger"), whom God entrusted with His counsel and commandments, walked unworthily of that trust; they were blind to His Word, ways, and works. The question is asked to quicken their remorse and repentance.

Many of the Lord's servants are spiritually blinded in five ways.

1. Blinded to the misery and eternal peril of the lost. Of Jesus, the Bible says, "When he saw the crowds, he felt sorry for them. They were confused and helpless, like sheep without a shepherd" (Matthew 9:36 CEV).

2. Blinded to the coldness and indifference of their own heart. "I have somewhat against thee, because thou hast left thy first love" (Revelation 2:4). "So then because thou art lukewarm, and neither cold nor hot, I will spue thee out of my mouth" (Revelation 3:16). "Gray hairs are here and there upon him, yet he knoweth not" (Hosea 7:9).

3. Blinded to the task God assigned to them. "Then I heard the voice of the Lord saying, 'Whom shall I send? And who will go for us?' And I said, 'Here am I. Send me!'" (Isaiah 6:8 NIVUK).

4. Blinded to the fleeting opportunities to make a difference for Christ in the home, job, and school. "Take advantage of every opportunity because these are evil times" (Ephesians 5:16 CEB). "Make the most of your chances to tell others the Good News. Be wise in all your contacts with them" (Colossians 4:5 TLB).

5. Blinded to all owed to Christ for the gift of salvation. "I am debtor both to the Greeks, and to the Barbarians; both to the wise, and to the unwise" (Romans 1:14). See Psalm 103:2–5. Spurgeon says, "But of the Christian, it can be said, that he does not owe God's justice a solitary farthing; for Christ has paid the debt His people owed. I am a debtor to God's love, I am a debtor to God's

grace, I am a debtor to God's power, I am a debtor to God's forgiving mercy; but I am no debtor to His justice—for He, Himself, will never accuse me of a debt once paid."[80]

What causes spiritual blindness?

1. Worldliness, indifference, callousness, and inattention to spiritual things.

2. Not using the eyes. Fish locked away in deep, dark caverns become blind because the eyes are unnecessary and, therefore, unused. Similarly, spiritual eyesight diminishes or dies if someone walks in "darkness rather than light" (John 3:19).[81]

3. Deaf ears to the truth revealed through evangelical ministers, the Scriptures, and the Holy Spirit.

Blindness is curable. "Hear, ye deaf; and look, ye blind, that ye may see" (Isaiah 42:18). Healing eye-salve is available at the foot of the Cross. Says Maclaren, "Apply the eye-salve. It will be keen; it will bite. Welcome the smart, and be sure that anything is good for you that takes away the veil that self-complacency casts over your true condition and lets the light of God into the cellars and dark places of your souls."[82]

"**Blindness and deafness in spiritual things are worse in those that profess themselves to be God's servants and messengers than in others. It is in them the greater sin and shame, the greater dishonor to God, and to themselves a greater damnation.**"[83]—Matthew Henry.

## 21
### "Wherefore Criest Thou Unto Me?"

"Wherefore criest thou unto Me?" (Exodus 14:15). Moses' cry or prayer is not stated but may have been one of despair over the Israelites' lack of faith (Exodus 5:22–23; 17:4).[84]

God asks of all that pray, "Why criest thou unto Me?"

We pray out of obedience. Jesus mandated prayer, saying, 'Enter into thy closet, shut the door and pray to thy Father' (Matthew 6:6).

We pray because it's part of worship (Psalm 95:6–7). We pray to have an intimate connection with and communion with God.

We pray, for prayer is the appointed means of receiving good things at God's hand (Ezekiel 36:37). We pray to attain mercy and grace (the supernatural power of God to supply comfort, consolation, strength, counsel, healing, peace, etc.) for every need (Hebrews 4:16).

We pray, for prayer is an exchange: "We leave our burdens, worries, and sin in the hands of God. We come away with the oil of joy and the garment of praise."[85]

We pray, for God attached to it divine promises (Matthew 7:7). Believers pray to acquire the power to defeat the wiles (tactics, strategies) of the Devil (Ephesians 6:11). Saith Spurgeon, "Prayer brings inner strength to God's warriors and sends them forth to spiritual battle with their muscles firm and their armor in place."[86] E. Stanley Jones said, "When prayer fades out, power fades out."

We pray to partner with God in advancing His kingdom on earth (Matthew 6:10). Moody said, "Behind every work of God, you will always find a kneeling form."

We pray to break down Satan's strongholds, thwart his devious and malicious work, and drive him back. Why pray? Pray to thrust needed workers into the harvest (Matthew 9:38).

We pray to solicit the power to bind up the brokenhearted, set the prisoner free, comfort all who mourn by giving them beauty for ashes and the garment of praise for the spirit of heaviness (Isaiah 61:1–3).

We pray to nourish and sustain the soul. Saith Andrew Bonar, "In order to grow in grace, we must spend a great deal of time in quiet solitude."[87]

We pray for prayer is a joy; it brings joy. "Until now you have asked for nothing in my name. Ask and you will receive, so that your joy may be complete" (John 16:24 CSB).

We pray because prayer changes things. Saith Hudson Taylor, "If we want to see mighty wonders of divine power and grace wrought in the place of weakness, failure, and disappointment, let us answer God's standing challenge, 'Call unto me, and I will answer thee, and show thee great and mighty things, which thou knowest not.'"

We pray to know God's plan and will. "When we are on our knees, then light flashes; then the intellect is clarified; then the conscience is aroused; then the spiritual sensibilities are quickened; and we can learn more of our duty and of His will than in hours of argumentation."[88]

The bottom line: We cry out to God, for He has promised to hear and answer the cries of our hearts. "Because He hath inclined His ear unto me, therefore will I call upon Him" (Psalm 116:2).

**"We do not bow the knee merely because it is a duty and a commendable spiritual exercise, but because we believe that into the ear of the eternal God we speak our wants, and that His ear is linked with a heart feeling for us and a hand working on our behalf. To us, true prayer is true power."**[89] – C. H. Spurgeon.

## 22

### "Get Thee Up; Wherefore Liest Thou Thus upon Thy Face?"

"Get thee up; wherefore liest thou thus upon thy face?" (Joshua 7:10). Joshua did well to humble himself and mourn Israel's defeat at the battle of Ai. Still, it is to end, "for God delights not in the grief of penitents when they afflict their souls further than as it qualifies them for pardon and peace; the days even of that mourning must be ended."[90] Joshua must "get up," for there is more to be done than to lie on the ground; a thief must be apprehended and judged.[91]

Prostrate yourself before God in time of need, cry out for help, soak in His Word and promises, gain strength to press on, and then in confident trust of God, "get thee up" and move on with life's responsibilities and its work. Matthew Henry says, "Weeping must not hinder sowing."[92] Trust in God (an entire reliance upon Him) is commanded (Proverbs 3:5–6) and is the antidote to despair, doubt, defeatism, and depression.

Protect this trust from the assault of companions, troublesome circumstances, and your own "understanding" (discernment, impressions, and impulsiveness). Nourish this trust by studying God's trustworthiness in history (Psalm 9:10). Treasure it above trust in another or provision afforded (Psalm 20:7). Grow it by its much use. Cleave to it relentlessly, unwaveringly, and explicitly. "Trust in Him at all times, you people; pour out your hearts to Him, for God is our refuge" (Psalm 62:8 NIV).

Spurgeon strikingly says, "It is a poor faith which can trust God only when friends are true, the body full of health, and the business profitable; but that is true faith which holds by the Lord's faithfulness when friends are gone, when the body is sick, when spirits are depressed, and the light of our Father's countenance is hidden. A faith that can say in the direst trouble, 'Though He slays me, yet will I trust in Him,' is Heaven-born faith."[93] He continues, "Believe! is the word which speaks life into a man, but doubt nails down his coffin."[94] See Isaiah 26:3–4.

"Why are you lying on your face on the ground?" Until prayer is answered, keep knocking, seeking, and asking (Matthew 7:7–8). But upon receiving the answer, "get thee up," trusting God to do what He promised ("walk by faith, not by sight").

"Those who know Him to be a God of inviolable truth and faithfulness will rejoice in His word of promise and rest upon that. Those who know Him to be the everlasting Father will trust Him with their souls as their main care and trust in Him at all times, even to the end."[95]—Matthew Henry

## 23
## "To Whom Then Will Ye Liken Me?"

"To whom then will ye liken Me?" (Isaiah 40:25). We must answer, like Jeremiah, saying, "No one is like you, Lord; you are great, and your name is mighty in power" (Jeremiah 10:6 NIV). Jehovah God is incomparable. "Whatever men may set in competition with Him," asserts Matthew Henry, "there is none to be compared with Him."[96]

1. None compare to God's mightiness and rule. "For who in the heaven can be compared unto the Lord? Who among the sons of the mighty can be likened unto the Lord?" (Psalm 89:6). "No other gods are like you; only you work miracles" (Psalm 86:8 CEV).

2. None compare to God's lovingkindness and mercifulness. The world embraces gods who will only exchange love and mercy for deeds done or a change in conduct. But Jehovah God shows mercy and love freely to all that call upon Him "without money and without price" (Isaiah 55:1). Spurgeon says, "He pours forth His love in plenteous streams to undeserving, ill-deserving, Hell-deserving objects."[97]

3. None compare to God's readiness to help. "God is our shelter and strength, always ready to help in times of trouble" (Psalm 46:1 GNT). Nothing compares to God's watchfulness over His own. "The LORD will watch over your coming and going both now and forevermore" (Psalm 121:8 NIV). Spurgeon says, "He observes them [His children] with approval and tender consideration; they are so dear to Him that He cannot take his eyes off them; He watches each one of them as carefully and intently as if there were only that one creature in the universe."[98]

4. None compare to God's gratification of man's thirst. He is "the fountain of living water" (Jeremiah 2:13a), from which flows joy, peace, hope, happiness, and meaning. No other fountain equals Him or approaches what He affords to man. He is the fountain that ever gushes, satisfying the thirst of man's soul; all other fountains are "broken cisterns, that can hold no water" (Jeremiah 2:13b).

5. None compare to God's protection. There is no Rock like our God that is a strong shelter in times of trouble (1 Samuel 2:2). "You are my mighty rock, my fortress, my protector, the rock where I am safe, my shield, my powerful weapon, and my place of shelter" (Psalm 18:2 CEV).

6. None compare to God's faithfulness. He is dependable, trustworthy, and reliable in every season. "So know that the Lord your God is God. He is the faithful God. He will keep his agreement of love for a thousand lifetimes. He does this for people who love him and obey his commands" (Deuteronomy 7:9 ICB).

7. None compare to God's salvation. It is an inimitable salvation. "I, even I, am the Lord; and beside me there is no savior" (Isaiah 43:11).

8. None compare to God's companionship. "For He hath said, 'I will never leave thee, nor forsake thee" (Hebrews 13:5). God is "a friend that sticketh closer than a brother" (Proverbs 18:24).

9. None compare to God's reality. "But the Lord is the only true God. He is the only God who is alive. He is the King who rules forever" (Jeremiah 10:10 ERV). He is unlike the fabricated gods of the world, made of wood and stone, formed from the imagination of man's heart. Matthew Henry asserts, "He is not a counterfeit and pretender, as they are, but is really what He has revealed Himself to be; He is one we may depend upon, in whom and by whom we cannot be deceived."[99]

10. None compare to God's wisdom. "Who would not fear thee, O King of nations? for to thee doth it appertain: forasmuch as among all the wise men of the nations, and in all their kingdoms, there is none like unto thee" (Jeremiah 10:7).

The bottom line: None compares to God in any respect. And "this God is our God for ever and ever; he will be our guide even to the end" (Psalm 48:14 NIV). Hallelujah!

**"What is the glory of the greatest prince or potentate, compared with the glory of him whose kingdom rules over all?"**[100]—Matthew Henry

24

"Where Did You Come From and Where Are You Going?"

Sarai's bitterness toward Hagar incited Hagar to run away, not knowing where to go, prompting the question to her by God, "Where did you come from and where are you going?" (Genesis 16:8 AMP). The question applies to the many meandering in life without purpose and direction.

How might peace, hope, and purpose be known? It takes four things.

1. A self to live with. A change of who a man is on the inside is required. Sin has marred God's intent (design) for man, leaving him miserable, captive to sin, hopeless, and wandering in the dark. Left to himself, the quest for meaning and purpose is futile.

2. A faith to live by. God says, "I'll give you a new heart, put a new spirit in you. I'll remove the stone heart from your body and replace it with a heart that's God-willed, not self-willed. I'll put my Spirit in you and make it possible for you to do what I tell you and live by my commands" (Ezekiel 36:26 MSG). This new heart (a Brand New You) and fresh start in life are afforded by Christ instantly at the moment of salvation through repentance of sin and confession of Christ as Lord and Savior (John 1:12). "When someone becomes a Christian, he becomes a brand new person inside. He is not the same anymore. A new life [of new meaning, purpose, and joy] has begun!" (2 Corinthians 5:17 TLB).

Apart from a personal relationship with Jesus Christ, life is empty and meaningless, resulting in depression, despair, and defeat that may ultimately lead to suicide. Note that there is a hole in our hearts that can only be filled with Christ. A round peg cannot fit in a square hole. Nothing can be substituted for personal faith in Christ Jesus. Just ask Solomon (Ecclesiastes 2:17).

3. A purpose to live for. Coupled with a self to live with and a faith to live by, there must be a purpose to live for. The invisible (eternal) in man, the soul, cannot be satisfied with the visible (temporal) of earth. God made man with personal design and

purpose. The Bible says, "The plans of the Lord stand forever. The plans of His heart stand through the future of all people" (Psalm 33:11 NLV). The Lord states, "I say this because I know what I have planned for you....I have good plans for you. I don't plan to hurt you. I plan to give you hope and a good future" (Jeremiah 29:11 ICB).

Lucado says, "You weren't an accident. You weren't mass-produced. You aren't an assembly-line product. You were deliberately planned, specifically gifted, and lovingly positioned on the Earth by the Master Craftsman." Happiness and meaning are linked to the Master's blueprint for one's life. Charles Stanley asserts, "The one supreme business of life is to find God's plan for your life and live it."

4. A future to look to. "Here on earth we don't have a city that lasts forever. But we are waiting for the city that we will have in the future" (Hebrews 13:14 ERV). Fulfillment, happiness, and meaning in life are inextricably tied to the hope of Heaven, where sorrows and troubles are unknown, perfect health is experienced, family and friends are reunited, and King Jesus sits on the throne. Such hope boosts perseverance in dark and difficult times, being a strong anchor to the soul (Hebrews 6:19). The person who does not possess this hope is 'to be pitied more than all men' (1 Corinthians 15:19).

**"Without God, life has no purpose, and without purpose, life has no meaning. Without meaning, life has no significance or hope."—Rick Warren.**

## 25

### "Who Put Wisdom in the Heart or Gave the Mind Understanding?"

"Who put wisdom in the heart or gave the mind understanding?" (Job 38:36 CSB). The question by God was rhetorically posed to show Job that he didn't qualify to criticize the One who was the root of all knowledge.

The question clarifies the source of wisdom (insight, judgment, discernment, understanding of the truth of the promises of God[101], and guidance to govern life) as being solely God, who bestows it through various means. Solomon says, "*All* wisdom comes from the LORD, and so do common sense and understanding" (Proverbs 2:6 CEV). Lawson said, "Experience, however long, observation, however close, human teaching, however skillful, can do nothing to supply us with true knowledge, without the influence of that Spirit which rested upon Christ as a Spirit of wisdom and understanding, and which is given by him to all his followers in their measure."[102]

*Wisdom is beneficial.* An acquisition of divine wisdom is the foundation of a sturdy house to live for life (Matthew 7:24–25).

1. Wisdom clarifies what is truth.

2. Wisdom enables the right choices.

3. Wisdom benefits life with "length of days," "riches," "honor," "pleasantness," "peace," "life," contentment and happiness (Proverbs 3:14–18).

4. Wisdom makes powerful its possessor; the more of it that is gained, the greater will be the strength (Colossians 1:9–11). Matthew Henry asserts, "A wise man will compass that by his wisdom which a strong man cannot affect by force of arms. The spirit is strengthened both for the spiritual work and the spiritual warfare by true wisdom."[103] Wisdom makes a person stronger than his adversaries (stronger than their evil schemes and attacks, nuclear missiles, and cannons), however inferior he may be in other respects.[104]

5. Wisdom gathered, digested, and applied throughout life bears benefit in old age. "Thy latter end should greatly increase" (Job 8:7). Daniel had wisdom in the latter end (when over 80 years old) to govern 120 provinces in the kingdom during the reign of King Darius (Daniel 6:1–3). Job states, "With the ancient [aged; elderly] is wisdom; and in length of days [long life] understanding" (Job 12:12). Mature wisdom (that which comes from a lifetime devoted to God, study of the Scripture, and acquired knowledge)

enables "increased" profitability to God, His people and causes, in old age.

6. Its possession is better than gold (Proverbs 16:16) and to be desired above that of rubies (Proverbs 3:14; 8:11). "What wisdom thus effects, riches cannot."[105] Gold is good, but wisdom is better. "To know Christ in the heart as a Savior, in the mind as a Teacher, in the life as a Pattern, and in all things as a King—this is wisdom. It is the fear of the Lord, the love of His law, faith in His Cross, the power of His Spirit, the hope in His Word."[106] In contrast to that, gold is not even in the ballpark.

"Happy is the man that findeth wisdom" (Proverbs 3:13). Seek it. The Bible offers great encouragement to its seeker, saying, "If you do not have wisdom, ask God for it. He is always ready to give it to you and will never say you are wrong for asking" (James 1:5 NLV). See 2 Chronicles 1:7–10. Find it. Keep it. Increase it. Share it. Pray that others will acquire it. Paul prayed, "that the God of our Lord Jesus Christ, the Father of glory, may give unto you [the reader] the spirit of wisdom and revelation in the knowledge of Him: The eyes of your understanding being enlightened; that ye may know what is the hope of his calling, and what the riches of the glory of his inheritance in the saints" (Ephesians 1:17–18).

**"For the things which make a man and woman truly rich and bring real joy and happiness, money is a worthless currency. Their price is wisdom."**[107]—K. T. Aitken.

## 26
### "What Is This That Thou Hast Done?"

"What is this that thou hast done?" (Genesis 3:13). Adam and Eve were ignorant of the momentous consequences of their sin.

1. They knew not that it would be the mother of all sin, causing not just physical death but, even worse, spiritual death (separation) from God for everyone. "When Adam sinned, sin entered the world. Adam's sin brought death, so death spread to everyone, for everyone sinned" (Romans 5:12 NLT).

2. They knew not it would usher evil, suffering, and sorrow into the world.

3. They knew not that its remedy would cost God His only Son and that Son His life through the death of a Cross (John 3:16). God's question, "What is this that thou hast done?" was to awaken Adam and Eve to the severe implications of their sin.

To him who sins, the Lord asks, "What is this that thou hast done?" Why? It prompts candid acknowledgment of the sin committed, honest reflection upon its ugliness and far-reaching consequences, and, hopefully, repentance.

All the Devil's apples have worms. "You will harvest what you plant" (Galatians 6:7 CEV). The serious contemplation of a sin's hideousness, its reproach to God, and its disparaging and destructive repercussions provides a convincing reason to turn away from it.

**"Be killing sin, or it will be killing you."—John Owen.**

## 27
### "Why Are You Angry?"

"Then the Lord said to Cain, "Why are you angry?" (Genesis 4:6 ESV). God's acceptance of Abel's offering and rejection of Cain's agitated Cain, flaring up his anger.

Anger at God implies that He is unjust, unfair, and uncaring. But the Bible says, "Righteousness and judgment are the habitation of his throne" (Psalm 97:2). God's fairness, rightness, and justness are incontestable.

Says Spurgeon, "There He abides, He never departs from strict justice and right, His throne is fixed upon the rock of eternal holiness. Righteousness is His immutable attribute, and judgment marks His every act. What though we cannot see or understand what He doeth, yet we are sure that He will do no wrong to us or any of His creatures."[108] Horder said, "We are not far-sighted enough to see how the ways of God are just and true. Some of them, because we see only a part, appear neither just nor true. But then we see only a fragment, and you cannot judge by a fragment any more than you can judge a house from a single brick. But we see enough of order, of law, of regularity, to be assured that, when the whole is revealed, we shall cry, 'Just and true are Thy ways, O thou King of saints.'"[109] Matthew Henry remarked, "The rules are just, and therefore His ways, according to those rules, must needs be equal."[110]

'His way is in the sea, and His path in the great waters, and His footsteps are not known' (Psalm 77:19). God's footsteps "in the sea" of man's adversities are inscrutable. The finite mind is incapable of understanding God's infinite plan and ways. "God's way is incomprehensible, though undoubtedly right: in His holiness lies the answer to the enigmas [conundrums, puzzlements]."[111]

The actions of God defy human comprehension and will remain, in part, a mystery until He chooses to interpret them. It is known that God promises to take the unexplainable, the bad and sad, seemingly senseless and unfair, and supernaturally use them for good in the lives of His children (Romans 8:28). This we accept by faith. Jerry Bridges says, "Confidence in the sovereignty of God in all that affects us is crucial to our trusting Him."[112]

"**[God] is doing right all the while, and in the end, he will show that in all cases he has been righteous.**"[113]—W. S. Plumer

## 28

### "To What Purpose Is the Multitude of Your Sacrifices unto Me?"

"To what purpose is the multitude of your sacrifices unto Me?" (Isaiah 1:11). Israel had become so sordid in sin that God addressed them as "rulers of Sodom [and] people of Gomorrah" (Isaiah 1:10). "Their hearts were empty of true devotion."[114] And their hands were polluted with grievous sin for which there was no repentance (Isaiah 1:6). Simeon says, "The Jews were prone to rest in compliance with the ceremonial law."[115] God, therefore, justly rejected their shallow and superficial religious observances, devotion, and worship.

The lesson. Outward religious observances and sacrifices are invalid apart from inward consecration to God.[116] No sacrifice compensates for the lack of obedience and devotion. Jesus said, "And to love him with all the heart, and with all the understanding, and with all the soul, and with all the strength, and to love his neighbour as himself, is more than all whole burnt offerings and sacrifices" (Mark 12:33). Matthew Henry asserts, "The most pompous and costly devotions of wicked people, without a thorough reformation of the heart and life, are so far from being acceptable to God, that really, they are an abomination to Him. Sacrifice, without obedience, is a jest, an affront and provocation to God."[117]

Samuel said, "Hath the Lord as great delight in burnt offerings and sacrifices, as in obeying the voice of the Lord? Behold, to obey is better than sacrifice, and to hearken than the fat of rams" (1 Samuel 15:22). Spurgeon, who thought these words by Samuel were "worthy to be printed in letters of gold,"[118] said, "Give as God has given to you, but remember God acts as well as gives. 'Go thou and do likewise.' Sacrifice, but also obey."[119]

Acceptable worship, service, and offerings, first, flow from clean "cups" (Matthew 23:26), cups washed white as snow inside-out through the blood of Christ. Prayers of the wicked, saith Jeremy Taylor, are likened to "the breath of corrupted lungs: God turns away from such unwholesome breathings." Second, it flows from hearts devoted and dedicated to Christ. First, bring the offering of surrender of self and holy submission, and be purified from sin, then, that of gifts. See Malachi 3:2.

**"Mere external religion is ever a cloak to cover iniquity. The conscience of a believer may become so seared that a person can practice religion while yet living in sin."[120]—W. E. Vine.**

## 29

## "How Long Wilt Thou Refuse to Humble Thyself Before Me?"

"How long wilt thou refuse to humble thyself before Me?" (Exodus 10:3). God's question, voiced through Moses, to Pharoah, applies to all who arrogantly and stubbornly refuse to bow in reverent submission to God's authority.

"Humble yourselves, therefore, under the mighty hand of God so that at the proper time He may exalt you" (1 Peter 5:6 ESV). Andrew Murray said, "Humility is the displacement of self by the enthronement of God"[121] and that it is "the disposition which prepares the soul for living on trust."[122]

1. The source of humility. The unknown author of *The Cloud of Unknowing* asserts that two things bring about humility in us: knowledge of our filth, wretchedness, and frailty (Isaiah 6:5) and knowledge of the glory of God, the "overabundant love and worthiness of God Himself, in view of which all nature quakes, all scholars are fools, and all saints and angels blind."

2. The signs of humility. True humility is expressed through sincere sorrow and grief for sins committed, by confession and repentance. It is expressed through acknowledgment of the bankruptcy of the soul ("in me...dwelleth no good thing"; "I am poor and needy"). It is exhibited through the prostration of self in surrender and obedience to the Lordship of Christ. It is manifested in the life that says, "He must increase, but I must decrease" (John 3:30). It is shown through submission to the circumstances in life, the good and bad, that God deems best. It is demonstrated through unending gratitude to Christ for the salvation He brought and wrought and His manifold goodness. It is portrayed through utter reliability upon the Lord for every care and need. The humble acknowledge the inability to cope with life's temptations, failures, pains, trials, and challenges apart from God's help and, therefore, seek it.

3. The spurning of humility. What causes man to balk at the call to humility, as did Pharoah? The love of sin. The pursuit of

self-made dreams. The refusal to believe in the sovereignty of God and His rule over their lives. The impact it would have on their social life, companionship, or political status. An unwillingness to surrender absolute control of their life to God. A highly inflated view of self (arrogance). "The wicked in his proud countenance does not seek God; God is in none of his thoughts" (Psalm 10:4 NKJV). C. S. Lewis said, "As long as you are proud, you cannot know God."[123]

4. The smack of pride. The proud will be humbled. "The arrogance of man will be brought low and human pride humbled; the LORD alone will be exalted in that day" (Isaiah 2:17 NIV). Matthew Henry said, "Men cannot punish pride, but either admire it or fear it, and therefore God will take the punishing of it into His own hands. Let Him alone to deal with proud men."[124] Man can either humble himself before God or be humbled by God. Just ask Pharaoh.

A kite flying high in the sky moved as stately as a person of royalty. Looking down with contempt at that below, it said, "What a superior being I am now! None has ever ascended as high as I. All are inferior to me." The kite shook its head in sneers and wagged its tail in pious arrogance as it moved onward and upward, expecting everything to make way for it. Then suddenly, the string broke, causing the kite's speedy descent and severe hurt in the fall.[125] With pride, what goes up always comes down. "Pride goeth before destruction, and a haughty spirit before a fall" (Proverbs 16:18).

"How long wilt thou refuse to humble thyself before Me?"

"Humility makes us ready to be blessed by the God of all grace."[126]—C. H. Spurgeon.

## 30

## "Is It a Time for You Yourselves to Live in Your Paneled Houses, While This House Lies in Ruins?"

"Is it a time for you yourselves to live in your paneled [luxurious] houses, while this house lies in ruins?" (Haggai 1:4 CSB). Instead of rebuilding the Temple, the people used their money to build elaborate, luxurious homes. "They preferred the material and temporal to the spiritual and religious."[127] The question prompted them to see their fault and prodded them to build the house of God (Haggai 1:14). Note, that the Jews are not reprimanded for building their own homes but for not building the house of God at the same time.[128]

The question may apply not just to the renovation or construction of the church building but to the Lord's work in general. It may be rendered in several ways: Is it a time for Christians to pursue earthly ambitions and pleasures while the work of God goes undone? Is it a time for the saved to sit at ease in Zion when spiritual darkness and decay are ever increasing? Is it a time for slothfulness among the saints when untold millions need the Gospel locally and globally? In whatever form the question is phrased, it condemns the neglect of Christian duty and support of the church for personal pursuits and sensual gratification.

To all guilty of neglecting the spiritual for love of the material, God says, "Consider your ways"—ponder the sin and its subsequent consequences, repent, and make God's interests and glory the priority of life (Haggai 1:5–6; Psalm 119:59).

"If men are selfish and keep their wealth to themselves, and rob God of His portion, they shall not prosper, or if they do, no blessing shall come of it."[129]—C. H. Spurgeon.

## 31
### "Why Do You Complain?"

"Why do you complain, Jacob?" (Isaiah 40:27 NIV). In light of the Israelites' knowledge of God, His faithfulness and lovingkindness and power, past works, and miracles, how could they have thought that He had forgotten them, was unaware of them, or was unable to help them? The question asks the reason for their foolish and unjust complaint.

The remembrance of four unchanging things prevents wrongful accusations against God.

1. God never grows weary or tired in caring for His own (Isaiah 40:28). If God grew tired and fainted, the universe would collapse, resulting in utter chaos, and man's existence would cease. But that will never happen, for He is the Creator, who neither sleeps nor slumbers (Psalm 121). Friends may grow tired of our infirmity and cease to care, but not God.

2. God is not to be compared to the young and strong who grow tired and fall (Isaiah 40:30). "Mortality means fickleness and caprice. His Name means constancy, faithfulness."[130]

3. God's ways are unsearchable and, at times, unknowable (Isaiah 40:29). Says George Horne, "The 'greatness' of Jehovah, whether we consider it as relating to His essence or His works, is never to be fully comprehended by His saints, whose delight it is to contemplate 'the breadth, and length, and depth, and height,' (Ephesians 3:18), the extent and duration of His being and His kingdom, the profundity of His counsels, and the sublimity of His power and glory. These are the inexhaustible subjects of divine meditation, transmitted from age to age."[131]

4. God keeps His Word. He said, "I will never leave thee nor forsake thee," and He can't lie. Though crushed and broken, the troubled soul can say with the Holy Spirit's help, "Though He slay me, yet will I trust in Him." What it must not do is to complain like the Israelites, accusing God of abandonment and uncaring concern.

"The man that measures things by the circumstances of the hour is filled with fear; the man who sees Jehovah enthroned and governing has no panic."—G. Campbell Morgan.

## 32

## "Have You Eaten from the Tree of Which I Told You Not to Eat?"

"Have you eaten from the tree of which I told you not to eat?" (Genesis 3:11 NLV). The divine inquiry is meant to prod Adam into confessing his guilt for the wrong he had done. Instead, Adam blames Eve and God for giving her to him (Genesis 3:12).

People tend to justify their sin by attributing it to the circumstances, the actions of others, upbringing, genes, and even God. But all such blame, as with Adam, will be rejected. God holds man personally accountable for his actions. The Bible says, "There is nothing that can be hid from God; everything in all creation is exposed and lies open before his eyes. And it is to him that we must all give an account of ourselves" (Hebrews 4:13 GNT).

When the voice of God awakens the conscience to a sin done, at once, own up to it and confess it. Don't excuse it. Don't justify it. Don't deflect blame to another for it. Don't deny it. But own it. Phillip Brooks asserts, "The only hope for any of us is in a perfectly honest manliness to claim our sins. 'I did it, I did it,' let me say of all my wickedness. Let me refuse to listen for one moment to any voice which would make my sins less mine."[132]

The frank admittance of sin and repentance for it ("Against Thee, Thee only, *have I sinned*," Psalm 51:3–4) is the first step to the gracious forgiveness of God (1 John 1:9–10). Matthew Henry said, "Though God knows all our sins, yet He will know them from us, and requires from us an ingenuous confession of them."[133] Says Spurgeon, "When the soul determines to lay low and plead guilty, absolution is near at hand."[134]

"Life-changing repentance begins where blame shifting ends."—Timothy Keller.

## 33

### "How Shall I Put Thee Among the Children?"

"How shall I put thee among the children?" (Jeremiah 3:19). Calvin makes it, "How can the race of Abraham be propagated again, being as it were dead?" Backslidden Israel's only means of restoration was to acknowledge God as "Father" and not to turn away from Him again. "Thou shalt call me, My father; and shalt not turn away from me" (Jeremiah 3:19).

How can a holy and righteous God allow transgressors and rebellious sinners into His royal family? How might the mighty chasm, created by sin, that separates man from God be forded? How might the just penalty of sin, eternal death, be resolved? How can loathsome, wretched man gain access to the presence of the righteous king?

The difficulty seems insurmountable. But God sovereignly, mercifully, and lovingly overcame it. He made a way when there was no way, though costly and woefully undeserved, for man to be reconciled to Himself and be made "the children of God." The Bible says, "When we were utterly helpless, with no way of escape, Christ came at just the right time and died for us sinners who had no use for him" (Romans 5:6 TLB). Christ's death at Calvary made possible the forgiveness and salvation of every sinner (that includes you) who confesses Christ as Lord and Savior (Romans 10:13; 1 Peter 1:18–20).

> It is the voice of Jesus that I hear;
> His are the hands stretched out to draw me near,
> And His the blood that can for all atone
> And set me faultless there before the throne.
> — S. J. Stone (1866)

The Duke of Argyll, facing punishment for rebellion in Scotland, was brought before James the Second, who said to him, "You know that it is in my power to pardon you?" Purportedly, the Duke replied, "It may be in your power, but it is not in your nature to forgive." The words cost him his life.

Thankfully, it is in the power and nature of God to forgive and save us and to make us His beloved children. The Bible says, "Behold, what manner of love the Father hath bestowed upon us, that we should be called the sons of God" (1 John 3:1). Spurgeon states that upon conversion, "We are as much loved as the children. We are treated as the children. We are forgiven as a father forgives his children. We are clothed, fed, and housed as children. We are taught, ruled, and chastened as children. We are honored and enriched as children."[135] And, "We are placed under filial obligation to love, honor, obey, and serve our Father."[136] Hallelujah! Oh, what a Savior who made this divine transaction and transformation possible!

"To those who question the possibility of their own salvation, God is able."[137]—Charles Simeon.

## 34

### "Wilt Thou Not from This Time Cry unto Me, My Father, Thou Art The Guide of My Youth?"

"Wilt thou not from this time cry unto me, My father, thou art the guide of my youth?" (Jeremiah 3:4). Impudently, in an attempt to abate the wrath of God, Israel uses hypocritical affection to address Him while practicing grievous sin (idol worship). God scorned and chided it. Note, that Jesus warns of heartless and insincere worship in the church, saying, "This people draweth nigh unto me with their mouth, and honoureth me with their lips; but their heart is far from me. But in vain they do worship Me, teaching for doctrines the commandments of men" (Matthew 15:8–9).

"Thou art the guide of my youth." It is prudent for young people to make God their guide and companion for several reasons.

1. Because the path of duty and what's best is often complex and challenging to find. Solomon advises, "Seek his will in all you do, and he will show you which path to take" (Proverbs 3:6 NLT).

2. Because the corrupt will seek their downfall. David asserts, "The wicked watcheth the righteous, and seeketh to slay him" (Psalm 37:32). Solomon says evil men seek to spoil and destroy the righteous (Proverbs 24:15).

3. Because the Devil has laid out landmines. David prayed as all youth ought, "Keep me from the snares which they have laid for

me, and the traps of the workers of iniquity" (Psalm 141:9 KJ21). Benson says, "Keep me from being taken in it: give me to discover and evade it."[138]

4. Because the heart's inclinations are evil and cannot be trusted. Jeremiah says, "The heart is deceitful above all things, and desperately wicked: who can know it?" (Jeremiah 17:9). Solomon says, "There is a way which seemeth right unto a man, but the end thereof are the ways of death" (Proverbs 14:12).

5. Because the way out of despair, sorrow, and defeat cannot be found elsewhere. The Bible says, "God will help those who live in darkness, in the fear of death. He will guide us into the path that goes toward peace" (Luke 1:79 ICB).

6. Because none other than Christ can authoritatively instruct a person how to get off the broad road that leads to destruction (Hell) and get on the narrow road that leads to life (Heaven). He said, "Go in through the narrow gate. The gate to destruction is wide, and the road that leads there is easy to follow. A lot of people go through that gate. But the gate to life is very narrow. The road that leads there is so hard to follow that only a few people find it" (Matthew 7:13–14 CEV). See John 5:40.

Following Christ is the sanest decision a youth (or adult) can make (Ecclesiastes 12:1). They who make the decision can say with the psalmist, "Thou shalt guide me with thy counsel, and afterward receive me to glory" (Psalm 73:24).

"He is infinitely wise and cannot lead you astray. He has conducted millions, and 'the wayfaring man, though a fool, has not erred' under His direction."[139]—William Jay.

## 35

### "Who Would Set the Briers and Thorns Against Me in Battle?"

"Who would set the briers and thorns against me in battle? I would go through them, I would burn them together" (Isaiah 27:4).

God uses the metaphor of briers and thorns to convey His enemy's weakness.

Man's effort to deter the wrath of Almighty God against their sin is a mere hedge of briers and thorns. "I would go through them, I would burn them together," saith the Lord (Isaiah 27:4). "Who can stand before his indignation? And who can abide in the fierceness of his anger?" (Nahum 1:6). "It is a terrifying thing to fall into the hands of the living God" (Hebrews 10:31 LSB). In the ISV, Isaiah 45:9 says, "Woe to the one who quarrels with his Maker." It's ludicrous to fight God, for He always wins.

Though God can easily defeat His enemies, He longs for them to make peace with Him. He says, "Let him take hold of my strength, that he may make peace with me; and he shall make peace with me" (Isaiah 27:5). A divine invitation is extended to be reconciled with God through that of His own doing, not man's ("my strength").

What a beautiful Old Testament presentation of the wondrous New Testament offering of salvation made possible through Christ Jesus, "the power [strength] of God" (1 Corinthians 1:24). Paul said, "It was through what his Son did that God cleared a path for everything to come to him—all things in heaven and on earth—for Christ's death on the cross has made peace with God for all by his blood" (Colossians 1:20 TLB).

Chalmers asserts, "We read of a mighty strength that had to be put forth in the work of a sinner's justification. Just in proportion to the weight and magnitude of the obstacle was the greatness of that strength which the Savior put forth in the mighty work of moving it away."[140] The Psalmist says, "God answers his anointed one from his heavenly sanctuary, answering with mighty acts of salvation achieved by his strong hand" (Psalm 20:6 CEB).

The worst of God's enemies, the most wretched and depraved, may most assuredly make peace with Him by complying with the stated condition, that of repentance and faith in Christ (Acts 20:21). Paul states, "We are made right with God by placing our faith in Jesus Christ. And this is true for everyone who believes, no matter who we are" (Romans 3:22 NLT). Says Vance Havner, "Not everyone who has made peace with God has realized the peace of God."

**"To be convinced in our hearts that we have forgiveness of sins and peace with God by grace alone is the hardest thing."**—Martin Luther.

## 36

### "Why Then Is This People…Slidden Back by a Perpetual Backsliding?"

"Why then is this people of Jerusalem slidden back by a perpetual backsliding [continual faithlessness]? They hold fast deceit, they refuse to return" (Jeremiah 8:5). The question is as timely today as when first asked of the nation Israel.

Backsliding is a departure from God to satisfy the worldly, lustful desires of the heart. It's not to be equated with a spiritual stumble that is only momentary.

Prompters to backsliding include improper associations (2 Corinthians 6:14), opposition and persecution from friends and family for living the Christian life (John 16:33), disappointment in a Christian we admired (1 Peter 2:21), unconfessed sin (Psalm 38:3–6), severe hardship and sorrow that despairs and discourages (Deuteronomy 1:27–36), neglect of abiding fellowship with Christ (John 15:4), persistent absenteeism from the church (Hebrews 10:25), change in priorities from the spiritual to the material (Matthew 6:33), busyness (Luke 9:57–62), habitual indulgence in a known sin (Song of Solomon 2:15), worldly pursuits (Philippians 2:21), 'weights' that easily entangle (Hebrews 12:1), unconcern for the lost (Acts 1:8), egotism (Proverbs 16:18), infrequent and unpassionate prayer (Luke 18:1), acts of moral impurity (Isaiah 52:11) and false teachers (Colossians 2:8).

Turning from God brings sorrow, havoc, unrest ("buyer's remorse"), and forfeiture of untold blessings. Packer wrote, "Unregenerate apostates are often cheerful souls, but backsliding

Christians are always miserable."[141] Says Spurgeon, "Remember that if you are a child of God, you will never be happy in sin."[142]

"Remember therefore from where you have fallen; repent and do the first works" (Revelation 2:5 NKJV).

*Remember* the spiritually healthy estate from which you have fallen. "Let's examine and probe our ways, and turn back to the LORD" (Lamentations 3:40 CSB). With desperation, cry out to God with Job, "Oh that I were as in months past" (Job 29:2).

*Repent,* turn away not just from the sins that caused the fall, but all sins. Jesus said, "If we confess our sins, he is faithful and just to forgive us our sins, and to cleanse us from all unrighteousness" (1 John 1:9). And then,

*Return,* "do the first works." Get back to communion with God, back to the Bible, back to the prayer closet, back to your "first love," back to working for God as you formerly did, back to giving, back to witnessing, and back to faithfulness to the church. "Return, ye backsliding children, and I will heal your backslidings" (Jeremiah 3:22). Bunyan said, "A returning penitent, though formerly bad as the worst of men, may by grace become as good as the best."[143]

> I've wandered far away from God;
>   Now I'm coming home.
> The paths of sin too long I've trod;
>   Lord, I'm coming home.
>                           – William J. Kirkpatrick (1892)

"If you want to know how to backslide, leave off going forward. Cease going upward, and you will go downward of necessity. You can never stand still."—C. H. Spurgeon.

## 37

### "No Man Repented Him of His Wickedness, Saying, What Have I Done?"

"No man repented him of his wickedness, saying, What have I done? everyone turned to his course, as the horse rusheth into the battle" (Jeremiah 8:6). With the reprimand of God over their sin ignored, the Israelites, without so much as asking, "What have I done?" continued in it. Man still fails to ask the question concerning the counsel and commandments of God.

*The unsaved fail to ask it.* None ask, upon rejection of Christ, "What have I done?" to the estate of their soul, future, influence, happiness, and hope of eternal life. Says Spurgeon, "There will be a time when you will ask the question, but it will be too late. If you only knew what they feel and could see what they endure, who have lost opportunity and lost themselves, you would, ere too late, pause and ask, 'What have I done?' As immortal spirits, bound for endless weal or woe, fly ye to Christ, seek for mercy at His hand, trust in Him, and be saved."[144]

*The religionists fail to ask it.* They fail to ask, "What have I done?" in trusting personal efforts and religious observances rather than the blood of the Lord Jesus Christ for the remission of sins.

*The Christian fails to ask it.* In response to God's rebuke of sin and call to repentance, instead of asking, "What have I done?" they rush out of His presence without considering their rebellious conduct and condition of heart.

*The worldly fail to ask it.* Amidst the rush and push for success, pleasure, fame, and wealth, the worldly fail to ask, "What have I done?" until it is often too late. How sad it is to live the whole of your life only to discover that the ladder you climbed was leaning against the wrong wall.

Stop in your tracks and ask, "What have I done?" with Jesus Christ, the offer of salvation, submission to His Lordship, the Bible, the church, His plan, and the commandments. In light of the answer, make confession and amendment of life.

"True repentance brings in a serious and impartial inquiry into ourselves, *what have we done*, arising from a conviction that we have done amiss."[145]—Matthew Henry

## 38
## "What Is Your Name?"

"'What is your name?' He said, 'Jacob'" (Genesis 32:27 WEB). Divulging that his name was Jacob revealed his character. He was a liar, cheater, trickster, and deceiver who had deceived his brother twice. Jacob's brother, Esau, said, "Jacob is the right name for him. He has tricked me these two times" (Genesis 27:36 NCV).

The divine encounter resulted in a radical change in Jacob's nature; no longer would he be a manipulator and liar but a new man with a new name, and destiny. The new name would bear witness to the changed man he had become. At the moment of salvation, a mighty, miraculous change occurs in the sinner's life. The Bible says, "When someone becomes a Christian, he becomes a brand-new person inside. He is not the same anymore. A new life has begun!" (2 Corinthians 5:17 TLB).

What is your name? Is it lust? Is it alcohol? Is it spiritual indifference? Is it greed? Is it fame? Is it money? Is it deception, like Jacob? Is it anger? Is it cowardice? Is it pornography? Is it immorality? Beneath the given name, what is your real name?[146] Christ stands ready to change it to that of holy, righteous, honorable, faithful, trustworthy, forgiven, and redeemed. "And he that sat upon the throne said, Behold, I make all things new" (Revelation 21:5). That newness is so encompassing that a new believer said, "Either the world is altered, or else I am."

"Thy name shall be called no more Jacob" (Genesis 32:28). No more Jacob, the liar, deceiver, and manipulator. But it shall be Israel, "God's fighter" and man of honor.

*What is your name?* Does it need to be changed to "Israel"?

**"Willpower does not change men. Time does not change men. Christ does."**—Henry Drummond.

## 39
## "In What Way Have You Loved Us?"

"I have loved you, saith the LORD. Yet ye say, Wherein hast Thou loved us?" (Malachi 1:2). The Israelites questioned God's love and favor, though it always was manifested to them, by saying, 'You say you love us. In what ways have you loved us?' The question is asked by many. How might it be answered? In what ways has God loved us? They are limitless.

1. By the substitutionary death of Christ at Calvary to save man from the condemnation of sin. The Bible says, "For God so loved the world, that he gave his only begotten Son, that whosoever believeth in him should not perish, but have everlasting life" (John 3:16 KJ21). "But God shows his love for us in that while we were still sinners, Christ died for us" (Romans 5:8 ESV). "Greater love hath no man than this, that a man lay down his life for his friends" (John 15:13). D. A. Carson said, "Christians have learned that when there seems to be no other evidence of God's love, they cannot escape the cross."[147]

2. By making us His children. "Behold, what manner of love the Father hath bestowed upon us, that we should be called the sons of God" (1 John 3:1). "I will be a Father unto you, and ye shall be My sons and daughters, saith the Lord Almighty" (2 Corinthians 6:18 GNV).

3. By not giving us what is deserved. God pours out blessings and benefits when we deserve the wrath of His judgment. "He hath not dealt with us after our sins, Nor rewarded us after our iniquities. For as the heavens are high above the earth, So great is his lovingkindness toward them that fear him. As far as the east is from the west, So far hath he removed our transgressions from us" (Psalms 103:10–12 ASV).

4. By the forgiveness of our sin. "You are the Lord our God. You show us your tender love. You forgive us" (Daniel 9:9 NIRV). God's enduring and patient love makes forgiveness possible, no matter how often requested (Psalm 86:15). C. S. Lewis remarked, "God's love is not wearied by our sins and is relentless

in its determination that we be cured at whatever cost to Him or us."

5. By hearing our prayers. God expresses love for us by hearing and answering prayer. "He will call on me, and I will answer him" (Psalm 91:15 NIV).

6. By correcting us when we do wrong. "God punishes us for our good so we will be holy as He is holy" (Hebrews 12:10 NLV). Love punishes the person loved for a wrong done to correct conduct and prevent future hurt.

7. By divine orchestration of our life. God's love is shown in His excellent plan for us. "The Lord will fulfill his purpose for me; your steadfast love, O Lord, endures forever. Do not forsake the work of your hands" (Psalm 138:8 ESV). "For I know the plans that I have for you,' declares the Lord, 'plans for well-being, and not for calamity, in order to give you a future and a hope" (Jeremiah 29:11 ISV).

8. By repeatedly telling of His love for us in the Bible. God's love is a fact, believed or not. "Though the mountains be shaken and the hills be removed, yet My unfailing love for you will not be shaken...says the LORD" (Isaiah 54:10 NIV) and "I will not take my love from him, nor will I ever betray my faithfulness" (Psalm 89:33 NIV).

9. By preparing Heaven for us. "And if I go and prepare a place for you, I will come again and will take you to myself, that where I am you may be also" (John 14:3 ESV). God wouldn't have made Heaven for us if God didn't love us.

10. By singing over us in joy. "The Lord your God is in your midst, a mighty one who will save; he will rejoice over you with gladness; he will quiet you by his love; he will exult over you with loud singing" (Zephaniah 3:17 ESV).

11. By our very life itself. Thomas Merton said, "Every breath we draw is a gift of God's love; every moment of existence is a grace." Paul states, "He is before all things, and by him all things hold together" (Colossians 1:17 CSB).

12. By His faithfulness to protect from harm, sustain in trial, supply need, and calm every sorrow. "Certainly the faithful love of the Lord hasn't ended; certainly God's compassion isn't through! They are renewed every morning. Great is your faithfulness" (Lamentations 3:22–23 CEB).

> O love of God, how rich and pure!
>    How measureless and strong!
> It shall forevermore endure—
>    The saints' and angels' song.
> – Frederick M. Lehman (1917)

"Let them give thanks to the LORD for his faithful love" (Psalm 107:31 CSB).

**"The great thing to remember is that though our feelings come and go, God's love for us does not."**—C. S. Lewis.

## 40

### "How Wilt Thou Do in the Swelling of Jordan?"

"If in the land of peace, wherein thou trustedst, they wearied thee, then how wilt thou do in the swelling of Jordan?" (Jeremiah 12:5b). If the petty trials, despite what was trusted, tripped Jeremiah up, how does he expect to withstand the catastrophic ones to come.

The same may be asked of you. If trusted human reliance and resources (cold and dry religion, personal courage and stamina, worldly philosophy, or possessions) failed to prevent you from being beaten down by the troubles, sorrows, temptations, and trials of life, how will they sustain you "in the swelling of Jordan," the hour of death? If you fail to keep up with the "footmen" (relatively minor adversity and affliction) without being overcome, how can you contend successfully with the "horses" (severe trouble and distress that is sure to come) or be ready for the "swelling of Jordan" (death)?

How will you deal with the swelling in Jordan? May it be met with Spurgeon's resolve: "When I come to die, how shall I do in the swelling of the Jordan? I hope I shall do as others have done before me, who have built on the same rock and had the same promises to be their succor. They cried, 'Victory!' So shall I, and after that, die quietly and in peace. If the same transporting scene may not be mine, I will at least lay my head upon my Savior's bosom and breathe my life out gently there."[148] May it be met, saying with Isaac Watts, "It is a great mercy that I have no manner of fear or dread of death. I could, if God pleases, lay my head back and die without terror this afternoon."

How will you meet death? May it be met, saying, with John Pawson, "I know I am dying, but my deathbed is a bed of roses. I have no thorns planted upon my dying pillow. Heaven is already begun!" May it be met, saying with Doddridge, "I am full of confidence. There is a hope set before me; I have fled, I still fly for refuge to that hope. In Him, I trust. In Him, I have strong consolation and shall assuredly be accepted in the beloved of my soul." May it be met saying with Adrian Rogers, "I am at perfect peace."[149]

How will you do in the approaching certain but uncertain (in its how, where, and when) hour of death? Will chilly Jordan be crossed with hope, comfort, confidence, and joyous anticipation because of faith and hope in Jesus Christ, or with fear, trembling, and great forebode because of stubborn unbelief? "Make your preparation for meeting God now," says Truett, "in order that you may be ready for life's end when such end shall come. And when will that end come? It may come before midnight tonight."[150]

How is the preparation to be made? Be washed in the blood of Jesus Christ. Live devotedly and obediently to the Lord's command. Stay at the post of duty to the end. Spurgeon said, "Preparation for death does not mean going alone into the chamber and retiring from the world, but active service, doing the duty of the day in the day. I have frequently thought that no happier place to die in could be found than one's post of duty."[151]

> When I come to the river at the ending of day,
>   When the last winds of sorrow have blown,
> There'll be somebody waiting to show me the way.
>   I won't have to cross Jordan alone.
>
> ~ Thomas Ramsey (1934)

Spurgeon states that when the saint is "dying, and the cold chilly waters of Jordan are gathering about him up to the neck, Jesus puts His arms around him, and cries, 'Fear not, beloved; to die is to be blessed. As the departing saint wades through the stream and the billows gather around him and heart and flesh fail him, the same voice sounds in his ears, 'Fear not; I am with thee; be not dismayed; I am thy God.' Thus strengthened and consoled, the believer is not afraid to die; nay, he is even willing to depart, for since he has seen Jesus as the morning star, he longs to gaze upon Him as the sun in his strength."[152] Amen, and amen.

As Augustine of Hippo was dying, he placed a big placard with Psalm 32 painted in large letters at the foot of his bed. Its wondrous words of God's mercy and forgiveness ministered hope and comfort as he prepared to cross chilly Jordan. A similar placard may prove consoling in your departure to Heaven.

"How wilt thou do in the swelling of Jordan?"

**"How awful to die out of Christ! How blessed to die in Christ!"**—William Tiptaft

# 41

"Where Were You When I Laid the Earth's Foundations?"

Job's protest of God's justice and fairness is met with a divine reprimand in the form of a question. "Where were you when I laid the earth's foundations?" (Job 38:4 NCB). "Jehovah claims not simply to have been the Framer of the mighty fabric of the globe but to have shared the honor of that stupendous achievement with no co-worker. Hence, certainly not with Job."[153] Criswell asserts, "A successful challenge of God's justice would presuppose that

Job, i.e., the challenger, had infinite knowledge of all relevant facts including the very nature of the act of creation itself."[154]

Like Job, we, too, may have moments when God seems unfair, unjust, and uncaring. In such times, remember that the complexity of creation and its maintenance proves beyond doubt the ability of God to faithfully, caringly, and justly govern the steps and circumstances of man's life to the minutest detail (Jeremiah 10:12). Charles Bridges says, "Every particle of the universe glitters with infinite skill."[155]

The Earth is just the right size—any smaller, an atmosphere would be impossible, like Mercury; any more extensive, its atmosphere would contain free hydrogen, like Jupiter. Earth is the only known planet to possess the right combination of gases in its atmosphere to sustain animal, plant, and human life. Earth is the perfect distance from the sun. The planets on either side of Earth, Venus and Mars, are too close to the sun and too far from it to support life as we see it on Earth. Earth's faithful rotation on its axis enables it to be properly warmed and cooled daily. Nature operates by inert, unchanging laws. The earth rotates the same distance every twenty-four hours, the speed of light is consistent, gravity remains the same, and day and night do not cease.[156]

If God can manage the universe's intricacy without error, He can govern man's life flawlessly and wonderfully (Romans 8:28).

**"Our grand effort ought to be to cultivate a loving trust in the Divine character rather than to comprehend the Divine procedure. Comprehend Him we never can."**[157]—Homilist

## 42
### "Where Is…Thy Brother?"

"And the Lord said unto Cain, 'Where is Abel thy brother?' And he said, 'I know not. Am I my brother's keeper?'" (Genesis 4:9 KJ21). The question challenged Cain to accept responsibility for his brother.[158] But insolently, he refused.

1. To be your Brother's Keeper means to provide for another's needs when it's within your means. Solomon says, "Don't withhold good from someone entitled to it when you have in hand the power to do it" (Proverbs 3:27 CJB).

Matthew Henry says, "A charitable concern for our brethren, as their keepers, is a great duty, which is strictly required of us but is generally neglected by us. Those who are unconcerned in the affairs of their brethren and take no care, when they have the opportunity, to prevent their hurt in their bodies, goods, or good name, especially in their souls, do, in effect, speak Cain's language."[159] Paul declares, "For none of us liveth to himself, and no man dieth to himself" (Romans 14:7).

2. To be your Brother's Keeper is to pursue peace and harmony with him. Paul said, "If it be possible, as much as lieth in you, live peaceably with all men" (Romans 12:18).

3. To be your Brother's Keeper is to apply the Golden Rule toward him. Jesus commands, "Therefore, all things whatsoever ye would that men should do to you, do ye even so to them; for this is the Law and the Prophets" (Matthew 7:12 KJ21).

4. To be your Brother's Keeper is to be governed by God's love for them. Thomson says, "The rights of men to our love and consideration rest upon an act of divine love. Their chartered right to our reverence is in these terms: that God loved them, and sent His Son to be the propitiation for their sins; and the Savior set to it His seal, and signed it with His blood."[160] Says Spurgeon, "Common feelings of humanity should lead every Christian man to feel an interest in the soul of every unsaved man."[161]

5. To be your Brother's Keeper is to bear his burdens and care with him. "Bear ye one another's burdens, and so fulfill the law of Christ" (Galatians 6:2).

6. To be your Brother's Keeper is restrictive in scope. We can challenge, comfort, counsel, and correct one another. We can bear the burdens, pain, and concerns of others. We can pray and lift another from their miry pit. But there are some things no man can do for another. No man can deal with another's sin before God. No

man can repent for another. No man can be saved or obey God for another. No man can stand in the stead of another at the Judgment of God. These things a man must do for himself. Finding another and bringing him to Christ is the height of being your "brother's keeper," but it cannot be done apart from his willingness to come to Christ.

> Am I my brother's keeper?
>   Or serving self alone?
> Are none around me better
>   Since I the way have known?
>
>                         – F. E. Belden (1886)

To whom might you be your "Brother's Keeper" today?

"I charge you because ye are men, and men are all your brothers, born of the same stock, and dwelling beneath the arched roof of the one eternal Father; therefore, care for the souls of others and be, each one of you, his brother's keeper."[162]—C. H. Spurgeon

## 43
### "Who Told You That You Were Naked?"

"Who told you that you were naked?" (Genesis 3:11 NIV). Why is your nakedness now a cause of shame when it never was? How is the garment of innocence and purity with which you were clothed defiled? What happened to the peace and delight you enjoyed? Why did you try to hide from Me? Who caused all this to happen to you? Who told you that you were naked?[163] The question was posed to get Adam and Eve to take personal accountability for and repent of the wrong they had done. G. Hughes said, "God's inquiries are invincible criminations on sinners."

Lessons gleaned from the first sin on earth are numerous.

1. The conscience condemns man when God's law is violated. "If our conscience condemns us, we know that God is greater than our conscience and that he knows everything" (1 John 3:20 GNT). Who told Adam and Eve that they had committed a grievous sin? In truth, nobody did. A sanctified conscience told them. It, undefiled and therefore undisturbed before the sin, was awakened to shame and guilt by the sin.

2. The prototype of all sin is the first sin. "All other sins are copies of it. Unbelief first, then disobedience; then corruption, then self-excusing; then the curse and the expulsion."[164]

3. People sin when enticed subtly and deceitfully by Satan. He who enticed the first couple to sin "was shrewder than any animal of the field" (Genesis 3:1 TLV). "That Satan's temptations are all beguiling, his arguments are all fallacies, his allurements are all cheats; when he speaks fair, believe him not."[165] James says, "Temptation comes from our own desires, which entice us and drag us away. These desires give birth to sinful actions. And when sin is allowed to grow, it gives birth to death" (James 1:14–15 NLT).

4. Sin interrupts or breaks fellowship with God. Adam and Eve, who walked in unbroken concord with God, now hid from God.

5. Man is prone to conceal sin. Adam and Eve covered themselves with fig leaves to conceal their nakedness. Man conceals his sin with the cloak of religion, charitableness, good deeds, and denial.

6. Guilt prompts fear. Adam and Eve, afraid of God, ran from God. Wiersbe says, "Guilt produces fear, and fear makes us want to run and hide."[166]

7. God takes notice of all that man does. Nothing is hidden from His observant eyes. Adam and Eve could not hide their sin from God, nor can any man (Hebrews 4:13). Matthew Henry states, "Though God knows all our sins, yet He will know them from us and requires from us an ingenuous confession of them; not that He may be informed, but that we may be humbled."[167]

8. Sin despoils peace, and delight and brings shame. Adam and Eve's utopia of happiness and tranquility ends when they eat the forbidden fruit. Criswell says, "Shame is the appropriate emotional attitude for those who have deliberately violated God's commands and ignored His purposes."[168]

9. The paramount consequences of sin are death and eternal separation from God (Genesis 3:19). "Therefore, just as sin entered the world through one man, and death through sin, and in this way death came to all people, because all sinned" (Romans 5:12 NIV).

10. God searches for man when he sins, rather than man searching for God. God sought out Adam and Eve. What a picture of the New Testament Gospel. God in love, through Christ, ever seeks out the erring one to rescue him from the plight and penalty of sin (to provide a covering for sin, the soul's nakedness). At the moment of salvation, by grace based on repentance and faith, God covers a person with the canopy of Christ's perfected righteousness (imputes).

From that moment forward, when He looks at that person, He sees Christ's righteousness (2 Corinthians 5:21), not that person's wretchedness. Saith Spurgeon, on behalf of Christ, "There, poor sinner, take My garment, and put it on; you shall stand before God as if you were Christ, and I will stand before God as if I had been the sinner; I will suffer in the sinner's stead, and you shall be rewarded for works that you did not do, but which I did for you."[169]

Man maintains free will to repent or not. J. C. Ryle asserts, "True repentance begins with KNOWLEDGE of sin. It goes on to work SORROW for sin. It leads to the CONFESSION of sin before God. It shows itself before a person by a thorough BREAKING OFF from sin. It results in producing a DEEP HATRED for all sin." The Bible says, "For as in Adam all die, even so in Christ shall all be made alive" (1 Corinthians 15:22).

**"Original sin is the only doctrine that's been empirically validated by two thousand years of human history."**—Gilbert K. Chesterton.

## 44

## "Can the Ethiopian Change His Skin, or the Leopard His Spots?"

To the Israelites, unwilling to admit their apostasy (Jeremiah 13:20), God asks, "Can the Ethiopian change his skin, or the leopard his spots?" (Jeremiah 13:23). The answer is crystal clear: no more could they change the wrong done by cloaking it with excuses and denial than the Ethiopian could change his skin color or the leopard his spots. The stain of sin is so embedded upon the soul and life of the sinner (inherent nature) that nothing short of a new birth can erase or change it (John 3:6–8).

1. Not amendment or alteration of life. Turning over a new leaf impacts the present; it fails to alter the sin of the past.

2. Not religious affiliation or activity.

3. Not baptism or drinking of the communion cup.

4. Not good deeds. The only hope for the soul stained with the filth and stench of sin is to be washed in the precious blood of Christ Jesus. "In Him we have redemption through His blood, the forgiveness of sins, according to the riches of His grace" (Ephesians 1:7 NKJV). The divine invitation to all is, "Come now, and let us reason together," saith the Lord. "Though your sins be as scarlet, they shall be as white as snow; though they be red like crimson, they shall be as wool" (Isaiah 1:18 KJ21). "When someone becomes a Christian, he becomes a brand-new person inside. He is not the same anymore. A new life has begun!" (2 Corinthians 5:17 TLB). It is written, "A new heart also will I give you, and a new spirit will I put within you" (Ezekiel 36:26).

It is an utter absurdity, foolishness, and folly for a person to deny sinning. John says, "If we say that we have no sin, we deceive ourselves, and the truth is not in us" (1 John 1:8). It is equally useless for him to try to remedy it by his doings. The outward appearance of the platter may be made clean and changed by resolve, but not its inside (Matthew 23:25). To conclude, Spurgeon says, "The question of the text is, 'Can the Ethiopian change his skin?' The answer is—no, no, no. Here is the other question: can the Ethiopian's skin be changed? The answer to that is yes, as emphatically as we have just now said no, no, no. Can the Ethiopian's skin be changed? Can the sinner's nature be renewed? Yes, for God can do everything."[170] And that's a game-changer.

**"The Ethiopian can wash or paint, but he cannot change that which is part and parcel of himself. A sinner cannot change his own nature."[171]** – C. H. Spurgeon

### 45
### "Why Have You Done This?"

"Why have you done this?" (Judges 2:2 NIV). The angel or messenger asking the question is seemingly the Lord Himself, who delivered the Israelites from Egyptian bondage.[172] Says Lightfoot, "Who but God and Christ could say, 'I made you to go up out of Egypt?'"[173] The question is a reprimand upon the people for violating two commandments: she entered into an alliance with the Canaanites, worshipped their gods (Judges 2:2a), and failed to destroy the Canaanites' altars to Baal (Judges 2:6–23). Instead of impacting the Canaanites for Jehovah God, they were infested by Canaanite idol worship and a detestable and despicable lifestyle. (Read Deuteronomy 6 for God's instruction about separation.)

The same happens with the church and its relation to the world today. It's getting difficult to differentiate the Christian from the non-Christian in the workplace, athletic arena, and schoolhouse. Instead of believers changing the ungodly to their likeness, the ungodly are making believers gradually more like them. Churches compromise foundational beliefs and mirror the world's views, standards, and tolerances more and more in the pulpit.

To all guilty of unholy alliances, compromise of belief, and carnality (worldliness), God sternly asks, "Why have you done this?" after being commanded to refrain from unequal yoking and mixing with the world. "What account can you give of this perverseness of yours at the bar of right reason? What apology can you make for yourselves, or what excuse can you offer?"[174]

Hear the Word of God with open ears and receptive hearts: "Don't become partners with those who reject God. How can you make a partnership out of right and wrong?...'Don't link up with those who will pollute you. I want you all for myself. I'll be a Father to you; you'll be sons and daughters to me.' The Word of the Master, God" (2 Corinthians 6:17 MSG).

One hundred forty years ago, Spurgeon addressed the religious compromise and moral and cultural tolerance of his day in the sermon "Bochim, or The Weepers," based on Judges 2:2. What he said mirrors the present day: "Whatsoever may be the law which God gives, either to the whole race or to His chosen, they will find their safety in keeping close to it. But Israel forgot this. Soldiering was hard work—storming cities and warring with men who attacked them with chariots of iron was heroic service. All this required strong faith and untiring perseverance, and in these virtues, the Israelites were greatly deficient; and so, in certain places, they said to the Canaanites, 'Let us be neighbors: let us dwell together.' Tolerance led to imitation, and Israel became as vile as the heathen whom the Lord had condemned, and the Israelites became a mixed race, in whose veins there flowed a measure of Canaanite blood. Yes, if you depart from God's Word by a hair's breadth, you know not where you will end. I would to God that in these degenerate times, we had back again somewhat of the stern spirit of the Cameroonians and the Covenanters; for now, men play fast and loose with God and think that anything they please to do will satisfy the Most High."[175]

Toleration of the Canaanites carried heavy consequences for Israel and will for us.

1. They would be powerless to drive the enemy from the land. "I will not drive them out from before you" (Judges 2:3a). A time comes when God says, "I will not do *for* you that which you will not do *with* Me." To pray for America's deliverance from cancel culture, worldliness, and anti-Christian values while being party to them is futile.

2. The very alliances with the world that promise pleasure and success, in time will be a vexation. "They shall be as thorns in your sides" (Judges 2:3b), and, "But if ye will not drive out the inhabitants of the land from before you; then it shall come to pass, that those which ye let remain of them shall be pricks in your eyes, and thorns in your sides, and shall vex you in the land wherein ye dwell" (Numbers 33:55).

3. It would give occasion to sin. "These people will become a problem for you. They will be like a trap to you. Their false gods will become like a net to trap you" (Judges 2:3c ERV). Some read it, "Their gods [their abominations] will be a snare to you; you will find yourselves wretchedly entangled in an affection to them, and it will be your ruin."[176] Is not all this happening before our very eyes?

The brief sermon met with little success. "And it came to pass, when the angel of the Lord spoke these words unto all the children of Israel, that the people lifted up their voice and wept. And they called the name of that place Bochim [that is, Weepers], and they sacrificed there unto the Lord" (Judges 2:4–5 KJ21). They wept, but they did not repent, and later returned to their disobedience practices, including idol worship. Matthew Henry remarks, "Many are melted under the word that harden again before they are cast into a new mold."[177] To that, every minister may sadly testify.

"The command to every one of us is to make no league with any one of our spiritual enemies—not with the world; on the contrary, we are to 'overcome it'; to 'come out from the people of it, and be separate'; to be 'dead to' all its cares and pleasures, 'being crucified to it, and esteeming it as crucified unto us': we are 'not to be of it, any more than Jesus Christ himself was of it.'"[178]—Charles Simeon.

## 46
## "Have I Not Commanded You?"

"Have I not commanded you?" (Joshua 1:9 NIV). At the death of Moses, Israel's new leader, Joshua, was met with the formidable task of organizing and leading the people to victory over the evil inhabitants of Caanan to possess the land as commanded by the Lord. With the challenge and appointment, Joshua was promised God's presence, power, and provision to encourage him and ensure the mission's accomplishment. "Have I not commanded you? Be strong and courageous! Do not be terrified nor dismayed, for the Lord your God is with you wherever you go....I will be with you; I will not desert you nor abandon you" (Joshua 1:9; 1:5b NASB).

"Have not I commanded thee?" The question prompts recall of God's promise to us ('I will not fail thee, or forsake thee') for encouragement, edification, and endurance, especially in the dark and challenging days of trial and duty.

"Have not I commanded thee?" A promise is only as good as its giver. Some make promises they are unable or unwilling to keep. But it is not so with the Giver of this promise, for He is "the faithful God, which keepeth covenant and mercy with them that love him and keep his commandments to a thousand generations" (Deuteronomy 7:9). "The inviolable faithfulness of the Promiser is good security for the accomplishment of the promise."[179]

His omnipotence, omniscience, immutability, and omnipresence assure that the promised thing can be done. Spurgeon said, "A promise is nothing unless I have good security that it shall be fulfilled. Here, every word of God is true. God has issued no more notes for the bank of Heaven than He can cash in an hour if He wills. There is enough bullion in the vaults of Omnipotence to pay off every bill that ever shall be drawn by the faith of man on the promises of God."[180] None but God may say truthfully, "I will be with thee: I will not fail thee, nor forsake thee," regardless of the circumstances of life.

God's promise of constant companionship and needed provision emboldens its possessor with courage, strength, and tenacity in the execution of duty, with comfort and hope in the hour of sorrow, most profound despair, and distress, with calmness and contentment in aloneness when friends wear out and abandon, and with peace in the crossing of Jordan into the promised land. The promise fully embraced by faith will be confirmed in experience, as it was for Joshua. "Satan has no dread of learning, or wisdom, or riches, but he does fear the courage of a soul resting in communion with God."[181]

In the assignments of God and struggles and conflicts met in the journey to Caanan, the saint will be borne up victoriously if he focuses on God and His reminding summons voiced in the question, "Have not I commanded thee?"

> The soul that on Jesus hath leaned for repose
> I will not, I will not desert to His foes;
> That soul, though all Hell should endeavor to shake,
> I'll never, no, never, no, never forsake.
> – attributed to George Keith (1787)

"If God be with our weakness, it waxes strong; if He be with our folly, it rises into wisdom; if He be with our timidity, it gathers courage."[182]—C. H. Spurgeon.

## 47
### "Will a Man Rob God?"

"Will a man rob God? Yet ye have robbed me. But ye say, wherein have we robbed thee? In tithes and offerings" (Malachi 3:8). The question and its frank answer reprimand the Israelites for defrauding God of that which belonged to Him, their tithes and offerings. Some failed to give at *all*, while others failed to give it *all*.

The sin of not practicing the tithe and free will offering, of defrauding or robbing the Sovereign God of that which is His, bears serious consequences.

1. It's a sin that blocks blessing. The windows of Heaven are shut up, at least to some degree, against the believer who begrudgingly and greedily withholds tithes and offerings from the Lord. Present adversity, says Criswell, is the result, not the cause, of the failure to tithe.[183] Windows closed up tightly because of this sin can be opened. "Bring ye all the tithes into the storehouse, that there may be meat in mine house, and prove me now herewith, saith the Lord of hosts, if I will not open you the windows of heaven, and pour you out a blessing, that there shall not be room enough to receive it" (Malachi 3:10).

God says, "Prove me! Show obedience, and I'll give you MY favor and a superabundance of blessings." Note, we only are to prove or test God at His invite and, then, never when our heart is not right (Malachi 3:15).[184] The reward or blessing to Israel for tithing was an agricultural success, rain to water the earth, rebuke of the locusts that devoured the fields, fruit from the vines at just the right time (Malachi 3:11), and a mark of God's favor (material prosperity) to the nations (Malachi 3:12; Amos 9:13–15).

To summarize, the tither and offering giver would have his Faith renewed, Foes rebuked, Fruitfulness (prosperity) restored, Favor enhanced among all people with godly impact ("the nations"), and Happiness heightened ("be a delightsome land"). Paul echoes a similar promise for giving in 2 Corinthians 9:6–12 and Philippians 4:19, as does Solomon, who declared, "It shall be health to thy navel, and marrow to thy bones. Honor the LORD with thy substance, and with the firstfruits of all thine increase: So shall thy barns be filled with plenty, and thy presses shall burst out with new wine" (Proverbs 3:8–10).

Five observations about the promised blessing:

a. The connection between obedience and blessedness cannot be severed.[185]

b. Blessings are bestowed not for the act but for demonstrating wholehearted obedience, allegiance, and subjection to the Lord.[186]

c. God's gifts (whatever the kind) are more than sufficient ("not be room enough to receive it") to supply man's need (2 Kings 4:6; Psalm 103:1–5).

d. First, the gift; then the blessing. Upon giving the gift, look for the opening of the windows of Heaven.

e. The overarching motive for giving isn't the blessing. It's love for Christ (2 Corinthians 8:8).

2. It's a sin that stagnates the soul. The discipline to deny selfish wants to supply kingdom needs develops spiritual muscle. Adrian Rogers states, "God doesn't need us to give Him our money. He owns everything. Tithing is God's way to grow Christians."

3. It's a sin that deprives kingdom work. The support of the priests and ministry of the Temple depended upon the tithes and offerings of the people. When it was witholden, both suffered. Likewise, the foundation of church and ministry support is the gifts of God's people. When withheld, the whole of their ministry is hampered. O. S. Hawkins said, "The principal hindrance to the advancement of the kingdom of God is greed."

4. It's a sin that deceives the heart. "Robbing God," says Matthew Henry, "is such a heinous crime that those who are guilty of it are not willing to own themselves guilty. They rob God and do not know what they do."[187] They never ask, "Wherein have we robbed thee." All are guilty of robbing God of honor, of reasonable service (Romans 12:1–2), of fellowship in His presence, of absolute allegiance, of precious time that belongs to Him spent doing other things, and of misapplying to something else money or possessions that rightfully belong to God. Let us not fail to ask the question the Israelites never did, "Wherein have we robbed thee?" "Lord, is it I?"

5. It's a sin that the Lord observes. The sin cannot be hidden or concealed from God. He watches what we give and the motive

with which it is offered. "Jesus sat near the Temple collection box and watched as people put money into it" (Mark 12:41 ERV). Matthew Henry asserts, "Our Lord Jesus takes notice of what we contribute to pious and charitable uses; whether we give liberally or sparingly; whether cheerfully or with reluctance and ill-will; nay, He looks at the heart; He observes what principles we act upon, and what our views are, in giving alms; and whether we do it as unto the Lord, or only to be seen of men."[188]

6. It's a sin that may be prevented. The sin may be avoided by giving cheerfully, willingly, not begrudgingly or legalistically (2 Corinthians 9:7) but systematically based upon ability—how God had "prospered him" (1 Corinthians 16:2). The tithe is the *floor* level of giving, not the *ceiling* (Haggai 2:8; Malachi 3:10). Criswell said, "Though stewardship may include more than the tithe, it is never less than the tithe."[189] Adrian Rogers asserts, "You'll always do more with nine-tenths and God as a partner than you will with ten-tenths by yourself. It's time we began to trust the Lord!"[190]

Sacrificial givers imitate Christ (John 3:16; 2 Corinthians 8:9).

They reveal where their treasure is stored (Matthew 6:19–21).

They show adherence to the Scripture (1 Corinthians 16:2).

They prove the genuineness of their love for Christ (2 Corinthians 8:8b). "Love is only expressed through giving. If there is no giving, there is no evidence that love exists."

They demonstrate the level of their faith (Luke 6:38; 2 Corinthians 8:5). William A. Ward says, "Giving is more than a responsibility—it is a privilege; more than an act of obedience—it is evidence of our faith." Adrian Rogers said, "A faith that hasn't reached your wallet probably hasn't reached your heart."

They resemble the members of the first-century church, who are our New Testament pattern (Acts 2:45).

They testify that giving is more blessed than receiving (Acts 20:35).

"Even if I give the whole of my worth to Him, He will find a way to give back to me much more than I gave."—C. H. Spurgeon.

## 48
### "What Seest Thou?"

"And the Lord said unto me, Amos, what seest thou? And I said, A plumbline" (Amos 7:7).

A plumb line (spiritual) measures man's compliance (straightness or perpendicularity) with God's teachings and commandments. Israel's failure to align with God's plumb line resulted in judgment (Amos 7:9).

The Bible, not creeds, culture, or church, is the infallible plumb line (standard) by which man is to examine and judge himself (Deuteronomy 4:2). Placed next to it, what saith it? Does it expose drifting, to one degree or another, from your first love, devotion, and allegiance to God? What saith it about your truthfulness, holiness, and separation from the world? What saith it about your faithfulness in duty? What saith it about your enduring suffering as a good soldier of Jesus Christ without murmuring or retreating? Preacher, what saith it to the biblical soundness of your preaching? If you find yourself wanting, amend your ways by aligning them with the plumb line, the Word of God. A life built non-perpendicular to the Scriptures will grow crooked, warped, and suffer a destructive fall (Matthew 7:27; Amos 7:9).

Six additional lessons may be drawn from the text.

1. A non-perpendicular wall (determined by God's plumb line) must first be demolished to give place to that which is perpendicular. "The first work of divine grace in the soul is to pull down all that nature has built up."[191] Jesus said, "New wine must be put into new wineskins" (Luke 5:38 TLB). Paul states, "Therefore if any man be in Christ, he is a new creature: old things are passed away; behold, all things are become new" (2 Corinthians 5:17).

2. A wall to stand perpendicular must be constructed on a good foundation. A house, even the most luxurious and admired, built on the shifting sands of possessions, pleasure, religion, merit, and good works will totter and fall (Matthew 7:27). The old foundation must be dug up (through confession of sin and repentance) and be replaced with that of a devoted relationship with Jesus Christ (through the New Birth). "For no man can lay another foundation than that which is laid, which is Jesus Christ" (1 Corinthians 3:11 KJ21).

3. Frequent inspection with the plumb line ensures a building's proper alignment. Periodically, the believer is to examine the straightness or rightness of his life by comparing it with the teachings of the Holy Scriptures (Job 23:12; Psalm 119:102 and Psalm 139:23–24). When the believer's life is not perpendicular to the Word, the "wood, hay, and stubble" part must be painstakingly removed. Paul says, "Put off [strip away] everything concerning the old way of life, that is, the old man who corrupts himself according to deceitful desires" (Ephesians 4:22 JUB). "Wash me thoroughly from mine iniquity, and cleanse me from my sin" (Psalm 51:2).

4. A rush in measurement may yield a false reading.

5. The plumb line never errs. The Scripture is an unprejudicial, flawless, and trustworthy measuring tool. It never needs calibration, for its standard never changes. It's always accurate. Spurgeon asserts, "Do not let us judge either ourselves or one another simply by the eye. I have frequently thought that a building was out of the perpendicular when it was not, and I have sometimes thought it was perpendicular when it was not. The human eye is readily deceived, but the plumbline is not; it drops straight down and at once shows whether the wall is upright or not."[192]

6. External factors (like the wind) may affect the plumb line's interpretation. The winds of perversion, prejudice, and preference impact man's accurate reading of God's plumb line. Quiet them before using them.

Note, the divine superintendent watches the construction of our house, monitoring its accuracy and alignment with His Word and plan until the topmost pinnacle is raised (Philippians 1:6). If we falter in building it, He will intervene with corrective measures (Amos 7:9).

**"God's standard is expressed in the Bible, and the ultimate example of that standard is Jesus Christ."**[193]—Billy Graham.

## 49
### "Hast Thou an Arm Like God?"

"Hast thou an arm like God?" (Job 40:9). Pride puffs man up like it did Job to believe he is the master of his fate and captain of his salvation.[194] But he, and all like him, are deceived. Only the mighty arm of God can stretch down into the miry pit of man's deepest need and bring him out. David testified, "He brought me up also out of an horrible pit, out of the miry clay, and set my feet upon a rock, and established my goings. And he hath put a new song in my mouth, even praise unto our God: many shall see it, and fear, and shall trust in the LORD" (Psalm 40:2–3).

How strong is the mighty arm of God?

1. The might of God's arm is unchangeable. It never diminishes in strength one iota despite being relied upon and used often. What He did yesterday, He easily repeats today. "I am the LORD, I change not" (Malachi 3:6).

2. The might of God's arm is incomparable. No human strength, not "Atlas" himself, nor the combined power of all men are equal to it. "No one can compare with you among the gods, Lord; No one can accomplish your work" (Psalm 86:8 ISV).

3. The might of God's arm is incontestable. It has the power to do whatever and accomplish whatever God wants. No man or nation can stay His hand when He acts. Isaiah says, "Who is there that can stop him? He has stretched out his hand. Who can turn it back?" (Isaiah 14:27 CJB). God says, "What I want to do, I will do" (Isaiah 46:10 EXB). Matthew Henry states, "He made the

heaven and the earth with his outstretched arm; and therefore, who can control Him? Who dares contend with Him? (Jeremiah 32:17)."[195]

> How strong thine arm is, mighty God!
> Who would not fear thy name?
> 
> – Isaac Watts (1806)

"The strong right arm of the Lord is raised in triumph. The strong right arm of the Lord has done glorious things!" (Psalm 118:16 NLT).

1. The might of God's arm is seen in the salvation of rebellious sinners such as you and me. "Every conversion is a display of omnipotence."[196] "The arm of the LORD is not too short to save" (Isaiah 59:1 NIV). It can open blinded eyes, humble the most arrogant, and break and penetrate the hardest of hearts.

2. The might of God's arm is seen in creation, in its splendorous beauty. "The heavens are thine, the earth also is thine: as for the world and the fulness thereof, thou hast founded them" (Psalm 89:11).

3. The might of God's arm is seen in the regulation of the universe. "He holds everything together through his powerful words" (Hebrews 1:3 NOG).

4. The might of God's arm is seen in the deliverances of His people from their enemy, infirmity, and adversity throughout history. "Remember the great terrors the LORD your God sent against them. You saw it all with your own eyes! And remember the miraculous signs and wonders, and the strong hand and powerful arm with which he brought you out of Egypt. The LORD your God will use this same power against all the people you fear" (Deuteronomy 7:19 NLT).

5. The might of God's arm is seen in the use of the frail and feeble to dispense the Gospel effectively. "What the world thinks is worthless, useless, and nothing at all is what God has used to

destroy what the world considers important" (1 Corinthians 1:28 CEV).

Joseph Parker says, "He who trusts in the Eternal is eternally safe. He has no need to reckon or compute or arrange as to contingencies and possibilities; he says, 'God is my refuge and strength, therefore will not I fear, though the earth be removed, and though the mountains be carried into the midst of the sea.'"[197]

Dependence upon secondary sources, 'chariots and horses' (Psalm 20:7)—human instrumentation for rescue and remedy—instead of God's mighty arm is not only sin, but proves futile. "The arm of flesh will fail you; you dare not trust your own." Note that God often uses secondary sources to accomplish healing and deliverance from trial. He did with Hezekiah (2 Kings 20:7). The wrong is not in their use but in relying upon them rather than God.

Personalize Isaiah's prayer for your present need: "Wake up, Lord, and help us! Use your power [mighty arm] and save us; use it as you did in ancient times" (Isaiah 51:9 GNT). Amen.

"Omnipotence is thine in smiting or uplifting."[198]—C. H. Spurgeon.

## 50
### "Who Hath Made Man's Mouth?"

"Who hath made man's mouth?" (Exodus 4:11). Moses' hesitation in speaking to Pharoah, at least in part, was due to the inability to speak fluently and eloquently (Exodus 4:10). The question God asked him was a stark reminder that He, who made the tongue, could enable it to articulately and effectively communicate His Word whenever and to whomever, king or peasant. "The meek Moses lost sight of the fact that God does not of necessity require good material."[199]

Five lessons may be drawn from the question and its applicable answer.

1. God transforms stammering tongues into instruments of eloquence and "maketh His...ministers a flame of fire" (Hebrews 1:7). Paul said, "God chose those who were regarded as foolish by the world to shame the wise; God chose those in the world who were weak to shame the strong" (1 Corinthians 1:27 NCB).

2. God promises to be with the tongue of the believer. "Now therefore go, and I will be with thy mouth" (Exodus 4:12). Jesus said, "For it is not you who will be speaking—it will be the Spirit of your Father speaking through you" (Matthew 10:20 NLT). See Jeremiah 1:9 and Luke 12:12. God used Moses' weak tongue and Aaron's to speak to Pharoah (Exodus 5:1–3). Note, that the Holy Spirit greatly enabled Paul's ineloquence in speech (2 Corinthians 10:10).

3. God often raises an Aaron to team with a Moses to compensate for his weakness. Matthew Henry observes, "The tongue of Aaron, with the head and heart of Moses, would make one completely fit for this embassy."[200]

4. Sometimes eloquence is withheld lest pride overtake the worker. Spurgeon says, "He will have it seen that the excellency of the power lies not in our speech, but in His Gospel."[201]

5. Where the ability to speak fluently is not given, another ability or gift is bestowed. J. S. Exell states, "If we have not eloquence, we have some other equally valuable talent in its place."[202]

**"Do not invent excuses to shift off your duty; but look up to God to direct you in His way, and to strengthen you for the performance of all His will."**[203] – Charles Simeon

## 51

### "Is the LORD's Hand Waxed Short?"

"Is the LORD's hand waxed short?" (Numbers 11:23). Moses was asked this question after questioning God's power to send meat to 600,000 men of Israel and their families for a whole month (Numbers 11:21–22). It may be paraphrased: Is God's hand too short to accomplish His purposes and maintain His works? Has it waned or diminished in strength?

1. The question is asked by the callous sinner in need of salvation. The Bible answers: No person is beyond God's forgiving grace and mercy. "He is able to save completely all who come to God through him" (Hebrews 7:25 TLB). Perhaps none were more wicked than King Manasseh (2 Chronicles 33:1–12), yet even he was not beyond the reach of the merciful hand of God.

2. It is asked by the shackled drunkard, gambler, pornographer, and drug addict in need of deliverance. The Bible answers: God hears the groaning of the prisoners and seeks to bring them out of their dungeon of captivity (Isaiah 42:7). God is the same great God that He was yesterday when, through His power, addicts and captives were set free. "For I am the LORD, I change not" (Malachi 3:6).

Spurgeon wrote a parable of how the Devil shackles man. A tyrant ordered a blacksmith to forge a chain. Upon its completion, the man presented it to the tyrant, who ordered him to make it twice the length. After arduous labor, the chain was brought to the tyrant. This time, the blacksmith was instructed to double the size of the chain. Upon returning with the lengthened chain, the tyrant commanded the servants to bind the man hand and foot with it and thrust him into prison. "That is what the Devil does with men," Spurgeon said. "He makes them forge their own chain, and then binds them hand and foot with it, casts them into outer darkness." Thankfully, God's hand is not too short to break their chains and set them free.

3. It is asked by the crushed and bruised heart in need of comfort, peace, hope, and consolation. The Bible answers: There is no sorrow or care beyond God's ableness to soothe and heal. "Cast your burden on the Lord, and He shall sustain you; He shall never permit the righteous to be moved" (Psalm 55:22 NKJV). Spurgeon states, "There is no balm in Gilead, but there is a balm in God. There is no physician among the creatures, but the Creator is Jehovah-rophi."[204]

4. It is asked by the doubter needing the assurance of eternal life. The Bible answers: Once reborn into the family of God, a person can never be unborn. "They shall never perish, neither shall any man pluck them out of my hand" (John 10:28). See Philippians 1:6.

5. It is asked by the righteous about God's might to thwart evil and punish evildoers. The Bible answers: The power of God to remedy evil and execute judgment upon the wicked has not diminished from the beginning. "Your right hand, O Lord, glorious in power, your right hand, O Lord, shatters the enemy" (Exodus 15:6 ESV).

Spurgeon asserts, "His hand is not waxed short; He is as strong to punish as when He bade the floods cover the earth, as powerful to avenge as when He rained hail out of heaven upon the cities of the plain. He is today as mighty to overtake and punish His enemies as when He sent the angel through the midst of Egypt or afterward smote the hosts of Sennacherib."[205]

The bottom line: "Whatever our unbelieving hearts may suggest to the contrary," says Matthew Henry, "it is certain that God's hand is not short; His power cannot be restrained in the exerting of itself by anything but His own will; with Him, nothing is impossible. That hand is not short which measures the waters, metes out the heavens (Isaiah 40:12), and grasps the winds (Proverbs 30:4)."[206]

**"It is impossible for that man to despair who remembers that his Helper is omnipotent."**—Jeremy Taylor.

52

"Who Put Wisdom in the Heart or Gave
Understanding to the Mind?"

"Who put wisdom in the heart or gave understanding to the mind?" (Job 38:36 GW). Did wisdom spontaneously happen? Is man responsible for it? Or is Elihu correct in saying, "There is a spirit within people, the breath of the Almighty within them, that makes them intelligent" (Job 32:8 NLT)?

"Who put wisdom in the heart or gave understanding to the mind?" (Job 38:36 GW). Wisdom is divine knowledge ascertained from the Holy Spirit through prayer (James 1:5), the Holy Scriptures (Psalm 119:130; Proverbs 2:6), instruction (Proverbs 19:20), and experience (Job 12:12) to govern life rightly, successfully, and pleasingly unto the Lord.

Elihu's question to Job counters the belief that wisdom is automatic and that man possesses it without seeking it. Isaiah warned of this danger, saying, "Woe unto them that are wise in their own eyes, and prudent in their own sight!" (Isaiah 5:21). William Law wrote nearly two centuries ago, "Man needs to be saved from his own wisdom as much as from his own righteousness, for they produce the same corruption."[207]

Philosophical reasoning, intelligence, and fleshly rationale are inapt, unfit guides to govern life. Of them, Paul warned, "Don't let anyone capture you with empty philosophies and high-sounding nonsense that come from human thinking and from the spiritual powers of this world, rather than from Christ" (Colossians 2:8 NLT). Horatius Bonar said, "Do not heed the jar of man's warring opinions. Let God be true and every man a liar. The Bible is the Bible still. If any man lacks wisdom, let him ask of God. You have an unction from the Holy One, and you know all things."

"Fools die for want of wisdom" (Proverbs 10:21). "My people are destroyed for lack of knowledge: because thou hast rejected knowledge" (Hosea 4:6). The man who hastily, rashly, and thoughtlessly lives life without wisdom errs in decisions that bring harm, distress, and failure to others, and himself. And, as Ironside remarks, it adds sin to sin.[208] Not until man distrusts "worldly" wisdom and depends utterly upon divine wisdom can life be governed and navigated happily and successfully. Guard against either foolishly or unthinkingly elevating your "wisdom" above the Lord's.

"Wisdom is the right use of knowledge. To know is not to be wise. Many men know a great deal and are all the greater fools for it. There is no fool so great a fool as a knowing fool. But to know how to use knowledge is to have wisdom."—C. H. Spurgeon

## 53
### "Have the Gates of Death Been Opened unto Thee?"

"Have the Gates of Death been opened unto thee?" (Job 38:17). God asks Job if he has visited the Gates of Death that border life in order to reveal Job's weakness and ignorance about the magnitude of creation and the power and intelligence needed to create it. He has not.

Observations about the Gates of Death:

1. The Gates of Death is every man's lot. "It is appointed unto men once to die, but after this the judgment" (Hebrews 9:27). "All mankind is sitting on death row."[209]

2. The Gates of Death is nigh to all. No person, young or old, is ever far from it. Small and large gravesites are scattered throughout every cemetery. Says Thomas Adams, "Death is as near to the young as to the old; here is all the difference: death stands behind the young man's back, before the old man's face." All can say, like David, "There is but a step between me and death" (1 Samuel 20:3).

3. The Gates of Death are many. The poet Robert Blair states, "Death's thousand doors stand open." The unexpected door often is its entry door.

4. The Gates of Death is kept by the Supreme Gatekeeper. God orders the time of man's birth and the hour of his death. The psalmist declared, "You saw me before I was born and scheduled each day of my life before I began to breathe. Every day was recorded in your book!" (Psalm 139:16 TLB). When talking about man's day of death, Jesus said, "The very hairs on your head are

all numbered" (Matthew 10:30 NLT). Henry Martyn said, "You are immortal until God's purpose for you is complete."

5. The Gates of Death open to two separate abodes. The "narrow gate" opens to rapturous joy and reunion with the redeemed in Heaven (Matthew 7:13a). The "wide gate" opens to misery and torment in Hell (Matthew 7:13b).

6. The Gates of Death is ticketed. Man's destiny is predetermined before death. The man stamped with saving grace—the blood of Christ—at the moment of death will gain entry into Heaven (Revelation 7:14). He, without it, will be cast into eternal darkness (Revelation 21:8). Spurgeon comments, "What I am when death is held before me, that I must be forever. When my spirit departs, if God finds me hymning His praise, I shall hymn it in Heaven; if He finds me breathing out oaths, I shall follow up those oaths in Hell."[210]

7. The Gates of Death grants hope of life beyond the grave. Gates bear entry to a place. They lead to somewhere, not to nowhere. To Christians, it promises a better land and life. Such is the reason Paul exclaimed confidently, "O death, where is thy sting? O grave, where is thy victory?" The sting of death is sin; and the strength of sin is the law. But thanks be to God, which giveth us the victory through our Lord Jesus Christ!" (1 Corinthians 15:55–57). Says Spurgeon to the believer, "When the time comes for you to die, you need not be afraid because death cannot separate you from God's love." Christians confidently can exclaim with Lyte, who, while dying of tuberculosis, wrote,

> I fear no foe with Thee at hand to bless;
> Ills have no weight and tears no bitterness.
> Where is death's sting? Where, grave, thy victory?
> I triumph still if Thou abide with me.

The hour is approaching when you, like Hezekiah, must say, "I shall go to the gates of the grave" (Isaiah 38:10). If it is today, which turnstile, Heaven or Hell, will you enter?

"Fit or not fit—we must all die, and we know not how soon. As death leaves us, the judgment must find us."—William Tiptaft.

## 54
### "What Have We Gained by Obeying His Commands?"

"You have said, 'What's the use of serving God? What have we gained by obeying his commands'" (Malachi 3:14 NLT). Israel hoped their service to God and obedience to rituals (which were cold and formal) would be paid back with prosperity. When that did not happen, they murmured against God, saying it wasn't profitable to serve Him.

Men tend to say it doesn't pay to serve God:

1. When the unrighteous prosper more than the righteous (Psalm 73:13).

2. When expectations are not realized.

3. When misfortune and suffering are experienced.

4. When ostracized and penalized for doing what is right.

5. When selfish motives are at play (Matthew 16:25).

But they are wrong. The profit of serving the Lord is seen in what He does with and for the Christian.

1. He pardons them of sin. "I, even I, am he that blotteth out thy transgressions for mine own sake, and will not remember thy sins" (Isaiah 43:25; Colossians 1:13).

2. He protects them in trouble. He is the believer's refuge in times of trials and tribulation (Psalm 46:1–2), a strong tower in times of personal conflict (Psalm 61:3), and a secure Rock in times of weakness and frailty (Psalm 31:2).

3. He preserves them to the end (Heaven is reached). Jesus said, "I kept them in thy name: those that thou gavest me I have kept, and none of them is lost" (John 17:12). George Wade Robinson wrote in the hymn "I Am His, and He Is Mine":

"His forever, only His—
  Who the Lord and me shall part?
Ah, with what a rest of bliss
  Christ can fill the loving heart!
Heav'n and earth may fade and flee,
  First-born light in gloom decline,
But while God and I shall be,
  I am His, and He is mine."

4. He prizes them as a treasure. "But God chose you to be his people. You are royal priests. You are a holy nation. You are God's special treasure [unique property or possession]" (1 Peter 2:9 NIRV). Matthew Henry asserts, "It is the honor of the servants of Christ that they are God's peculiar [special] people. They are the people of His acquisition, choice, care, and delight."[211]

5. He provides them with all they need. "But my God shall supply all your need [not wishes and wants] according to his riches in glory by Christ Jesus" (Philippians 4:19). He has provisions equal to whatever the need. Says Spurgeon, "The riches of nations are as rags and rottenness in comparison with His resources."[212] Note, that God determines the need and means of its supply, not us.

6. He promises them a reward. "He is a rewarder of them that diligently seek him" (Hebrews 11:6). For a life of faith and obedience to God, the believer is rewarded with peace, love, satisfaction, joy, eternal life, and reunion with the saints in Glory.

No devoted Christian has ever said, "It is vain to serve God" (Malachi 3:14). But instead, he testifies:

It pays to serve Jesus; it pays every day;
It pays every step of the way.
Though the pathway to glory may sometimes be drear,
You'll be happy each step of the way.
– Frank C. Huston (1909)

"O taste and see that the LORD is good" (Psalm 34:8), for it will prove that it pays to serve God. Many see but do not taste His goodness and walk away counting a life lived for Him futile and wasted. When a person tastes the Lord's goodness, he discovers the benefit of following Him.

Taste the forgiveness He gives in failure, comfort He gives in sorrow, deliverance He gives from a sin's bondage, friendship He gives in desolation, hope He offers in despair, and calm He provides in the storm, and you will be made to trust in Him. The truth about the value and profit of serving God awaits those who refuse to hear without seeing and to hear and see without tasting. Brady wrote,

"Oh, make but trial of His love;
   Experience will decide.
How bless'd are they—and only they—
   Who in His truth confide."

"Satisfaction. A rare word! The richest man in England [or elsewhere] has not found it. The greatest conqueror has never won it. The proudest emperor cannot command it. It is a spiritual blessing, a divine grace that comes from *the great satisfying God—the God who is Himself all sufficient to fill the human heart.*"[213]—C. H. Spurgeon.

## 55
### "What Seest Thou?"

"Amos, what seest thou? And I said, A basket of summer fruit" (Amos 8:2). Baskets of summer fruit indicated the end of the harvest in Palestine. To Amos, it pictured the inevitable end of a nation. It had sown corruption; it would reap destruction. The metaphor of the basket of summer fruit teaches four lessons about the coming judgment that determines man's everlasting abode in Heaven or Hell.

1. You get what you plant. What a man sows, that shall he reap (Galatians 6:7).

a. Reaping is not divorced from the sower. Man reaps his sowing, the consequences of his sin—an eternal abode in Heaven or Hell.

b. Reaping is not divorced from the sowing. Nature's law of reaping decrees you get in "like-kind" to the seed sown. He that sow's wheat (good, godliness) will reap wheat; he that sow's briers and thistles (bad, evil) will reap briers and thistles. The person who sows to the flesh (worldliness and disdain for Christ) will reap corruption and damnation. He that sows to the Spirit (godliness and devotion to Christ) will reap blessings and everlasting life.

A man asked his servant to sow barley. The servant sowed oats. The master asked why he sowed oats. The servant replied, "I hoped to grow barley."

The master said, "What a foolish idea! Who ever heard the like!"

The servant replied, "You yourself constantly sow seeds of evil and yet expect to reap the fruits of virtue."[214]

2. You only get what you plant. F. W. Robertson said, "No man can have two harvests for one sowing."[215] You cannot live the life of the unrighteous and die the death of the righteous. Balaam couldn't have it both ways (Numbers 23:10). No man can. Paul says, "He that soweth to his flesh shall of the flesh reap corruption; but he that soweth to the Spirit shall of the Spirit reap life everlasting" (Galatians 6:8).

3. You can change what you plant now. Christ summons, "Come now, and let us reason together, saith the LORD: though your sins be as scarlet, they shall be as white as snow; though they be red like crimson, they shall be as wool" (Isaiah 1:18). The only thing necessary to obtain abundant and eternal life, and an everlasting state free from sin, sickness, and suffering, is to "come" to Jesus. Just "come"—not to the church, not to a minister or priest, but to Jesus Christ. The promise, although certain, calls for a response by "coming."

How might you come? Come with a repentant (godly sorrow) heart over sin in simple childlike trust, receiving Christ's gift of forgiveness and abundant and eternal life through prayer. John says, "As many as received him, to them gave he power to become the sons of God, even to them that believe on his name" (John 1:12). "Behold, now is the accepted time; behold, now is the day of salvation" (2 Corinthians 6:2). See Amos 8:2 and Proverbs 29:1. John Dobell wrote,

> Now is the accepted time,
>   Now is the day of grace;
> O, sinners! Come, without delay,
>   And seek the Savior's face.

4. You cannot change what you plant at death. At death (the harvest), the outcome of what is planted cannot be altered (Galatians 6:8). What it is, at the time of harvest, it is and ever will remain. Where the tree falls, it will lie (Ecclesiastes 11:3). Will it be a harvest of corruption or blessing, damnation or glory for you?

> Delay not, delay not, O sinner, to come,
>   For mercy still lingers and calls thee today.
> Her voice is not heard in the vale of the tomb;
>   Her message, unheeded, will soon pass away.
>                  – Thomas Hastings (1831)

"Ignorance of the kind of seed sown will make no difference to the crop."—D. L. Moody.

## 56

### "And the LORD Said to Satan, Whence Comest Thou?"

"And the LORD said unto Satan, Whence comest thou?" (Job 1:7). The dialogue between God and Satan, initiated by God, indicates the existence and nature of Satan. Note, the primary witness to the reality and existence of Satan is not experience or even the repulsive, shameful, perverted, depraved, and degenerate acts of man, but the testimony of Scripture. Both the Old Testament and New Testament unequivocally affirm Satan's reality.

It's important to understand that Satan is not omnipresent. He cannot be everywhere at the same time. In response to God's question, Satan answered, "From going to and fro in the earth, and from walking up and down in it." The New Testament text of Job 1:7 is 1 Peter 5:8: "Your adversary the devil, as a roaring lion, walketh about, seeking whom he may devour."

1. Satan's purpose is to destroy. He is behind all the evil that exists. Jesus said, "The thief [the Devil] cometh not, but for to steal, and to kill, and to destroy" (John 10:10). Give Satan the just desert for the suffering and evil in the world.

2. Satan is subject to limitations. God has a hedge of protection about the believer, which Satan cannot penetrate without permission (Job 1:10–12). Paul asserts that God will not allow Satan to tempt the believer beyond his ableness to endure (1 Corinthians 10:13).

3. Satan possesses tremendous power. Spurgeon said, "Only omnipotence itself keeps off the fiery darts of Satan."[216] Look at the havoc he caused Job (Job 1:13–19). He is a foe not to be taken lightly. Remember, in the battle against him, "Greater is He that is in you than he that is in the world" (1 John 4:4 ASV). Adrian Rogers said, "You might as well be throwing snowballs at the rock of Gibraltar as come against Satan in your own strength."[217]

4. Satan is subject to the sovereignty of God. Jesus said, "The ruler of the world is coming [Satan]. He has no power over me" (John 14:30 CSB). As Augustine of Hippo reminds us, "The whole world therefore, from the highest heavens to the lowest earth, is subject to the Creator, not to the deserter; to the Redeemer, not to the destroyer; to the Deliverer, not to the enslaver; to the Teacher, not to the deceiver."

5. Satan is a defeated foe. Calvary was Satan's Waterloo (Romans 16:20). The day is nigh when "the devil that deceived them was cast into the lake of fire and brimstone" (Revelation 20:10). Adrian Rogers says, "Satan is a decided fact and a destructive force, but he is also a defeated foe."[218]

**"The devil rages the more when his empire is, the nearer to its end."**[219]—C. H. Spurgeon

## 57
### "Did Ye at All Fast unto Me, Even to Me?"

"Did ye at all fast unto me, even to me?" (Zechariah 7:5). The reproof to the Israelites was necessary to expose the formalism of the fast (cold ritualism), the superstition of the fast (it was believed fasting produced God's blessing), and the hypocrisy of the fast (outward worship apart from inward devotion) they observed for seventy years. What they did was right. How they did it was wrong. "They had not an eye to God in their fasting."[220]

1. Who fast? Followers of Christ are expected to fast, provided health permits (Matthew 9:15). Note that Jesus said, "When ye fast," not if you fast (Matthew 6:16).

2. Why fast? Fast to bring the body into subjection to the Spirit (1 Corinthians 9:27), to prevail with God (Ezra 8:23; Mark 9:29), to liberate from the "yoke" of guidance in decision-making (Nehemiah 1:4), to express mourning and repentance for personal or corporate sin (Ezra 9:5; Joel 2:12–13), to give strength to follow through victoriously with Holy Spirit-led decisions (Esther 4:16), to reveal God's plan for life (Acts 10:10), to intercede for another when he/she falls into sin (1 Kings 21:27), to drive Satan and the demons of Hell back (Mark 9:17–29), to intercede for a personal enemy (Psalm 35:12–13), to humble the soul (Psalm 69:10; 1 Kings 21:27–29), to break the bondage of physical appetite (1 Corinthians 6:12–13), to gain strength in spiritual warfare (Psalm 18:39) and to express love and devotion to God (Luke 2:37). Fasting apart from spiritual design or objective is no more than a

diet. David Livingstone said, "Fastings and vigils without a special object in view are time run to waste."

3. How fast? In secret. Jesus says, "When you fast, brush your hair and wash your face. Then you won't look like you are fasting to people, but only to your Father who is present in that secret place. Your Father who sees in secret will reward you" (Matthew 6:17–18 CEB). Don't do it legalistically like the Pharisees (Luke 18:12).

4. When fast? Practice it when prompted by spiritual hunger and pressing need. Engage in it to praise and thank God (Joel 2:12–13). D. L. Moody said, "If you say, 'I will fast when God lays it on my heart,' you never will. You are too cold and indifferent to take the yoke upon you."

5. How long to fast? Jesus did not state how often and how long (Luke 5:33–35). Therefore, the duration and intervals are discretionary.

6. Ways to fast? The word "fast" in Scripture refers to the abstinence from food and drink, not material things. That said, denying a hobby or entertainment to bring the body under submission to God is legitimate.

"The purpose of fasting is to loosen to some degree the ties which bind us to the world of material things and our surroundings as a whole, in order that we may concentrate all our spiritual powers upon the unseen and eternal things."—Ole Hallesby.

## 58
### "Have I Been a Wilderness unto Israel?"

"Have I been a wilderness unto Israel?" (Jeremiah 2:31). Joseph Parker says, "The very inquiry is a defense; the very method of the inquiry means it is impossible to answer this but in one way."[221] And that way is by saying, "Absolutely not!"

A wilderness suggests a lonely, gloomy, uncaring, and miserable place. It's where God is absent, prayers go unanswered, devotion is unrewarded, happiness is diminished, and His goodness is suspended. Israel unjustly treated God as if He were such a wilderness. Many are guilty of the same offense.

1. They who acclaim God to be a wilderness have relied on religion, instead of Him, for happiness and satisfaction. Religion fails to do what is only possible with God for man.

2. They who acclaim God to be a wilderness have flawed theology. The prosperity gospel's failure to deliver has prompted many to say God is "a wilderness."

3. They who acclaim God to be a wilderness protest His works. God's failure to work as man wants or on his timetable brings revolt and remonstration.

4. They who acclaim God as a wilderness do so on hearsay, not experience. David urges, "O taste and see that the LORD is good: blessed is the man that trusteth in him" (Psalm 34:8).

5. They who acclaim God to be a wilderness possess faulty memory (Deuteronomy 8:14). They fail to remember the goodness of the Lord. They fail to recall that God gave them His only Son to be their Savior; the Holy Spirit to be their comforter, enabler, preserver, and guide; the Holy Bible to be their instructor and shining light in the darkness to show the way to go; precious promises to be their stay in times of trouble and service; answered prayers; saints to encourage and assist; and a thousand other blessings (Psalm 103:1–5).

They fail to remember that "The LORD'S kindness never fails! If he had not been merciful, we would have been destroyed. The LORD can always be trusted to show mercy each morning" (Lamentations 3:22–23 CEV). They fail to remember that no good thing doth He withhold from those who seek it at His hands (Psalm 84:11). "Remember the former things of old; for I am God, and there is none other; I am God, and there is none like Me" (Isaiah 46:9 KJ21).

God did not deserve the demeaning allegation of the rebellious Israelites. Nor does He deserve it from us (Psalm 27:3). God is not "a wilderness" but a Paradise (Luke 23:43), not a barren terrain but a green pasture (Psalm 23:2)—a land flowing with milk and honey (Deuteronomy 26:9), not a *hireling* but a Shepherd who faithfully cares for the sheep of His fold (John 10:12). This they who trust Him fully find to be wholly true.

**"None of those who have had any dealings with God ever had reason to complain of him as a wilderness."**[222]—Matthew Henry.

## 59
### "Why Did Sarah Laugh?"

"Why did Sarah laugh?" (Genesis 18:13 NIV). God told Abraham that he would father a son. His wife, Sarah, laughed at the news, counting it to be humanly impossible at their age. Sarah's laugh of skepticism resounds loudly in universities, Hollywood, the government, the media, and liberal-minded churches.

At what does the skeptic laugh? He laughs at the belief that God created the world in seven days (he says the world and all in it originated from a "Big Bang"). He laughs at the existence of Hell (he says a God of love would never create such a place). He laughs at the miracle of the Red Sea (he says the sea was parted by the force of a strong wind blowing from one direction). He laughs at Jonah's experience in the belly of a great fish (he says it's but a myth, folklore). He laughs at Bible-thumping preachers and teachers with indignation. He laughs and sneers at churchgoers. Not a doctrine in the whole of Scripture has not been attacked with the skeptic's mockery, disdain, insults, and ridicule.[223] And yet, it stands firm and unshakeable.

Peter warns of scoffers and laughers at the Truth, saying, "First, I want to remind you that in the last days there will come scoffers who will do every wrong they can think of and laugh at the truth. This will be their line of argument: 'So Jesus promised to come back, did he? Then where is he? He'll never come! Why, as far back as anyone can remember, everything has remained exactly as it was since the first day of creation'" (2 Peter 3:3-4 TLB).

T. De Witt Talmage asserts, "Oh, what an awful thing it is to laugh in God's face and hurl His revelation back at Him! After a while, the day will come when they will say they did not laugh. Then all the hypercriticisms, all the caricatures, and all the learned sneers…will be brought to judgment, and…God will thunder, 'But thou didst laugh!' The meanest laughter ever uttered is the laughter of the skeptic."[224]

They may laugh now, but the laughter will be turned into wails of anguish at the Judgment. The skeptic's laughter can never drown out the voice of truth.

**"Skepticism is unbelief in cause and effect."**—Ralph Waldo Emerson.

### 60
### "How Long Will You Mourn?"

"How long will you mourn?" (1 Samuel 16:1 NIV). God asks the question of Samuel, who was mourning Saul's dethronement as King of Israel. Here are some lessons about mourning.

1. Mourning and grief are different. In contrast, grief is the internal feeling of sorrow (how a person thinks and feels), and mourning is its outward manifestation (tears, anxiety, fear, isolation). Swanson says mourning is "an [outward] emotional reaction of sorrow to a sad situation."[225]

2. Mourning is an instrument of God that brings comfort, relief, and healing to broken hearts. MacArthur asserts, "Human sorrow is a natural emotion. It is a God-given relief valve for the pain and sorrow in this fallen world and promotes the healing process."[226] Paul says that God's only prohibition regarding sorrow is that we're not to "sorrow as those who have no hope" of the resurrection (1 Thessalonians 4:13 NLV).

3. Mourning is not to be suppressed. It is a medicine. The mourning process must not be short-circuited. There is "a time to mourn, and a time to dance" (Ecclesiastes 3:4). Don't attempt to escape or skip the pain and distress part. Samuel Johnson said, "While grief is fresh, every attempt to divert only irritates. You must wait till it be digested." Longfellow wrote, "Well has it been said, that there is no grief like the grief which does not speak."

Don't bottle in the sorrow and pain; express it. Grief is never remedied entirely until it is expressed fully.[227] Ron Dunn said, "It is right and essential to express the pain of our souls. Sometimes the suffering can be endured only when the pain can be articulated."[228]

4. Everyone grieves or mourns differently. The absence of tears does not indicate that one person's grief is less horrendous than that of another. Never imitate another's pattern of grief. It's a unique process for each person.

5. Help to cope with grief and mourning is available. "Blessed are those who mourn, for they shall be comforted" (Matthew 5:4 ESV).

a. Coping strength is found in the help of the Holy Spirit. Jesus said, "And I will ask the Father, and he will give you another Helper, to be with you forever" (John 14:16 ESV). The Holy Spirit is the believers' Paraclete, "one who is called alongside," to help, support, and comfort "forever."

b. Coping strength is found in abiding trust and communion in Christ. Stowell states, "Even though your heart is breaking and tears are clouding your eyes and staining your cheeks, God does give us something worth trusting in tough times—and that's Him, and Him alone."[229] Stott said, "Stronger than any chemical tranquilizer is trust in our all-knowing God."[230]

c. Coping strength is found in the Holy Scripture. Spurgeon says, "There is not a promise—not a word in the Bible—that is not ours. In the depths of tribulation, it will comfort. In the midst of waves of distress, it will cheer; when sorrows surround, it will be our helper."[231]

d. Coping strength is found in saints who have been comforted. Saints who have been comforted by God are His ministers of comfort to others who grieve. Paul said, "Blessed be the God and Father of our Lord Jesus Christ, the Father of mercies and God of all comfort, who comforts us in all our affliction, so that we may be able to comfort those who are in any affliction, with the comfort with which we ourselves are comforted by God" (2 Corinthians 1:3–4 ESV).

6. Mourning will lessen. "The good news," states Spurgeon, "is that, by God's grace, in time, the sorrowing sadness will lessen more and more, giving way to sweet sadness. Though sorrow will never be completely erased, by God's promises and the testimonies of others who have walked the same path, it will evolve into a life of heightened peace, hope, and joy....Sorrow is not a stage you get through but rather a process you live with."

The intensity of a crushing hurt diminishes. The Bible says: "He brought them out of their gloom and darkness and broke their chains in pieces" (Psalm 107:14 GNT), "[I will give] them beauty for ashes, the oil of joy for mourning, the garment of praise for the spirit of heaviness" (Isaiah 61:3), and "I will turn their mourning into gladness; I will give them comfort and joy instead of sorrow" (Jeremiah 31:13 NIV).

Brooks elucidates upon Psalm 30:5, "Their mourning shall last but till morning. God will turn their winter's night into a summer's day, their sighing into singing, their grief into gladness, their mourning into music, their bitter into sweet, their wilderness into a paradise."[232]

7. Tranquility and joy follow the deep night of sorrow and mourning. "Weeping may endure for a night, but joy cometh in the morning" (Psalm 30:5). Sorrow is wrenching and despairing. Hopes and dreams crumble. Life is shattered into a million pieces. The darkness eclipses the light. All is gloomy. Faith is challenged. Doubts assail. A new, unwanted journey begins. But on its coattail, unseen, is a renewal of hope, peace, strength, purpose, and sprouting happiness.

8. Grief's duration or time cycle does not reflect spirituality.

9. The clock of grief ticks according to the person. It cannot be sped up. Recovery time from the mourning process is unique to the individual and cannot be based on another's experience. Grief has to work through whatever stages or passages are necessary for healing.

10. Duty often works as an antidote to grief. "Fill your horn with oil and be on your way" (1 Samuel 16:1 NIV). Ministry to others assuages (soothes and calms) sorrow and mourning. Abraham Lincoln said, "To ease another's heartache is to forget one's own." Bind up the wounds of others despite bleeding yourself (2 Corinthians 12:10). "My health fails; my spirits droop, yet God remains! He is the strength of my heart; he is mine forever!" (Psalm 73:26 TLB).

11. Sorrow and mourning can become immoderate. Steel asserts, "Sorrow, however reasonable and becoming, may be carried too far. It may be indulged until it unfits us for duty or darkens our hope in God; it may disturb our peace and weaken our energies; it may be made an occasion of our halting and of our neglecting public duty."[233] Mourning and grief that goes awry may need addressing by a trained Christian clinical therapist.

"'Come,' saith Christ, 'and I will give you rest. I will not *show* you rest nor barely *tell* you of rest, but I will *give* you rest. I am faithfulness itself and cannot lie; I will give you rest. I that have the greatest power to give it, the greatest will to give it, the greatest right to give it—come, laden sinners, and I will give you rest.'"[199]—Thomas Brooks

## 61
### "Who Makes the Mute or the Deaf, or the Seeing or the Blind?"

"Who makes the mute or the deaf, or the seeing or the blind? Is it not I, the Lord?" (Exodus 4:11 AMP). God counters Moses' excuse ("I stutter") for not speaking to Pharoah as commanded with a declaration of His miraculous power to regulate man's tongue, hearing and sight. Six lessons may be drawn from the attestation.

1. God determines man's abilities and disabilities.[234] "Who makes him…"

2. The disabled, in their weakness or deficiency, do incredible feats for the glory of God (1 Corinthians 1:27). Fanny Crosby, blinded at six weeks old, wrote over 7,000 hymns that have stirred the church. George Matheson, yet blind (he could only see shadows and forms), wrote the beloved hymn "O Love That Wilt Not Let Me Go," and pastored churches.

When General William Booth's eyesight began to leave him, his son Bramwell said, "Dad, you are going to be permanently blind."

Booth responded, "You mean that I am going to live the rest of my life in physical blindness?"

"I fear you must reckon with that fact," said Bramwell.

"Shall I never see your face again?" Booth asked.

"No," said Bramwell, "probably not in this world."

Booth then moved his hand slowly forward until he found Bramwell's hand. He grasped his son's hand and said, "I have done what I could for God and the people with my eyes. Now I shall do what I can for God and the people without my eyes!" Booth, despite losing his eyesight, refused to quit.

3. View disability through the lenses of God. Picasso states, "There is only one way to look at things until someone [God through the Holy Spirit, Scriptures, and caring saints] shows us how to look at them with different eyes."

4. God gives grace to cope with the handicap experienced when yielded to Him. He says, "My grace is all you need. Only when you are weak can everything be done completely by my power" (2 Corinthians 12:9 ERV).

5. Murmuring about a handicap is thwarted when the heart trusts God about it and with it. "And we know that all things work

together for good to them that love God, to them who are the called according to his purpose" (Romans 8:28).

6. No believer is ever put on the shelf due to a handicap. Jack Wellman says, "There is no point in a person's life when they are no longer useful to God or the church. It doesn't matter to God if you're disabled or not. God is the One Who enables the disabled and the rest of us too."[235]

C. S. Lewis remarks, "Every disability conceals a vocation, if only we can find it, which will 'turn the necessity to glorious gain.'"

"A bend in the road is not the end of the road. Unless you fail to make the turn."—Helen Keller

## 62
### "What Seest Thou?"

"Moreover the word of the LORD came unto me, saying, Jeremiah, what seest thou? And I said, I see a rod of an almond tree" (Jeremiah 1:11). The almond tree is "the wakeful tree" because throughout the weary winter, it anticipates and longs for spring when the radiant sun shines down upon it, and the birds nestle in its branches, sounding forth their glad song.

The illustration or parable reminds Jeremiah (and us) that God is watching over His Word to ensure its promises are fulfilled to His people at the right time. No promise will be left unfulfilled. That which is grasped in faith will become sight. "For I am the LORD. I speak, and the word which I speak will come to pass;...I will say the word and perform it" (Ezekiel 12:25 NKJV).

Unfulfilled promises (the second coming of Christ, reign of righteousness on earth, binding of Satan in eternal darkness forever, reunion with the saints, abolishment of sorrow, suffering, death, and tears in Heaven, etc.) are not unkept promises—just budding almonds awaiting their season to blossom. Find hope and consolation in the words of Christ: "Heaven and earth shall pass away, but my words shall not pass away" (Matthew 24:35).

"The spring cometh and also the summer. God watches over His Word to perform it" (see Jeremiah 1:12). Gladstone says, "Yes, as God watches over the almond blossoms to open their beautiful leaves, and to gladden the eyes of men, so will He open the promises and prophecies of His Word to fill men's hearts with joy and peace."[236]

"God makes a promise; faith believes it; hope anticipates it; and patience quietly awaits it."[237]—D. L. Moody

## 63

### "How Shall We Know the Word Which the LORD Hath Not Spoken?"

"How shall we know the word which the Lord hath not spoken?" (Deuteronomy 18:21). How might it be known if a prophet's (an appointed messenger, spokesman of God) words are the Word of God? Upon asking the question, God immediately answers (Deuteronomy 18:22).

The credibility of the prophet or messenger is manifested in his words.

1. Their words align with the Bible (1 John 4:1–3). Teachings that fail to mesh with the Scripture are false. Paul says, "Stay away from those who cause divisions and are upsetting people's faith, teaching things about Christ that are contrary to what you have been taught. Such teachers are not working for our Lord Jesus" (Romans 16:17–18 TLB).

2. Their words don't mix truth and lies (2 Peter 2:1–3). MacArthur said, "Mixing sacred truth with myths corrupts the Word of God. And the cults have done it for years."[238]

3. Their words do not contradict Scripture.

4. Their words about the future come to pass with flawless accuracy (Deuteronomy 18:20–21).

5. Their words are forthright. They refuse to whitewash the sin or condemnation that God pronounces, regardless of audience (2 Samuel 12:7; 2 Timothy 4:3–4).

6. Their words are God's words. Like Luther, the faithful messenger of God, says, "My conscience is captive to the Word of God."

7. Their words are borne witness to by their life. Jesus warned, "Beware of false teachers....You can detect them by the way they act, just as you can identify a tree by its fruit" (Matthew 7:15–16 TLB). Matthew Henry asserts, "By the fruits of their persons, their words and actions, and the course of their conversation. If you would know whether they be right or not, observe how they live; their works will testify for them or against them."[239]

Don't accept, at face value, a prophet (messenger of God). John counsels, "Beloved, believe not every spirit, but try the spirits whether they are of God: because many false prophets are gone out into the world" (1 John 4:1). Note, false teachers creep in unawares in some of the most conservative of churches, colleges, and seminaries. Jude asserts, "For there are certain men crept in unawares, who were before of old ordained to this condemnation, ungodly men, turning the grace of our God into lasciviousness, and denying the only Lord God, and our Lord Jesus Christ" (Jude 4).

"Beware of false prophets because their influence may distort one's own embrace of the teaching of Jesus."[240]—J. Nolland

## 64
### "Can a Woman Forget Her Nursing Child?"

"Can a woman forget her sucking child, that she should not have compassion on the son of her womb? Yea, they may forget, yet will I not forget thee" (Isaiah 49:15). Babylon's captivity prompted the Israelites to claim that God had forsaken them. The rhetorical question denounces the allegation. As a mother's disposition is to nurse and protect her baby relentlessly, come what may, God's nature is to abide with and care for His own endlessly. He said, "I will not forget you." Solomon says, "The steadfast love of the Lord never ceases; his mercies never come to an end; they are new every morning; great is your faithfulness" (Lamentations 3:22–23 ESV).

The Bible says, "For he hath said, I will never leave thee, nor forsake thee. So that we may boldly say, The Lord is my helper" (Hebrews 13:5–6). Note the four parts of the promise.

1. The pledge of the promise. Christ promises, "I will never leave thee, nor forsake thee." He pledges to walk with the saint ("never leave thee"), being their helper in every life circumstance. In a letter to his friend Charles Heetwood, John Owen says, "Live and pray, hope and wait patiently, and do not despond; the promise stands invincible that He will never leave nor forsake us."

2. The Promiser of the Promise. "For he hath said." A promise is only as good as its giver. Some make promises they are unable or unwilling to keep. But it is not so with the Promiser of this promise, for He is "the faithful God, which keepeth covenant and mercy with them that love him and keep his commandments to a thousand generations" (Deuteronomy 7:9). "The inviolable faithfulness of the Promiser is good security for the accomplishment of the promise." None but God may say truthfully, "I will never leave thee, nor forsake thee."

3. The perimeter of the promise. Wherever the locale—hospital, assisted living facility, land or sea, prison, home, or foreign soil—the promise stands. Whatever the circumstance—sickness, suffering, loneliness, grief, utter hopelessness, fear, deathbed—it is included in the promise. Whenever the time—now, tomorrow, or anytime ('never will I leave thee')—the promise applies. It pertains to all times of the believer's life—good or bad, ups and downs, joys and sorrows.

4. The profit of the promise. The assurance of Christ's unwavering companionship secures peace amid life's storms, averts the fear of His abandonment, assures His help in the hour of need, emboldens with strong courage and bravery to face the

darkest of trials, and fills the heart with satisfying contentment, knowing the Great Physician and the Holy Comforter are always available. Maclaren says, "Peace comes not from the absence of trouble, but from the presence of God."

> I know not where His islands lift
>     Their fronded palms in air;
> I only know I cannot drift
>     Beyond His love and care.
>
> ~ John G. Whittier

"We (Christians) are always in the presence of God. There is never a non-sacred moment! His presence never diminishes. Our awareness of His presence may falter, but the reality of His presence never changes."—Max Lucado.

## 65
### "Can a Woman Forget Her Nursing Child?"

"Can a woman forget her sucking child, that she should not have compassion on the son of her womb? Yea, they may forget, yet will I not forget thee" (Isaiah 49:15). The love of Jehovah for His children is greater than a mother's maternal love. Even that may perish, but never His loving affection.

1. The pledge that He makes is never to forget. "Yet will I not forget thee." Friends and family may forsake and abandon, but never God: "Even if my father and mother abandon me, the Lord will hold me close" (Psalm 27:10 NLT). Throughout the scriptures, God promises, "O Israel, thou shalt not be forgotten of me" (Isaiah 44:21).

> No, never alone,
> No, never alone,
> He promised never to leave me,
> Never to leave me alone"
>
> – Ludie Pickett (1897)

2. The proof that He gives never to forget. "I have graven thee upon the palms of My hands; thy walls are continually before Me" (Isaiah 49:16). God will not forget his children because He has engraved them (not just their name but image, anxieties, temptations, and needs) upon the palms of His hands in permanent ink. Spurgeon says, "The Lord's loving word of rebuke should make us blush; He cries, 'How can I have forgotten thee when I have graven thee upon the palms of My hands? How dares thou doubt my constant remembrance when the memorial is set upon my very flesh?'"[241]

Spurgeon relates a time in history when a friend's image was imprinted onto the hand out of the person's dearness and desire to keep them close to the heart. The person never had to retrieve such a picture from an album, for he always had it.[242] Similarly, the Lord always has His children with Him stamped upon His palms as a memorial of remembrance. When you doubt the presence and love of God, look at His hands.

3. The profit to those He does not forget. The person who God does not forget is nourished and cherished all his days with the tenderness and care of a mother to her nursing child. Saith God, "As one whom his mother comforteth, so will I comfort you" (Isaiah 66:13). Matthew Henry says, "Note, God's compassions to his people infinitely exceed those of the tenderest parents towards their children."[243]

J. I. Packer remarked, "I am graven on the palms of His hands. I am never out of His mind. He knows me as a friend, One who loves me, and there is no moment when His eye is off me or His attention distracted for me, and no moment, therefore, when His care falters. This is momentous knowledge. There is unspeakable comfort—the sort of comfort that energizes, be it said—not enervates—in knowing that God is constantly taking knowledge of me in love and watching over me for my good."[244]

"His setting them as a mark on His hand, or a seal upon His arm, denotes His being ever mindful of them."[245]—Matthew Henry.

## 66
### "Have I Any Pleasure at All That the Wicked Should Die?"

"Have I any pleasure at all that the wicked should die, saith the Lord God, and not that he should return from his ways and live?" (Ezekiel 18:23 KJ21). To the question, Clarke answers, "No! That is foreign to Him whose name is love, and whose nature is mercy. On the contrary, He 'wills that he should return from his evil ways and live.'"[246] Why has God no pleasure in the death of the wicked?

1. They are objects of His love. God loves those who spurn His love.

2. God's character or nature rules it out. God could no more take pleasure in the suffering of a person in Hell than a parent could in the deserved punishment of their wayward son.

3. At death, the sinner's day of salvation, which God yearns for, is forever passed. In Hell, the sinner's cries for mercy are unheard.

4. God does not relish the thought of reprisal for man's rebellion toward Him. Bonar says, "He did not kindle Hell in order to gratify His revenge. He does not cast sinners headlong into its endless flames in order to vent to His blind fury. He will finally condemn the unbelieving, but not because He delights to do so, but because He is the righteous Lord that loveth righteousness."[247]

The divine assertion is proven in four ways.

1. God's graciousness to save all that believe proves it. He keeps as many as possible from Hell. If He found delight in the sinner's punishment in Hell, no effort would be made to keep him out of its torment.

2. Calvary proves it. God's displeasure in the death of the wicked was manifest on the Cross. He let His only Son die rather than allow sinners to be thrust into Hell without hope of salvation. "God didn't spare his own Son but handed him over to death for all of us" (Romans 8:32 NOG). If He took pleasure in the death of the wicked, no avenue of escape or recovery from it would have been provided. See John 3:16. As long as breath is in a man, God's

pleasure is to expend every effort and means to save him from the just death that awaits (2 Peter 3:9).

3. God's longsuffering toward sinners proves it. The Bible says, "The Lord is not slack concerning his promise, as some men count slackness; but is longsuffering to us-ward, not willing that any should perish, but that all should come to repentance" (2 Peter 3:9).

4. God's own Word proves it. He says, 'I have no pleasure in the death of the wicked.'

The bottom line: God's pleasure is not in the destruction of the wicked but in their repentance and salvation. Although God's justice calls for severe punishment upon the unrepentant, He prefers and yearns to do everything possible to grant mercy and salvation (2 Peter 3:9).

The Bible says, "This is good, and pleases God our Savior, who wants all people to be saved and to come to a knowledge of the truth" (1 Timothy 2:3–4 NIV). C. S. Lewis said, "All that are in Hell, choose it. Without that self-choice, there could be no Hell."

**God did not kindle the fire in Hell to delight in the suffering of the wicked but as a just punishment for their sin.**—Frank Shivers.

## 67

### "Are Ye Not as Children of the Ethiopians unto Me, O Children of Israel?"

"Are ye not as children of the Ethiopians unto Me, O children of Israel?" (Amos 9:7). The rhetorical question was intended to clarify that Israel (the Northern Kingdom, now pronounced as "the sinful kingdom") was just as accountable before God as any other nation.[248]

God judges and punishes the believer for wicked conduct as He does the heathen. Israel was banking on a false security in their rebellion against God. They thought that since He delivered them from Egyptian bondage, His favor would remain with them despite their idolatrous practices. The question revealed the assumption wrong; they had become no better than the ungodly Ethiopians who surrounded them and would face judgment (Amos 9:8; 3:1–2).

How saddening it is when the children of God act like the ungodly Ethiopians, when the devoutly religious "throw off their profession and become as bad as the worst,"[249] and think God will wink at their sin and still bless them. Do not be deceived; no person or nation is beyond the judgment of God for repeated and unrepentant sins.

Note, God loves the believer with everlasting love and saves him from the wrath to come. Nevertheless, the believer who lives carnally and sinfully will suffer judgment. "Be sure your sin will find you out." "The eyes of the LORD are on the righteous, and his ears are attentive to their cry" (Psalm 34:15 NIV). However, "The face of the Lord is against those who do evil" (Psalm 34:16 NIV).

To align with the practices of the ungodly is to distance oneself "afar off" from God, His favor, and to be judged severely as them (Amos 9:8). To the wayward Israelites, Amos declared, "Seek the Lord and live, or else he will sweep like fire through Israel and consume her, and none of the idols in Bethel can put it out" (Amos 5:6 TLB). The same promise of restoration and pronouncement of judgment applies to all who behave like the ungodly.

"It is a thing to be greatly lamented that the children of Israel often become as children of the Ethiopians."[250]—Matthew Henry.

## 68
### "Do Not My Words Do Good to Him That Walketh Uprightly?"

"Do not My words do good to him that walketh uprightly?" (Micah 2:7b). The question argues for Israel's obedience to God's Word, which promises to benefit those who walk in its truth. Five facts about the Holy Scripture and its promise are indicated or suggested.

1. The intention of God's Word is to bring good to His people. "This Book of the Law shall not depart out of thy mouth, but thou shalt meditate therein day and night, that thou mayest observe to do according to all that is written therein. For then thou shalt make thy way prosperous, and then thou shalt have good success" (Joshua 1:8 KJ21).

2. The promise of the benefit of the Word of God belongs to the upright (Psalm 119:30). If the Word of God fails to do good, the fault lies within man, not it. It is the righteous man who may lean upon the pledge of God in Isaiah 55:11: "So shall My word be that goeth forth out of My mouth: It shall not return unto Me void, but it shall accomplish that which I please, and it shall prosper in the thing whereto I sent it."

3. The good that proceeds from the Word of God sown on fertile soil is plenteous. It gives divine knowledge and understanding, God's counsel, sanctification, correction of error, direction to life, comfort to sorrow (a healing balm to a broken heart and troubled soul), illumination about God's will and plan, inner strength and power, courage and boldness, peace, purpose, hope, happiness, and instruction about spiritual growth.

> Now, let a new and better hope
>   Within our hearts be stirred;
> The Lord hath yet more light and truth
>   To break forth from His Word.
>             – George Rawson (1807–1889)

4. The good that the Word of God gives is not gained elsewhere. There is no Book like the Bible. No other book possesses the treasures the Bible contains or the help that, through the Holy Spirit, it gives.

5. Whatever the Word of God says profits the ready receiver. Every flower in God's Garden, even those given to another, that clash with one's views and conduct and bring pain, bear

enrichment to him that inhales deeply its heavenly fragrance and practices it.[251]

To experience the good benefits and blessings of God's Word, walk uprightly, receive it gladly, and implement it quickly.

"'Do not My words do good to him that walketh uprightly?' Yes, they do good. When they are translated, not into languages and creeds, but into living deeds."[252]—the Homilist

## 69
### "Is the Spirit of the LORD Straitened?"

"Is the Spirit of the LORD straitened?" (Micah 2:7a). "Is the Holy Spirit less an Enlightener, a Sanctifier, and a Guide now than He was in the days of Abraham, or David, or Paul? Is He less powerful? Is He less willing? Is He less gracious in His promises?"[253] The answer is a resounding no. He changes not. The same power and attributes He possessed with them at Pentecost and on the first Easter morning exist today and will last forever.

1. The saint often acts and works like the Spirit is straitened. How? When they expect nothing supernatural to result in their preaching and teaching. When they depend upon methodology and gimmickry to convert the lost. When they faint before the enemy of Christ. When they write some men and churches off as hopeless. When they allocate His work to particular times and events (like Sunday mornings or revivals).[254] When they expect little or no benefit from prayer. When they set boundaries on the Spirit's power to provide what is needed. When they fail to plead for His mighty touch to be upon work done for Christ. When they prioritize duty and other things above Him. When they count themselves too frail to be used by Him.

2. Evil forces cannot straighten the Holy Spirit. Despite Satan's best efforts to impede the Spirit in His work, it falters. He cannot quarantine the wind of the Spirit that "blows everywhere *[He]* wants to" (John 3:8 ERV).

3. Proof that the Spirit is not straightened is witnessed each time a soul is converted; the preacher preaches with great power and efficacy, sinners respond to the altar call, hardened sinners become convicted, the flame of revival sweeps through the congregation, an unspeakable peace is given to the grief-stricken soul, and a soul is refreshed and renewed at the hearing of the Word. Rely by faith more upon the agency of the Holy Spirit to accomplish great and mighty things for the glory of God.

> Come, Spirit, come in mighty power,
>   As on the blessed day of old
> When fell the Pentecostal shower
>   That gathered thousands to the fold.
>         – Fanny Crosby (1820–1915)

"We must have the Holy Spirit, and if we have Him not, all our machinery will stand still; or if it goes on, it will produce no effect whatever."[255]—C. H. Spurgeon.

## 70

### "Is Not This a Brand Plucked out of the Fire?"

Satan's accusation against Joshua, the high priest, was met with the Lord's defensive question: "Is not this a brand plucked out of the fire?" (Zechariah 3:2). The question is descriptive of the sinner's vile condition, dangerous plight, and miraculous rescue by God's unmerited grace and mercy through Jesus' death and resurrection. It is the testimony of the redeemed and the attestation of the Savior to Satan. Note:

1. A brand plucked out of the fire once abode within the fire.

a. The godliest of saints once abode in the fire of vileness and worthlessness [morally bankrupt and at the bottom of the barrel; natural depravity] fit for nothing but to be consumed by its flame. "But ye are washed, but ye are sanctified, but ye are justified in the name of the Lord Jesus, and by the Spirit of our God" (1 Corinthians 6:11). Never, dear child of God, forget from whence you were fallen and rescued. But for God's grace, you would be still in the fire.

b. All men abide in the fire of sin, its condemnation until delivered. David declared, "Behold, I was shaped in iniquity, and in sin did my mother conceive me" (Psalm 51:5 KJ21). Paul said, "Wherefore, as by one man sin entered into the world, and death by sin; and so death passed upon all men, for that all have sinned" (Romans 5:12).

c. There is no better concise testimony for the saved than to say, "I am a brand plucked out of the fire"! It is spot on.

2. A brand plucked out of the fire bears marks of being in the fire. The saved retains marks of his unregenerate estate. The conscience still accuses. The flesh still tempts. The marring scars of sin remain. Bad habits try to resurrect. It is to the glory of God that the saved bear such marks, bearing witness to His power to change vile and sinful creatures into His trophies of grace.

Spurgeon asserts, "We have here a 'brand plucked out of the fire.' Sinners these, who though they have still within them the propensity to sin, are no longer in the fire of sin. They have been taken away from it. They sin through infirmity, but willful sin they do not commit. The fire that once burned within them has been quenched. They are rescued from that fire which once threatened their everlasting destruction. They are brands still, but brands no longer in the fire."[256]

3. A brand plucked out of the fire escapes the destructive consequences of the fire. The person plucked from the fire may have been scorched and pained by the fire (fruit of sin) but is delivered from its bitterest fruit of eternal despair, misery, destruction, and damnation. James says, "And sin when it is finished, bringeth forth death" (James 1:15 GNV).

> What a wonderful change in my life has been wrought
>     Since Jesus came into my heart!
> I have light in my soul for which long I had sought,
>     Since Jesus came into my heart!
>                     – Rufus H. McDaniel (1914)

4. A brand plucked out of the fire was delivered and rescued by another. Can a brand save itself? Can it quicken itself to life? Can it remove itself from the fire? Absolutely not. All efforts to save oneself are futile. Apart from God's hand snatching a person out of the fire, he will suffer and perish forever in Hell.

5. A brand plucked out of the fire can never be put back in it. Its deliverance is permanent. The words "plucked out of the fire" affirm the believer's inalterable conversion. Plucked out of the fire (sin and the wrath of God) by the nail-scarred hand of Christ, the believer is kept from falling back into it. Peter says believers "are kept by the power of God through faith for salvation" (1 Peter 1:5 KJ21). Matthew Henry states, "They have been wonderfully delivered out of the fire, that God might be glorified in them; and will He then cast them off and abandon them? No, He will not."[257] See John 10:28–29.

6. A brand plucked out of the fire differs from when in the fire. A brand plucked from the fire doesn't behave like one still in the fire. Paul says, "Therefore if any man be in Christ, he is a new creature: old things are passed away; behold, all things are become new" (2 Corinthians 5:17). The change at salvation is so emphatic and evident that people who know the person best say, "Is this not a brand plucked from the fire?"

Bring home two questions to your soul. The first question is, "Am I a brand plucked out of the burning?" If uncertainty exists, ensure salvation through repentance of sin and acceptance of Christ as Lord and Savior (Romans 10:9–13). Charles Wesley wrote,

> O Jesus, of thee I require,
>   If still thou art able to save,
> The brand to pluck out of the fire,
>   And ransom my soul from the grave.

The second question is, "What is the responsibility of brands plucked out of the fire?" It is to rescue those who are still in it. Jude exhorts, "Save others by snatching them from the fire of hell.

Show mercy to others, even though you are afraid that you might be stained by their sinful lives" (Jude 23 NOG). Richard Baxter said, "I remember no one sin that my conscience doth so much accuse and judge me for as for doing so little for the saving of souls and for not dealing with the lost soul ones more fervently and earnestly for their conversion."[258]

"A converted soul is a brand plucked out of the fire by a miracle of free grace, and therefore shall not be left to be a prey to Satan."[259]—Matthew Henry.

## 71
### "Where Is Mine Honor?"

"A son honoureth his father, and a servant his master: if then I be a father, where is mine honour? and if I be a master, where is my fear? saith the Lord of hosts unto you, O priests, that despise my name. And ye say, Wherein have we despised thy name" (Malachi 1:6). The priests' conduct clashed with their confession. They claimed God as their Father but failed to honor and revere Him as His children through worship, priesthood duties, and personal conduct. Their hypocrisy is widespread today. Of them, Jesus says, "This people draweth nigh unto me with their mouth, and honoureth me with their lips; but their heart is far from me" (Matthew 15:8).

Marks of the hypocrite:

1. The religious hypocrite is the person who parades before others an identity not their own. The word *hypocrite* refers to an actor on stage who wears a mask to portray the character being played. The audience sees the masked actor, not his true identity beneath the mask. They are mere pretenders of the character played.

2. Hypocrites make hollow, insincere, and pompous confessions of love and honor to God. Says Brooks, "How many threadbare souls are to be found under silken cloaks and gowns!"

3. Hypocrites live in the contradiction between what is said and what is done. They resemble a safety pin that points one way but heads another. They mirror a character in Bunyan's book *Pilgrim's Progress* named "Mr. Facing Both-Ways," a man, it is presumed, who talked one way but walked another. Spurgeon asserts, "A fellow who howls with the wolves and bleats with the sheep gets nobody's praise unless it is the Devil's. To carry two faces under one hat is, however, very common. Many roost with the poultry and go share with Reynard the Fox. Holding with the hares and hunting with the hounds is still in fashion."[260] Says A. B. Simpson, "A divided heart loses both worlds." Stephen Charnock states, "It is a sad thing to be Christians at a supper, heathens in our shops, and devils in our closets."[261]

The cure for hypocrisy is found in possessing a pure and untainted love for God and consistency in obeying His rule. It is to pray with John Calvin, "My heart I offer to you, O Lord, promptly and sincerely." Jeremy Taylor counsels, "Do not burn false fire upon God's altar; do not pose and pretend, either to Him or to yourself, in your religious exercises; do not say more than you mean, or use exaggerated language that goes beyond the facts, when speaking to Him whose word is truth."

**"The house built on the sand may oftentimes be built higher, have more fair parapets and battlements, windows and ornaments, than that which is built upon the rock; yet all gifts and privileges equal not one grace."—John Owen.**

## 72

"And Ye Say, 'Wherein Have We Despised Thy Name?'"

"Saith the Lord of hosts unto you, O priests, who despise My name. And ye say, 'Wherein have we despised Thy name?'" (Malachi 1:6 KJ21). The priests denied the accusation of profanation of God's name, and they asked for proof of the charge. Matthew Henry asserts, "It is common with proud sinners, when they are reproved, to stand thus upon their justification. These priests had most horridly profaned sacred things, and yet, like *the adulterous woman*, they said that they had done no wickedness; they were so inobservant of themselves that they remembered not or reflected not upon their own acts."[262]

Though not obliged to do so, God, as a prosecutor in a trial, states irrefutable evidence of the priests' guilt.

1. The priests were so worldly that not even one would attend to God's work without the promise of pay (Malachi 1:10). *Application:* Preachers who only preach and serve God for personal gain indicate a corrupt spirit and a mistaken call. Jesus called them "hirelings" (John 10:12).

2. The priests gave God sickly sacrifices (Malachi 1:13). Torn (injured), lame, and sick sacrifices were given to God when He deserved and required the best. *Application:* Shepherds and flocks are guilty of giving God sick gifts. Cold formalistic prayers, songs without sincerity, work without heart, mechanical worship, sickly sermons, offerings that cost them nothing to give, and ill-prepared Sunday school lessons.[263] What profanation of God's name it is to give God that which is sickly. "Give of your best to the Master." He asks no less. He deserves far more.

3. The priests compromised their service (Malachi 1:14). The law required that the flour offering be made of "fine flour" (Leviticus 2:1), but the priest brought "polluted bread." *Application:* The minister's task must be performed biblically without allowance for "polluted bread." He must keep the table of the Lord sacred and free from the world's pollution and adulteration (Malachi 1:12).

4. The priests served God perfunctorily (Malachi 1:10). Lacking a heart of devotion and reverence to God and their sacred calling, they served Him slothfully, indifferently, and deplorably to the degree the "church" (Temple) and people would have been far better off without them. *Application:* Churches with preachers like these priests ought to expel them or shut their doors (they would be better off!). Saith the Lord, "Woe be unto the pastors that destroy and scatter the sheep of my pasture! Saith the LORD. Therefore, thus saith the Lord God of Israel against the pastors that feed my

people; Ye have scattered my flock, and driven them away, and have not visited them: behold, I will visit upon you the evil of your doings, saith the LORD" (Jeremiah 23:1–2).

Addressing the preachers at his London Bible College, Spurgeon said, "It will matter eternally how we have discharged our work during our lifetime. 'Thou art weighed in the balances, and art found wanting'—will that be the verdict on any one of us when we stand before the Lord God Almighty who trieth the hearts and searcheth the reins of the children of men?"[264] "The gates of hell shall not prevail against it [the church]" (Matthew 16:18). Note, God says, despite the hypocrisy and deception of the priests and the sins of His people, that "My Name shall be great" (magnified and glorified) throughout the earth (Malachi 1:11). God always has a remnant who will not cave to godliness and worldliness but bear His banner in battle victoriously.

5. The priests failed to hold the people accountable to God's standards (Malachi 1:13). The people did not fail to bring their sacrifices. However, the sacrifices were the worst they had and served only to mock and profane God. Instead of rejecting them, the priests accepted them, violating the Law (God's standard). *Application:* Preachers are to hold God's people to His standard without wavering or faltering, regardless of cost or consequence. The shepherd is God's watchman over the souls of the flock to hold them accountable to God's precepts and rules (Hebrews 13:17).

6. The priests profaned God's name (Malachi 1:6). Not just what they did in ministerial duty, but their very person profaned God's name. Matthew Henry asserts, "God's name is all that whereby he has made himself known—His word and ordinances; these they had low thoughts of and vilified that which it was their business to magnify. His purity cannot be polluted by us, for He is unspotted, but His name may be profaned, and nothing profanes it more than the misconduct of priests, whose business it is to do honor to it."[265] *Application:* There is no greater offense than for a minister to profane (to treat with irreverence, disdain, disrespect) God's sacred name. Spurgeon says, "It is a terribly easy matter to

be a minister of the Gospel and a vile hypocrite at the same time."[266]

7. The priests murmured that their duty was weariness (Malachi 1:13). "Ye said also, Behold, what a weariness is it!" The priests bemoaned the very ministry that priests before them enjoyed and did gladly.[267] The former priests, in seeing what was happening in God's house, lamented, "My heart is breaking as I remember how it used to be: I walked among the crowds of worshipers, leading a great procession to the house of God, singing for joy and giving thanks amid the sound of a great celebration" (Psalm 42:4 NLT). *Application:*

a. It is a bad sign when the preacher considers worship and work weariness.[268] The minister who serves God out of love and sacred calling finds the work, despite its exhausting demands, a grand pleasure and reward. "They go from strength to strength, every one of them in Zion appeareth before God" (Psalm 84:7).

b. Retired ministers who served well, remembering how things used to be in the church, lament the work that some who followed them perform.

"**I am no advocate for an idle and ill-deserving ministry.**"[269]— C. H. Spurgeon

73
"What Seest Thou?"

"What seest thou?" (Jeremiah 1:11). Jeremiah is informed through a vision of a budding almond of future things, the meaning of which God explained.

Amidst the deluge of evil and abandonment of God, do you see the budding of the almond leaves (the promises of God unfolding to make things better)? Wickedness and lawlessness rage, bringing heartache and havoc. Is there any hope of a soon remedy? What saith the promises of God? "What seest thou?"

Is there any hope for man's salvation and reconciliation with God, or is he hopelessly lost and damned to an eternity in Hell? Has he passed the point of no return? What says God's Word? "What seest thou?"

Is man annihilated at death? "If a man dies, shall he live again?" Is there nothing beyond the cemetery, the grave, and the casket? What says the Holy Scripture? "What seest thou?"

What prophesy is coming to pass on the world stage? What saith God's Word? "What seest thou?"

In brokenness and sorrow, is there not comfort and hope, a balm in Gilead to be found to heal and console? What saith the promises? "What seest thou?"

Will the day come when people "shall beat their swords into plowshares, and their spears into pruning hooks; nation shall not lift up sword against nation, neither shall they learn war anymore"? What saith God's Word? "What seest thou?"

Looking into the future, "What seest thou?" Is there any hope for a better day? Is the King coming to take His children without fear, pain, or crying to a land of reunion, where all things are made new? What says the truth in the sacred book? "What seest thou?"

A vision of what will unfold (the budding of the almond) stems from sound theological knowledge. "As people understand your word, it brings light to their lives" (Psalm 119:130 ERV). "What seest thou?"

1. Some see more than others because they choose to see it. Closed eyes ignore and avoid the truth and the revelation of God. He is never so blind as he who will not see. Henry Van Dyke said, "No amount of energy will take the place of thought. A strenuous life with its eyes shut is a kind of wild insanity."

2. Some see more than others because of their spiritual estate. "It is to us, however, that God has revealed these things. How? Through the Spirit. For the Spirit probes all things, even the profoundest depths of God" (1 Corinthians 2:10 CJB). It is to the believer that the Holy Spirit reveals the mysteries and operations of

God. Unbelievers are inapt to see the budding of the almond leaves, for Satan, "the god of this world," has blinded their eyes (2 Corinthians 4:4).

Two sisters sought to describe a dress in a storefront window to their blind sister. Despite their best effort, they failed. The believer's effort to describe and explain the splendor of salvation to the lost, apart from the Spirit's miraculous work of opening their blinded eyes, is equally futile. Spurgeon asserts, "The only hope for them is to believe in Jesus who can give sight to the spiritually blind as easily as He gave sight to the physically blind when He was here in the flesh."[270]

3. Some see more than others because of their spiritual plane. The profoundly spiritual see more than the brazenly shallow or carnal. This is why it appears some Christians march to a different drumbeat.

4. Some see more than others because they seek to see. They are not content with limited eyesight; they yearn to see more. Thus, they pray, "Open my eyes to see wonderful things in your Word" (Psalm 119:18 TLB).

> Open my eyes that I may see
> Glimpses of truth Thou hast for me.
> Place in my hands the wonderful key
> That shall unclasp and set me free.
> Silently now I wait for Thee,
> Ready, my God, Thy will to see.
> Open my eyes; illumine me,
> Spirit divine!
>
> – Clara H. Scott (1895)

5. Some see more than others because of the hardship experienced. Crises in life (death, divorce, business failure, life-threatening disease, suffering) thrust the eyes open to a fuller grasp of spiritual truth and its application.

6. Some see more than others for divine purposes. God enabled Elisha to *see* the mountains full of horses and chariots of

fire surrounding them, while his servant only saw, at first, the mighty army that stood against them (2 Kings 6:15).

7. Some see more than others because of their in-depth study of the Scripture. The diligent student of the Word sees more than its casual reader.

"What seest thou?" "What seest thou?" How's your eyesight? The kind of lenses or glasses worn determine what is seen and the clarity and accuracy of what is seen. "I counsel thee to…anoint thine eyes with eyesalve [Holy Spirit illumination], that thou mayest see" (Revelation 3:18). Don't fail to see the budding of the almond (the opening and fulfilling God's promises to His people). Turn the focusing dial of the telescope upon His promises until all is seen clearly and accurately. "For thou wilt light my candle: the LORD my God will enlighten my darkness" (Psalm 18:28).

May "the eyes of your understanding [be] enlightened; that ye may know what is the hope of his calling, and what the riches of the glory of his inheritance in the saints, And what is the exceeding greatness of his power to us-ward who believe, according to the working of his mighty power, Which he wrought in Christ, when he raised him from the dead, and set him at his own right hand in the heavenly places, Far above all principality, and power, and might, and dominion, and every name that is named, not only in this world, but also in that which is to come" (Ephesians 1:18–21). Amen, and amen.

**"The first step to overcoming spiritual blindness [or distortion] is to acknowledge its existence."—Unknown.**

## 74

### "Is There a God Beside Me?"

"Is there a God beside me? yea, there is no God; I know not any" (Isaiah 44:8). When God didn't act according to the Israelites' expectations, they sought a god who would. God responds by saying that He alone is God; there is none other, and He substantiates the assertion in four ways.

1. Graven images are lifeless statues made by man's hands. God says of them that they "shall not profit; and they are their own witnesses; they see not, nor know" (Isaiah 44:9), cannot display compassion and love or answer man's cry for help or deliver him from his troubles (Isaiah 44:17; Isaiah 46:7). In time, the graven images of stone crumble into dust, and those of wood decay or are consumed by the fire. In contrast, Jehovah God is the Almighty God, a mighty deliverer, redeemer, helper, counselor, and compassionate Father who reigns forever and ever. "Mark how this glorious self-existent Being is subject to none, exists in Himself, the source of all being, and subject to no other beings."[271]

2. God's ability to predict the future accurately proves He is the true and living God. He said, "Do not tremble, do not be afraid. Did I not proclaim this and foretell it long ago? You are my witnesses" (Isaiah 44:8a NIV). MacArthur comments, "Israel's God repeatedly predicted the future accurately, enabling Israel to witness to His truthful accuracy (Isaiah 43:10), and thus the reality that He was the only eternal, living God."[272] Only Him, who is God, can accurately predict what will happen.

Spurgeon says, "All things in Heaven and earth are full of voices bearing witness for the living God. The universe, human history, governments, philosophy, science, art, and institutions are witnessing for God."[273] But most significantly, the Christian is called to testify to the fact that God is the only God and man's only Savior (Isaiah 43:12; Acts 1:8). Matthew Henry says, "God's people are witnesses for Him, and can attest, upon their knowledge and experience, concerning the power of His grace, the sweetness of His comforts, the tenderness of His providence, and the truth of His promise."[274]

3. Further proof that Israel's God was the living God is proved by a challenge from God to the idols. God says, "who among them can declare this, and shew us former things? let them bring forth their witnesses, that they may be justified: or let them hear, and say, It is truth" (Isaiah 43:9). They are challenged to substantiate their claim that they are God, not the God of Israel, with witnesses to prove their omniscience and omnipotence. If proof is

forthcoming, they shall be justified in their claim. If not, they must say, "It is truth" that Israel's God is God alone.[275] The graven images lost the challenge. Matthew Henry attests, "The cause of God is not afraid to stand a fair trial; but it may reasonably be expected that those who cannot justify themselves in their irreligion should submit to the power of the truth and true religion."[276]

4. God's declaration that He is the only God is proven by His miracles and works. God says, "But what my prophets say, I do; when they say Jerusalem will be delivered and the cities of Judah lived in once again—it shall be done! When I speak to the rivers and say, "Be dry!" they shall be dry. When I say of Cyrus, "He is my shepherd," he will certainly do as I say; and Jerusalem will be rebuilt and the Temple restored, for I have spoken it" (Isaiah 44:26–28 TLB).

Remember the contest between Baal and God at Carmel (1 Kings 18:24). The God that sent fire upon the altar would be acclaimed as the true God. The priests of Baal went first but without success. "So they shouted louder and slashed themselves with swords and spears, as was their custom, until their blood flowed. Midday passed, and they continued their frantic prophesying until the time for the evening sacrifice. But there was no response, no one answered, no one paid attention" (1 Kings 18:28–29 NIV).

When it came Elijah's time to ask the God of Israel to send the fire, buckets of water first soaked the altar until the trench was full. This was to remove any doubt that if the fire came, it would be at the hand of Jehovah God. Elijah then prayed, "Answer me, LORD, answer me, so these people will know that you, LORD, are God, and that you are turning their hearts back again. Then the fire of the LORD fell and burned up the sacrifice, the wood, the stones and the soil, and also licked up the water in the trench" (1 Kings 18:37–38 NIV). "When all the people saw this, they fell prostrate and cried, 'The Lord—he is God! The Lord—he is God!'" (1 Kings 18:39). Had the song been written, they would have in mighty chorus sung, "There is no God like Jehovah; there is no God like Jehovah."

"God has no competitor or equal. He alone is God. He alone holds this unique position."[277]—J. Vernon McGee.

75

"Who Hath Begotten the Drops of Dew?"

"Who hath begotten the drops of dew?" (Job 38:28). God, being the Father of the dew (its only maker and giver), reveals His superiority over Job and every man. Dewdrops easily bear several spiritual contrasts. After reviewing them, hopefully, you will never look at the morning dew with the same eyes. I won't.

1. Dewdrops picture the goodness of the Lord. The dew reminds us that God's blessings and goodness to His people are new each morning and innumerable. "The faithful love of the Lord never ends! His mercies never cease. Great is his faithfulness; his mercies begin afresh each morning" (Lamentations 3:22–23 NLT). "I will be as the dew unto Israel [and to all His children]: he shall grow as the lily, and cast forth his roots as Lebanon. His branches shall spread, and his beauty shall be as the olive tree, and his smell as Lebanon" (Hosea 14:5–6). Matthew Henry says, "He rains righteousness upon us and is Himself as the dew unto Israel."[278]

2. Dewdrops picture the work of the Spirit. Spurgeon says, "Without the Spirit of God, I am a dry and withered thing. I droop; I fade; I die. How sweetly does this dew refresh me! When once favored with it I feel happy, lively, vigorous, elevated. I want nothing more. The Holy Spirit brings me life, and all that life requires. All else without the dew of the Spirit is less than nothing to me: I hear, I read, I pray, I sing, I go to the table of communion, and I find no blessing there until the Holy Ghost visits me. But when He bedews me, every means of grace is sweet and profitable."[279]

3. Dewdrops picture the transiency of life. Dewdrops are here and then quickly gone. They dissipate and dry up unless absorbed

by flowers and grass. The dew teaches us to live in the present moment, redeeming its opportunities to its fullest use. Micah said of the dew that it "tarrieth not for man, nor waiteth for the sons of men" (Micah 5:7).

4. Dewdrops picture the resurrection. Dew is life-giving. Just as the earth brings forth its dew, it shall bring the dead to new life. Isaiah said, "But those who die in the Lord will live; their bodies will rise again! Those who sleep in the earth will rise up and sing for joy! For your life-giving light will fall like dew on your people in the place of the dead!" (Isaiah 26:19 NLT).

5. Dewdrops picture church unity. "How wonderful and pleasant it is when brothers live together in harmony!... Harmony is as refreshing as the dew from Mount Hermon that falls on the mountains of Zion" (Psalm 133:1, 3 NLT). As Hermon and Zion would wither apart from the dew (the dew God sent in the coolness of the night in Palestine was the only thing that sustained vegetation), so would the church. "Every kingdom divided against itself is brought to desolation; and every city or house divided against itself shall not stand" (Matthew 12:25). Says Spurgeon, "Holy concord is as dew, mysteriously blessed, full of life and growth for all plants of grace."[280] Knight comments, "It [unity] offers us true life, for it is life together with others, not the half-life of a Robinson Crusoe."[281]

6. Dewdrops picture influence. Dewdrops bear a refreshing, gentle, all-pervading influence upon that which they touch. "Dew helps plants accelerate their metabolism and increase plant biomass." Christians are to use their influence for good, instilling life, vitality, and hope in withering lives. Dewdrops on a leaf picture influence on a life, which soon passes or dissipates unless absorbed (applied, heeded) by the plant (person).

7. Dewdrops picture fluctuating love for God. Hosea complained that the 'goodness of Israel goeth away as the early dew' (Hosea 6:4). Israel's love and obedience to God vacillated. Craige says, "Love that is like a morning cloud is eventually a mockery of true love, for it promises, but never delivers; it offers hope, but no fulfillment."[282]

Who identifies with Israel? They who:

a. Love God superficially.

b. Harbor secret sin.

c. Fail to count the cost of being a disciple of Christ (Luke 14:28).

d. Neglect regularity and steadiness in prayer, Bible study, worship, and service.

e. Love the pleasures of the world, like Demas, more than God (2 Timothy 3:4; 2 Timothy 4:10).

f. Embrace bitterness toward God for something experienced. Constancy in the walk with the Lord prevents transitory goodness and devotion.

8. Dewdrops picture humility. They work silently; they cannot be heard working on earth among the flowers and grass. They don't bring attention to themselves with pomp and circumstance. Note, humility shrinks back into the shadow when praised; pride looms toward its limelight. Humility does not seek attention or applause for the good that is done.

"He is a stupid Christian who thinks so much of the printed and bound Bible that he neglects the Old Testament of the fields, nor reads the wisdom and kindness and beauty of God written in blossoms on the orchard, in sparkles on the lake, in stars on the sky, in frost on the meadows."[283]—T. De Witt Talmage

## 76
### "Should I Not Have Compassion on Nineveh?"

"Should I not have compassion on Nineveh?" (Jonah 4:11 AMP). Jonah's attitude toward the lost in Ninevah and resentment toward God for sparing them suggests several lessons for the believer to heed.

1. Don't begrudge God's mercy and pardon toward the undeserving sinner. Jonah was angered that God spared Ninevah

from destruction. Fairbairn says, "Whenever and wherever God is pleased to manifest His grace and goodness, it is our part to acknowledge and rejoice in the manifestation."[284] Don't pout, but shout over a sinner's salvation. Note, the elder son (Luke 15) pictures Jonah. He resented the father's display of mercy to the outrageous sinner his brother had become in the Far Country.

2. Don't devalue the worth of a soul. Jonah grieved over the withering of a single gourd but resented the preservation of an estimated 600,000 people in Ninevah. Christians are prone to value objects of temporal pleasure (various types of "gourds") far more than eternally perishing souls.

How valuable is a soul? Jesus answers that it is more valuable than all the world's riches, fame, successes, comforts, and pleasures combined (Mark 8:36).

How valuable is a soul? So valuable that God gave His only Son to the cruel death at Calvary to save man from sin's ruinous and damnable results.

3. Never count the hand of God too short to save the vilest offender. No man, despite the filthiness and ugliness of his sin, is beyond the reach of grace. God saved Paul, the chief of sinners (1 Timothy 1:15), the thief on the cross (Luke 23:39–43), the adulterous woman at Jacob's well (John 4), the wicked King Manasseh (2 Chronicles 33:1–21).

From God's perspective, no person is beyond His forgiving grace and mercy. "He is able to save completely all who come to God through him" (Hebrews 7:25 TLB). "Whoever comes to me I will certainly not turn away" (John 6:37 CJB). "The LORD says, "Now, let's settle the matter. You are stained red with sin, but I will wash you as clean as snow. Although your stains are deep red, you will be as white as wool" (Isaiah 1:18 GNT).

"We have a glorious testimony," says John R. McDuff, "in the case of Manasseh, that no sinner needs to despair. Manasseh is now stooping over the walls of Heaven in company with Saul the blasphemer, Zacchaeus the extortioner, the Magdalene of the Pharisee's house, the dying felon of Calvary and proclaiming that for the vilest sinner, there is mercy. Yes, although this man had defied his God, had scorned pious counsels, had added bloodshed and cruelty to rampant unbelief and lawless lust, yet when the blast of God's trumpet sounded over the apparently impregnable citadel of his heart, it fell to the dust; and from that hour in which grace triumphed, its walls became 'salvation and its gates praise.' And that grace which saved Manasseh can save every one of us—the poorest, the vilest, the most desponding."[285]

4. Don't be cold-hearted toward sinners. Jonah, the first foreign missionary, proves it's possible to be God's worker and not be concerned for the lost. J. Vernon McGee asserts, "God is saying to a great many people today, 'I want you to go and take the Word of God to those who are lost.' And they say, 'But I don't love them.' God says, 'I never asked you to love them; I asked you to go.' I cannot find anywhere that God ever asked Jonah to go because he loved the Ninevites. He said, 'Jonah, I want you to go because *I* love them. I love Ninevites. I want to save Ninevites. And I want you to take the message to them. So many people are waiting to be motivated by emotional things. Take the Word of God to them because God loves them, and if you'll do that, I will guarantee that you will learn to love them also."[286] Pray that the weight of lost immortal souls (burden, concern, interest) that Christ possesses will be known experientially by you.

It is strongly supposed that Jonah finally understood, by the Word of the Lord, why God is merciful to all who seek Him, even the wicked Ninevites, and became convinced that sparing them was just and proper.

"Our great aim is conversion—the conversion of transgressors. Be content with nothing short of the conversion of men."[287]— C. H. Spurgeon.

## 77

### "Will You Say That I Have Done Wrong, That You May Be Made Right?"

Job sought to vindicate himself of wrong by showing God guilty of treating him unfairly (Job 9:20). Criswell says, "Often one may attempt to accuse God of injustice in order to justify and maintain his own righteousness."[288] God responds with a question: "Will you say that I have done wrong, that you may be made right?" (Job 40:8 NLV). Job is asked if he could make a case for being more righteous than God because his suffering was thought to be more than justice demanded. Further, Job is told that if he thinks he knows what's best for himself and not God, he ought to take over being God (Job 40:9–14).[289] "That for a puny creature to find fault with God is an amazing act of presumption."[290]

Note, arrogant presumption and impudence second guess God's actions and put man in the place of God. God's judgment and governance of the affairs of man are regulated by inerrant truth. Therefore, they cannot be unfair, unjust, and unrighteous or be annulled or overruled. Octavius Winslow remarks, "How constantly is the human mind tempted to speculate and philosophize and reason about divine truth [or happenings]! To attempt to sound that which is unfathomable, to unveil that for which there is no clue, to understand that which baffles speculation, transcends reason, and, like Him whose truth it is, enfolds itself in inexplicable and awful mystery. Let reason give way to faith; and pride to humility; and vain speculation to adoring wonder, gratitude, and love."

When tempted to act like Job, disannulling God's judgment for his own, heed God's response. "Do you presume to tell me what I'm doing wrong? Are you calling me a sinner so you can be a saint? Do you have an arm like my arm? Can you shout in thunder the way I can? Go ahead, show your stuff. Let's see what you're made of, what you can do. Unleash your outrage. Target the arrogant and lay them flat. Target the arrogant and bring them to their knees. Stop the wicked in their tracks—make mincemeat of them! Dig a mass grave and dump them in it—faceless corpses in an unmarked grave. I'll gladly step aside and hand things over to you—you can surely save yourself with no help from me!" (Job 40:8–14 MSG).

Trust God's goodness, justness, and righteousness. Say with Habakkuk, "Although the fig tree shall not blossom, neither shall fruit be in the vines; the labour of the olive shall fail, and the fields shall yield no meat; the flock shall be cut off from the fold, and there shall be no herd in the stalls: Yet I will rejoice in the Lord, I will joy in the God of my salvation. The Lord God is my strength, and he will make my feet like hinds' feet, and he will make me to walk upon mine high places" (Habakkuk 3:17–19).

All my trust on Thee is stayed,
    All my help from Thee I bring;
Cover my defenseless head
    With the shadow of Thy wing.

                        – Charles Wesley (1740)

"That we cannot vie with God for power; and therefore, as it is great impiety, so it is great impudence to contest with Him, and is as much against our interest as it is against reason and justice."[291]—Matthew Henry.

## 78
### "Who Is This That Darkeneth Counsel by Words Without Knowledge?"

"Who is this that darkeneth counsel by words without knowledge?" (Job 38:2). Job was guilty of speaking of the spiritual out of ignorance, without knowledge, to the confusion of those to whom he spoke. "He had obscured and misrepresented the prearranged plan and underlying principles of the Divine administration."[292]

1. Danger lurks in a superficial knowledge of the Christian faith. Agrippa knew much about the Jewish religion, the prophets, and Christ's death and resurrection.[293] He also appears to have understood what it meant to be a Christian, a term he used (Acts 26:28). Says Maclaren, "And was he any better for it? No, he was

a great deal worse. It stood in the way of his apprehending truths which he thought he understood."[294]

Though multitudes know more about Jesus and the Gospel than Agrippa did, the same thing stands true. A superficial knowledge of Christ "darkens" their ability to comprehend the whole. Maclaren asserts, "Superficial knowledge is the worst enemy of accurate knowledge, for the first condition of knowing a thing is to know that we do not know it. I believe that there is nothing that stands more in the way of hundreds of people coming into real intelligent contact with Gospel truth than the half-knowledge that they have had of it ever since they were children."[295] Note that Job thought he understood the deep things of God but was grossly mistaken. A superficial knowledge of Christ and the Gospel (a fragment of the Gospel) blinds and confines many to ignorance of the truth that can set them free.

2. Christians must study the Word to enunciate it clearly and accurately. Let none go to Hell on the coattails of flawed doctrine you espouse. Paul declares, "Teach the truth so that your teaching can't be criticized. Then those who oppose us will be ashamed and have nothing bad to say about us" (Titus 2:8 NLT). Says Wiersbe, "God didn't question Job's integrity or sincerity; He only questioned Job's ability to explain the ways of God in the world."[296] Alden states, "We all speak 'words without knowledge' unless they are the properly understood and interpreted words of the Bible."[297]

3. False teachers capitalize on a person's superficial knowledge to allure them into their deceptive web (Galatians 1:8; 1 John 4:2; 1 Timothy 1:6–7).

"Give yourself to prayer, to reading and meditation on divine truths: strive to penetrate to the bottom of them and never be content with a superficial knowledge."—David Brainerd.

## 79
## "What Men Are These with Thee?"

"What men are these with thee?" (Numbers 22:9). Balak sent messengers to Balaam to ask that he prophesy a curse against Israel. Instead of immediate refusal, Balaam puts the men up for the night to give him time to decide. At night, God asks Balaam, "What men are these with thee?" The question helps Balaam see the error of his judgment.[298] God instructs him not to go with the men or curse the nation (Numbers 22:12). Balaam obeys.

A second time, Balak sent messengers to Balaam (this time, more honorable men), promising him a position of great honor to curse Israel (Numbers 22:16–17). He said no to the proposal and invited them to lodge the night while he consulted the Lord. This time, God tells him to go with the men and only do what He told him. Difficulties arose—Balaam's mule balks and talks. But Balaam remained faithful to God.

Note five lessons that might be drawn from the narrative.

1. We set ourselves up for failure when we keep the wrong company. "Do not be deceived: 'Bad company ruins good morals'" (1 Corinthians 15:33 ESV). Gurnall asserts, "Thou canst not be long among unholy ones, but thou wilt hazard the defiling of thy soul, which the Holy Spirit hath made pure."[299] Solomon said, "He that walketh with wise men shall be wise: but a companion of fools shall be destroyed" (Proverbs 13:20). Evil associates influence one's conduct and bring havoc into their life.

2. It is best to let people know where you stand at the outset of a relationship.

3. Something wrong must be rejected immediately. No delay, consultation, or debate can make something that is wrong today right tomorrow.

4. Time spent musing over a temptation opens a cracked door to it wider, possibly resulting in a serious fall.

5. Satan doesn't stop with one effort to bring a believer down. He will present the temptation again, garbed with greater

enticement and allurement. "Wherefore let him that thinketh he standeth take heed lest he fall" (1 Corinthians 10:12).

"Friendship is the balm of life when it is entered into with discretion—but it is a plague and a snare when it is injudiciously contracted."[300]—George Lawson.

### 80
### "Who Then Is Able to Stand Before Me?"

"Who then is able to stand before me?" (Job 41:10). The terrible and frightful sea creature or monster (Job 41:1–4) described may have been the crocodile, whale, or one that was well known in the time of Job, but extinct now.[301] Though its identity is uncertain, the lesson stands true: man's inability to control it reveals his stupidity in challenging or contending with God, its Creator.[302] Note, the same point is made concerning the sea creature (Behemoth) in Job 40:15 (perhaps the hippopotamus). Job, and man in general, would better fight with one of these sea monsters than contending with God.

"Who then is able to stand before me?"

1. The wicked cannot. "God is angry with the wicked every day" (Psalm 7:11).

2. The religionist cannot.

3. The unbeliever cannot.

4. The moralist cannot.

5. The atheist and agnostic cannot.

Only he whose garments are washed white in the blood of the Lord Jesus Christ through repentance and faith stands accepted (justified, acquitted, reconciled) before God. No man not attired in the wedding garment of Christ's righteousness at the Judgment will gain access to Heaven. Jesus used a parable to present that truth: "And when the king came in to see the guests, he saw there a man who did not have on a wedding garment. And he said unto him, 'Friend, how camest thou in hither not having a wedding garment?' And he was speechless. Then said the king to the servants, 'Bind him hand and foot and take him away, and cast him into outer darkness: there shall be weeping and gnashing of teeth'" (Matthew 22:11–13).

> When the Bridegroom cometh, will your robes be white?
>   Are you washed in the blood of the Lamb?
> Will your soul be ready for the mansions bright,
>   And be washed in the blood of the Lamb?
> ~ E. A. Hoffman (1878)

"The fact that Jesus will sit upon the throne of judgment will be the consternation of His enemies and the consolation of His people."—John Owens.

# PART 2
## Questions Asked by Jesus in the New Testament

### 81

### "If the Salt Has Lost His Savor, Wherewith Shall It Be Salted?"

"Ye are the salt of the earth, but if the salt has lost his savor, wherewith shall it be salted? It is thenceforth good for nothing, but to be cast out and to be trodden under foot of men" (Matthew 5:13 KJ21). Christians, as salt, are to be the antidote to the corruption and decay of the world. This they are by the bold and daring profession and declaration of the faith, protest of the deeds of darkness, and life of godliness.

Note three unique qualities of salt to which Christ likens the believer.

1. Salt purifies. As salt, the believer cleanses society of the causes of its stinking decay—sin and evil. It diminishes its presence and power.

2. Salt preserves. As salt, the believer has a preserving influence on what is good, just, and honorable in society.

3. Salt makes food tasty. Food without salt is bland and repulsive. Barclay says, "Christianity is to life what salt is to food. Christianity lends flavor to life."[303] The Christian as salt is the antidote to the tastelessness of life in the world. They permeate the world with sweetness, joy, peace, hope, love, and cheer, making it more palatable (enriching and enjoyable).

Matthew Henry asserts, "What great blessings they are to the world. Mankind, lying in ignorance and wickedness, was a vast heap of unsavory stuff, ready to putrefy, but Christ sent forth His disciples, by their lives and doctrines, to season it with knowledge and grace and so to render it acceptable to God, to the angels, and to all that relish divine things."[304]

To be effective salt to the world, the Christian must maintain his saltiness through personal purity and abiding in Christ.

(Believers who have lost their saltiness are good for nothing—their testimony is trampled beneath the feet of men, bearing no good impact.) He must be shaken onto the world as salt, not stored up in a salt cellar (church). Havner says, "Salt must be brought into close contact with whatever it is meant to affect if it is to do any good. Christians are the salt of the earth. We must be willing to be rubbed into the decaying carcass of an unregenerate society. Most of us are content to sit in our little saltshakers, far removed from a needy and lost humanity."[685]

**"The power of the kingdom citizen is in his difference from the world, just as salt is different from that into which it is placed."**[305]—W. A. Criswell.

## 82
### "Will Ye Also Go Away?"

"From that time, many of His disciples went back and walked no more with Him. Then Jesus said to the twelve, Will you also go away?" (John 6:66–67 NMB). The question suggests another question: Why do people walk away from Jesus? On the occasion of the text, people walked away from Christ, counting His teachings too strenuous to accept. Since that moment, multitudes, upon hearing the call of Christ to follow Him, have likewise walked away. Matthew Henry asserts, "Though the faith of some be overthrown, yet the foundation of God stands sure."[306] Why do people walk away from Jesus?

1. Some walk away due to the hard sayings of Christ. Christ's teachings and prohibitions are offensive and repugnant to some sinners (John 6:60).

2. Some walk away due to a lack of clarity of salvation. A fourteen-year-old student was saved following the presentation of the Gospel. Afterward, he said, "That was simple. I just needed someone to explain it to me." Many would be saved if presented with the clear, simple gospel message.

3. Some walk away due to distraction. The magnets of pleasure, popularity, and possessions pull people away from Christ (2 Timothy 3:4). But Jesus warns, "What shall it profit a man, if he shall gain the whole world, and lose his own soul?" (Mark 8:36).

4. Some walk away due to doubt. Doubts and questions about Christ and the Bible hold many back from salvation. These, however, could be resolved if probed to their very depth. God promises to give the necessary light to clarify man's religious questions and difficulties if sought honestly and earnestly (John 7:17).

5. Some walk away due to discouragement. The hypocritical lifestyle of believers, the godless influence of companions, the misrepresentation of what it means to be saved, and the high cost of being a disciple of Christ keep people back from being saved.

6. Some walk away due to doctrinal distortion. Distorted truth about Christ keeps people from the faith (Matthew 24:11). The real Christ must be displayed before the world (John 12:32).

7. Some walk away due to deception. A man blinded by Satan perceives not the danger of his soul and need for the salvation Christ affords (2 Corinthians 4:4).

8. Some walk away due to fear. Fear of push-back from family and friends prevents some from following Christ. "The fear of man bringeth a snare."

9. Some walk away due to delay. Procrastination is not only the thief of time but of the soul. "Behold, now is the day of salvation!" (2 Corinthians 6:2).

"Will ye also go away?" The same testing and challenging question is asked of all followers of Christ. As Christ sees some who are 'tossed to and fro and carried about with every wind of doctrine by the sleight of men and their cunning and craftiness,' as He sees others who are "lovers of pleasures more than lovers of God," as He marks others who have 'left their first love,' He says to you and me, "Will ye also go away?"[307]

May we answer passionately with Peter, "Lord, to whom shall we go? Thou hast the words of eternal life, and we believe and are sure that Thou art that Christ, the Son of the living God" (John 6:68–69). Paul admonishes, "So you must continue to be strong in your spirits, my Christian friends that I love. Do not let anything move you away from your faith. Continue to work hard as you serve the Lord" (1 Corinthians 15:58 EASY).

Defections happen, but don't let them hinder your faith. "They went out from us, but they were not of us; for if they had been of us, they would no doubt have continued with us: but they went out, that they might be made manifest that they were not all of us" (1 John 2:19).

**"We will not forswear the sun till we find a better light, nor leave our Lord until a brighter lover shall appear; and, since this can never be, we will hold Him with a grasp immortal, and bind His name as a seal upon our arm."**[308]—C. H. Spurgeon.

### 83
### "Lovest Thou Me More Than These?"

"Jesus said to Simon Peter, 'Simon, son of Jonah, lovest thou Me more than these?'" (John 21:15 KJ21). The inquiry is based on the intensity and degree of Peter's love, not for others, hobbies (like fishing), or the ministry, but Christ.

1. The reason for it. Peter had impetuously declared that he would not desert the Lord, even if others did (Matthew 26:33). But he did, not once, but three times (Matthew 26:67–75). The inquiry, a compassionate reprimand, forced Peter to examine the real depth and degree of love he possessed for Christ.

2. The repetition of it. The repetition sought to ensure that Peter's answer would not be a "tongue in cheek," brash answer like previously (Matthew 26:33) but one thoroughly and sincerely pondered.

3. The response to it. Peter answers the question each time not by stating that his love supersedes the other disciples but by

appealing to Jesus' knowledge of it. "'Yes, Lord,' he said, 'you know that I love you'" (John 21:15 NIV). Beasley states, "He could only appeal to the Lord's totality of knowledge, which included His knowledge of Peter's heart; more than all people could tell that he was speaking the truth. He really did love Him, and more than that, he could not say."[309] And no more needed to be said, for the Lord accepted the declaration as accurate, despite his failure in the courtyard. Matthew Henry remarked, "Being satisfied in his sincerity, the offense was not only forgiven, but forgotten, and Christ let him know that he was as dear to him as ever."[310]

4. The reflection of it. Jesus tells Peter, based on his love for Him, to "feed my sheep" (John 21:16). The believer's love for Christ is not to be idle but proven through work. Spurgeon asserts, "Many professing Christians give no proof of love to Christ, except that they enjoy sermons. But now, if you love Him as you say you do, prove it by doing good to others."[311]

The bottom line:

1. A deeply rooted love for Christ is an adhesive to sticking to what is done for Christ.[312] "Men often leave what they like, but never what they love."[313] Spurgeon cautions, "If your heart is not true to Christ, you will not be able patiently to endure for His Name's sake."[314]

2. Periodically, the question should be directed to every believer due to man's spurious love for Christ.

3. Love for Christ, despite the cost and consequence, will be expressed and manifested in Christian service and loyalty to His cause.

"This question was asked three times as if to show that it is of the first, of the second, and of the third importance, as if it comprised all else. This nail was meant to be well fastened, for it is smitten on the head with blow after blow."[315]—C. H. Spurgeon.

## 84
## "What Do You Want Me to Do for You?"

"What do you want me to do for you?" (Luke 18:41 NIV). What a powerful and personal question Jesus asked the blind beggar. It's a question in truth He passionately asks of all, for no one is without need for Christ to do something for them of which they are incapable.

There are four possible replies to the question.

1. Some reply, "Nothing now or ever." They tell Christ, the lover of their soul, to leave them alone. As the most tremendous favor Diogenes could bestow on Alexander, he wished for him to "stand out of my sunshine." The Devil deceives man into believing Christ stands between them and the sunshine.[316]

2. Some reply, "Nothing now, but later." They know Christ provides what is needed to live life to its fullest and best and to gain eternal life, but they delay asking for it. Note, the blind man seized the opportunity to be healed, realizing that another may not come. Don't let the opportunity afforded now to be saved be eternally lost by delay.

3. Some reply, "Nothing spiritual, but temporal." Man is prone to want the benefits Christ affords without allegiance to Him. They want to live the life of the unrighteous and, at the same time, enjoy the blessings of the righteous (Numbers 23:10). They want what Christ affords without a change of heart (Matthew 5:8). "They wish for 'bread enough,' but it is not the bread of life for which they hunger; they would like much to be wealthy, but they are not careful to be 'rich toward God.'"[317]

4. Others reply precisely, "Cleansing of sin and rightness with God." Like Bartimaeus, they ask for sight. Like the leper, they ask to be made clean. Like the woman who touched Jesus' garment, they ask to be made whole. Like the woman at Jacob's well, they ask for the emptiness of their soul to be satisfied. Like the Philippian jailer, they ask to be saved. And upon the asking, they are cured and made whole through the blood of Christ.

Note that when a person makes the right reply and places faith in Christ as Savior and Lord, evidence of the miracle will be manifested immediately in his 'following Jesus, praising God' (Luke 18:43). Other people, in seeing the miraculous healing, will praise God, too.

Despite the crowd's rebuke, Bartimaeus refused to be discouraged from going to Jesus (Luke 18:39). Let not opposition from foe, family, and friends hinder your coming to Christ.

"Though Christ knows all our wants, He will know them from us: 'What wilt thou that I shall do unto thee?'"[318]—Matthew Henry.

## 85
### "But Whom Say Ye That I Am?"

"And He said unto them, "But whom say ye that I am?" (Mark 8:29 KJ21). The question is asked in all four Gospels. Peter, as the spokesman of the twelve, answered, "Thou art the Christ."

"But whom say ye that I am?" Christ's identity rests upon the answer to this question. MacArthur states, "No question is more important than, 'Who is Jesus Christ?' It is of ultimate significance because how people respond to the Lord Jesus determines their eternal destiny."[319] Christ's sinlessness, miraculous works, redemptive mission, power to forgive sin, substitutionary death, and resurrection all verify Him to be the Son of God and Savior of the world.

It is a question that has only one answer. "And Peter answered and said unto Him, "Thou art the Christ" (Mark 8:29). Gill states, "This confession of Peter's in which all the apostles agreed with him speaks out what Jesus really was, and exceeds the most exalted sentiments which the people had of Him: He was not the harbinger of the Messiah but the Messiah Himself; not Elias in whose Spirit His forerunner was to come and did come, nor any one of the prophets; but He who was spoken of by all the holy prophets, which have been since the beginning of the world."[320]

Jerry Vines says we are pushed to one of four views about Jesus' identity: "Jesus was a legend; He never existed. Jesus was a liar; He was lying about who He claimed to be. Jesus was a lunatic; He was crazy and didn't know what He was doing. Jesus is Lord."[321] C. S. Lewis cautions, "Either this man was, and is, the Son of God or else a madman or something worse. You can shut Him up for a fool, you can spit at Him and kill Him as a demon, or you can fall at His feet and call Him Lord and God. But let us not come with any patronizing nonsense about His being a great human teacher. He has not left that open to us. He did not intend to."

It is a question whose answer must not be delayed. T. Croskery says, "Upon many questions, we can afford to suspend our judgment, but not upon this. It makes all the difference to the world, it makes all the difference to ourselves, whether or not Jesus be the Savior from sin and the Lord of righteousness and life."[322] It is a question whose true answer brings satisfaction.

Jesus gives life all that is needed for its meaning, happiness, and peace (John 10:10). Calvin said, "The whole life of man until he is converted to Christ is a ruinous labyrinth of wanderings." Brooks says, "It is only an infinite God, and an infinite good, that can fill and satisfy the precious and immortal soul of man." Samuel Rutherford said, "Jesus Christ came into my prison cell last night, and every stone flashed like a ruby."

Others may consider Him to be "John the Baptist; but some say, Elias; and others, One of the prophets" (Mark 8:28). But knowing His person, work, and words, let us unhesitatingly and promptly attest with Peter and the other Apostles, "Thou art the Christ."

**"Jesus Christ, the condescension of divinity, and the exaltation of humanity."**—Phillip Brooks

## 86
## "What Think Ye of Christ?"

"What think ye of Christ?" (Matthew 22:42). Based on their study of Old Testament prophesy, the Pharisees fully expected Messiah to come. Jesus pointedly asked their opinion of the Messiah, specifically of His ancestors and progenitors.

"What think ye of Christ?" The health of your soul, happiness of life, and hope of Heaven hinge upon your answer to the question.

1. What think ye of His cradle? The birth of Christ in Bethlehem's manger was prophesied by Micah 700 years in advance (Micah 5:2). Its manner, prophesied by Isaiah (Isaiah 7:14), was to be conception without physical contact with a man ("Behold, a virgin shall conceive, and bear a son"). This allowed Jesus to be born sinless (Romans 5:12), a trait necessary to be man's substitute at Calvary to make payment (atonement) for his sin.

Note, Criswell asserts that the word *almah* (rendered "virgin" in KJV) in its seven uses in the Old Testament (including Isaiah 7:14) always refers to a "virgin."[323] Millard Erickson says, "If we do not hold to the virgin birth despite the fact that the Bible asserts it, then we have compromised the authority of the Bible, and there is, in principle, no reason why we should hold to its other teachings. Thus, rejecting the virgin birth has implications reaching far beyond the doctrine itself."[324]

2. What think ye of His conduct? Christ was not only born without sin, but He also lived sinlessly. Paul says, "Christ had no sin" (2 Corinthians 5:21 ICB). Peter says, 'In him, there was no deceit' (1 Peter 2:22). The author of Hebrews says, 'We have a high priest who was tempted in every point like we are, yet without sin' (Hebrews 4:15). Pilate, an enemy of Christ, said, "I find no fault in him" (John 19:6). Piper states that "He needed to be a spotless lamb, and he was a spotless lamb."[325] Adrian Rogers asserts, "From birth to the cross, Jesus lived a perfectly sinless life because of how He dealt with the sin around Him. He fought sin

perfectly through the use of prayer, the Word, and seeking God's will entirely."[326]

3. What think ye of His crucifixion? Crucifixion involved the hammering of seven-inch iron spikes through the victim's feet and hands, fastening them to a wooden cross. This torturous act, with other painful inflictions, Jesus endured at Calvary for man's forgiveness and salvation. Thomas Brooks said, "Our sins are debts that none can pay but Christ. It is not our tears but His blood; it is not our sighs, but His sufferings, that can testify for our sins. Christ must pay all, or we are prisoners forever." See 1 John 2:2.

Stephen Charnock said, "Let us look upon a crucified Christ, the remedy of all our miseries. His cross hath procured a crown, His passion hath expiated our transgression. His death hath disarmed the law, His blood hath washed a believer's soul. This death is the destruction of our enemies, the spring of our happiness, and the eternal testimony of divine love."

4. What think ye of His conquest? Death could not hold Christ prisoner, and on Easter morning, He broke its chains and arose, a mighty victor over it, sin, and the Devil. There were more than 1,500 eyewitnesses to His resurrection (1 Corinthians 15:3–6), including:

- Mary Magdalene (John 20:11–18),
- Other women (Matthew 28:9–10)
- Peter (Luke 24:34; 1 Corinthians 15:5)
- Two disciples on the Emmaus Road (Luke 24:13–35)
- Ten disciples (Luke 24:36; John 20:19–25)
- Thomas (John 20:26–31)
- Seven disciples on the Sea of Galilee (John 21:1–25)
- The eleven disciples at the giving of the Great Commission (Matthew 28:16–20)
- The five hundred [only men were numbered in New Testament times; factoring in women and children, this number could easily have exceeded 1,500] (1 Corinthians 15:6)
- James (1 Corinthians 15:7)
- Those at His ascension (Acts 1:9–10)
- Stephen (Acts 7:55–60)

- Paul on the way to Damascus (Acts 9:3–6)
- Paul in the Temple (Acts 22:17–21)
- Paul on the ship going to Rome (Acts 23:11)
- John (Revelation 1:10–18).

"The appearances of Jesus," says Michael Green, "are as well authenticated as anything in antiquity....There can be no rational doubt that they occurred." Said Spurgeon, "The resurrection of Jesus Christ from the dead is one of the best-attested facts on record. There were so many witnesses to behold it that if we do in the least degree receive the credibility of men's testimonies, we cannot, and we dare not doubt that Jesus rose from the dead."

5. What do you think of His claims? Christ claimed that He existed before Abraham and was the Jehovah of the Old Testament (John 8:56–59). He declared Himself to be the only Way or Door to Heaven (John 14:6; 10:9) and said that "my kingdom is not of this world" (John 18:36). Jesus said that "he that believeth in me, though he were dead, yet shall he live: And whosoever liveth and believeth in me shall never die" (John 11:25–26). He claimed equality with God, saying, "He that seeth me seeth him that sent me" (John 12:45) and "I and my Father are one" (John 10:30). Further, Jesus claimed to be the one (the Messiah) spoken of by the prophets in the Scripture (Matthew 24:25). Jesus backed his claims up with action.

> If ask'd what of Jesus, I think,
>     Although my best thoughts are but poor;
> I say he's my meat and my drink,
>     My life, and my strength, and my store,
> My shepherd, my husband, my friend,
>     My savior from sin and from thrall,
> My hope from beginning to end,
>     My portion, my Lord, and my all.
>                     – John Newton (1725–1807)

What think ye of Christ? Do not ignore the question or delay answering it. Eternity is at stake. Do you believe Him to be who He claims, the Son of God? Do you think He was sinless in His birth in Bethlehem and all His deeds? Do you believe He was God's Son who took upon Him your sin at Calvary to make possible your justification with God? Do you think God raised Him from the dead? Do you believe Him to have the power and authority to forgive your sin and save your soul from Hell? If so, surrender your all to Him at this moment.

J. C. Ryle asserts, "What others think about Him is not the question now. Their mistakes are no excuse for you—their correct views will not save your soul. The point you have before you is simply this: "What do you think yourself?"[327]

"**Remember, if our views of Christ be wrong, our state is wrong.**"[328] – C. H. Spurgeon.

## 87
### "What Think Ye of Christ?"

"What think ye of Christ?" (Matthew 22:42).

1. Some think of Christ only in times of crisis. In times of grave need, Christ is sought; otherwise, He is virtually ignored and unwanted.

2. Some never think of Christ. They have no opinion or conviction about Christ. Spurgeon says, "With other questions, they push off the main question and keep far from them the soul-saving truth."[329] To evade the question is to place the soul in peril. Note, believers sometimes have to force the question when the sinner fails to ask it of themselves.

3. Some think of Christ with erroneous facts and warped theology. Misconceptions about Christ's identity and redemptive work taught by false teachers keep people from knowing the real Jesus. Peter warns, "There were indeed false prophets among the people, just as there will be false teachers among you. They will bring in destructive heresies, even denying the Master who bought them, and will bring swift destruction on themselves" (2 Peter 2:1 CSB). Make sure what is believed about Christ is the truth, not man's erroneous teaching (2 Timothy 1:13).

4. Some think of Christ with adversarial intention. The aim of some is to obliterate Christ and His teaching from the face of the earth by whatever means necessary. With the angry mob, they cry, "Crucify Him, crucify Him."

5. Some think of Christ with cruel mockery. God told Abraham that he would father a son. His wife, Sarah, laughed at the news, counting it to be humanly impossible at their age. Sarah's laugh of skepticism and mockery resounds loudly in universities, Hollywood, the government, the media, and liberal-minded churches. At what does the skeptic laugh?

He laughs at the virgin birth of Christ (he says it is biologically impossible). He laughs at the Bible, which bears witness to the identity of Christ as the Son of God (he says its origin was with man, not God). He laughs at Jesus' blood-bought salvation (he says the blood of Jesus has no more power to save than that of a chicken). He laughs at the resurrection of Christ (he says it never happened; Christ is still in the tomb). He laughs at Christ's claim to be the Son of God. He laughs and sneers at Christ's 'gullible' followers.

6. Some think of Christ with closemindedness. A close-minded person is unwilling to consider that Christ is the Son of God and man's only Savior from sin. The Pharisees were close-minded to Jesus and the apostles (Matthew 10:13–15). Solomon says, "A [closed-minded] fool does not delight in understanding, but only in revealing his personal opinions [unwittingly displaying his self-indulgence and his stupidity]" (Proverbs 18:2 AMP). The only reason anyone accepts Christ as the revealed Son of God and their Savior is that they become open-minded enough to weigh the preponderance of evidence citing that He is.

7. Some think of Christ as a myth of history. Did Jesus exist? Proof of one's existence in antiquity was not provided by DNA but by historians' documentation. "There are at least 39 sources outside of the Bible (e.g., Flavius Josephus; Cornelius Tacitus; Thallus) within 150 years of Jesus' life that reveal more than 100 facts about His life, teachings, death, and resurrection."[330]

Flavius Josephus, the Jewish historian who was born in A.D. 37, stated: "Now there was about this time Jesus, a wise man if it is lawful to call Him a man, for He was a doer of wonderful works, a teacher of such men as receive the truth with pleasure. He drew over to Him both many of the Jews and many of the Gentiles. He was the Christ, and when Pilate, at the suggestion of the principal men among us, had condemned Him to the cross, those who loved Him at first did not forsake Him, for He appeared to them alive again on the third day, as the divine prophets had foretold these and ten thousand other wonderful things concerning Him. And the tribe of Christians, so named from Him, are not extinct at this day."[331]

Also, "Roman government officials such as Pliny the Younger and even two Caesars, Trajan and Hadrian, wrote intriguing letters mentioning Jesus and early Christian origins."[332] The myth that Jesus never existed is just that, a myth, for a preponderance of evidence exists to the contrary.

8. Others think of Christ with wholehearted receptivity and acceptance. "O taste and see that the LORD is good: blessed is the man that trusteth in him" (Psalm 34:8). Many see but do not taste the Lord's goodness and walk away in disbelief or disdain. "To *taste* is to make proof by experience,"[333] says W. S. Plumer. It was when Jonathan tasted the honey that his eyes were enlightened. When a person tastes the goodness of the Lord, he discovers Him to be all He claims. Gill asserts, "Every taste now influences and engages trust in the Lord."[334]

It matters what you think of Christ.

"The tendency of a life in which there is no regard for God and eternity is to produce unbelief far more blighting than that of disbelief, which is the result of misguided thinking."[335]—T. Stephenson

## 88

### "Are Ye Able to Drink of the Cup That I Shall Drink Of?"

"Are ye able to drink of the cup that I shall drink of?" (Matthew 20:22). The bitter cup to which Jesus referred was that of His impending suffering and torturous crucifixion for man's sins. Barnes paraphrases the question: "Are ye able to suffer with me—to endure the trials and pains which shall come upon you and Me in endeavoring to build up My kingdom? Are you able to bear it when sorrows shall cover you like water, and you shall be sunk beneath calamities as floods in the work of religion?"[336]

What was James and John's reply? "They say unto him, we are able" (Matthew 20:22b). Clarke responds to their answer, "Strange blindness! You can? No; one drop of this cup would sink you into utter ruin unless upheld by the power of God."[337] And it would sink us, too, apart from that same power. Peter said, "Be happy as you share Christ's sufferings. Then you will also be full of joy when he appears again in his glory" (1 Peter 4:13 GW).

> Are ye able, said the Master
>    To be crucified with me?
> Yea, the sturdy dreamers answered
>    To the death, we follow Thee.
>
> Lord, we are able,
>    Our spirits are Thine.
> Remold them, make us,
>    Like Thee, divine.
>
> – Earl Marlatt (1926)

"We know not what we ask when we ask for the glory of wearing the crown and ask not for grace to bear the cross in our way to it."[338]—Matthew Henry.

## 89
## "Can Any of You Live a Bit Longer by Worrying About It?"

"Can any of you live a bit longer by worrying about it? (Matthew 6:27 GNT). The question intends to caution the disciples about the futility of anxiety and worry.

Reasons not to worry:

1. Worrying cannot change things. It has been said, "Worry is like a rocking chair. It will give you something to do but won't get you anywhere!" Darlow Sargeant comments, "What is the use of worrying? It never made anybody strong, never helped anybody do God's will, never made a way of escape for anyone out of perplexity."[339] Spurgeon remarks, "By anxious thought, you cannot add an inch to your stature nor turn one hair white or black; take no anxious thought for the morrow, for the morrow shall take thought for the things of itself. Lean upon your God and remember His promise that as your day is, so shall your strength be."[340]

2. Worrying is distrust in God's promises of care. It slanders every promise of God. What does He promise His children? He promises that everything that happens will work together for their good. He promises grace to sustain us when things happen that we prayed wouldn't. He promises that what happens only happens with His permission. He promises nothing shall separate them from His love and care. Thomas à Kempis said, "Oh, how great peace and quietness would he possess who should cut off all vain anxiety and place all his confidence in God."[341] "Thinking God's thoughts" will replace worried, anxious concerns."[342]

3. Worrying feeds fear. Arthur Somers Roche (1883–1935) remarked, "Worry is a thin stream of fear trickling through the mind. If encouraged, it cuts a channel into which all other thoughts are drained."[343]

4. Worrying robs of peace and joy. "Worry is putting tomorrow's possible cloud over today's sunshine."[344] Adrian Rogers said, "There are two days that can steal joy from today. One is yesterday, and the other is tomorrow. Both are days in

which we as Christians should refuse to live."[345] Worry is the gong that takes away the song. It fills the heart with fear, making the outlook weary and drear.

5. Worrying bears a false witness against God. Beecher said, "This way of life, devoid of cheer, is bearing false witness against your Master."[346] Anxiety cannot be hidden. Sargeant said, "People know you live in the realm of anxious care by the lines on your face, the tones of your voice, the minor key in your life, and the lack of joy in your spirit."[347]

6. Worrying negatively impacts others. "It does not take more than one smoky chimney in a room to make it intolerable."[348]

7. Worrying does not gain a greater notice of God. He cares for us the same regardless of it. There is no promise made to worry.[349]

8. Worrying is useless. If there were any good to worry, Jesus never would have told us to get rid of it.[350]

The cure for worry is to cast all your care and concerns upon the Lord, trusting Him to do what is best (1 Peter 5:7). In doing this, "the peace of God, which passeth all understanding, shall keep your hearts and minds through Christ Jesus" (Philippians 4:7). "Scale the heights of a life abandoned to God, then you will look down on the clouds beneath your feet."[351]

> The worried cow
> Would have lived till now,
>    If she had saved her breath;
> But she feared her hay
> Wouldn't last all day,
>    And she mooed herself to death.
>
> – Unknown

"The load of tomorrow added to that of today makes the strongest falter. Shut off the future as tightly as the past."[352]— William Osler.

## 90
### "What Shall a Man Give in Exchange for His Soul?"

"What shall a man give in exchange for his soul?" (Matthew 16:26). The reason for His coming death and resurrection, Jesus tells the disciples, is the value of a soul to God (John 3:16).

The person who exchanges his soul's relationship with Christ for worldly happiness, honor, possessions, riches, and pleasure makes a foolish bargain. Why?

1. The salvation of the soul outweighs earthly gain. Jesus asked, "What is a man profited, if he shall gain the whole world, and lose his own soul?"

2. That gained in the exchange of the soul for evil will be lost. An end will come to the pleasure, fame, and partying. "And the world passeth away, and the lust thereof: but he that doeth the will of God abideth forever" (1 John 2:17). The well of the world will dry up.

3. Transient pleasures cannot compensate for the loss of Heaven, reunion with the redeemed, and the torment of eternity in Hell. Matthew Henry asserts, "Many a one has ruined his eternal interest by his preposterous and inordinate care to secure and advance his temporal ones. It is the love of the world, and the eager pursuit of it, that drowns men in destruction and perdition."[353]

4. The imaginary good in the gain of worldly stuff is only a pipe dream and fantasy. Solomon says it is like a bubble that bursts (Ecclesiastes 1:2).

5. The soul that is exchanged for carnal, selfish appetites at death is irreparable and unretrievable. Nothing at the Judgment Seat of Christ can buy back the opportunity lost to do the right thing with the soul (Proverbs 11:4). There is no salvation beyond the grave.

6. Eternal misery, the gnawing of a reflective conscience that indicts over a wrong decision, and torment in the fire of Hell that never will be quenched will prove, all too late, that the exchange of

the soul for this world's dainties was a miserable bargain. Matthew Henry states, "If the soul is lost, it is the sinner's own losing; and his blood is on his own head."[354]

> What will you give in exchange for your soul?"
> What will it profit you, sinner,
> To gain the whole world and then lose your own soul?
> Shall I miss it—be lost forever?
> ~ Barney E. Warren (1897)

Don't foolishly exchange your soul's health and eternal welfare for temporal objects of pleasure.

**"The man, then, that gains the whole world for a time and loses his soul for eternity, can gain no profit."**[355] —R. Newton.

## 91
### "What Man of You, Having a Hundred Sheep?"

"What man of you, having an hundred sheep, if he lose one of them, doth not leave the ninety and nine in the wilderness, and go after that which is lost, until he find it?" (Luke 15:4). The shepherd's search for the lost sheep pictures that of the soulwinner's for the lost sinner.

1. It was an immediate search. Upon discovering a missing sheep, without hesitation, the shepherd launches an all-out search for it. Note, sheep are ignorant of their condition and danger and incapable of finding their way home. They depend on being rescued by the shepherd. The lost sinner is equally unconscious of his soul's lost estate and dangerous peril and depends on the believer's rescue.

2. It was a targeted search. The sole object of the search was for one particular lost sheep. Spurgeon says the shepherd goes after it and after nothing else.[356] Like the shepherd, the soulwinner must identify the lost sinner and go after him with tunnel vision.

3. It was a personal search. The shepherd doesn't dispatch another to find the sheep but goes himself. Seeking and winning souls cannot be done by proxy. Christ has given the task to all believers (Acts 1:8; Matthew 28:19). Spurgeon says, "You must go into the fire if you are to pull others out of it, and you will have to dive into the floods if you are to draw others out of the water."[357]

4. It was a persistent search. The shepherd relentlessly pursued the sheep despite the drudgery, difficulty, danger, and darkness. Soulwinning is hard work. "As things are," said William Newell, "soulwinning is just about the toughest task to which man can put his hand."

5. It was a monopolizing search. The shepherd's search absorbed his fullest attention and energies. The one consuming thought of the shepherd was the welfare of the lost sheep and finding it before harm befell it. "Seeing the crowds, He felt compassion for them, because they were distressed and downcast, like sheep without a shepherd" (Matthew 9:36 NASB). Pray that the weight of lost immortal souls (burden, concern, interest) that the Good Shepherd possesses will be manifested in every believer.

6. It was a costly search. The shepherd left the comfort and safety of home to pursue the lost sheep. Spurgeon says to the believer, "Are you not willing to pass through every ordeal if by any means you may save some? If this be not your spirit, you had better keep to your farm and to your merchandise, for no man will ever win a soul who is not prepared to suffer everything within the compass of possibility for that soul's sake."[358] The Bible says of Christ, "Who for the joy that was set before Him endured the cross, despising the shame" (Hebrews 12:2).

7. It was a thorough search. The shepherd sought the lost sheep over the abysses, through thorns, over mountains, and beside dangerous cliffs. No spot was left unsearched. Don't be content to fish in the same pond. Venture out to other streams and lakes, even the more treacherous.

8. It was an undeterred search. The shepherd's past non-successes didn't impede his effort to find the lost sheep. To be

rescued, a lost soul must want to be found. Some are impossible to find and win because of their obstinacy. Past failures mustn't impede present efforts.

9. It was a successful search. With rejoicing, the shepherd found the sheep, placed it upon his shoulders, and brought it home safely. Pursue each soul "until [you] find it."

"Never forget that the whole drama of Redemption—the Incarnation, the Ministry, the Cross, the Resurrection, the Ascension—was all but one long search for the lost sheep, and carrying it home rejoicing."[359]—Archdeacon Farrar.

## 92

### "My God, My God, Why Hast Thou Forsaken Me?"

"My God, my God, why hast thou forsaken me? (Psalm 22:1). David's prophesy of Messiah's crucifixion, written nearly 1,000 years before the event, is exactly and explicitly foretold, as if he had witnessed it. How is that possible? God revealed it to him. Jesus, in fulfilling the prophecy, substantiated His claim to be Messiah, the anointed one sent from God to save His people from their sins. The prophecy depicts scenes from the crucifixion. "The significant point is that David wrote this Psalm long before crucifixion was even adopted as a means of execution."[360]

"My God, my God, why hast Thou forsaken me?" The words speak of Jesus' abandonment upon the Cross at Calvary by God (Matthew 27:46). Plumer says, "This desertion was a judicial act on the part of God towards sin."[361] Spurgeon says, "No other place so well shows the griefs of Christ as Calvary and no other moment at Calvary is so full of agony as that in which His cry rends the air—"My God, my God, why hast Thou forsaken me?"[362] The cry, Kidner asserts, "is not a lapse of faith, nor a broken relationship, but a cry of disorientation as God's familiar, protective presence is withdrawn."[363]

Writing of the *desertion* of Jesus by God on the Cross, Caldwell states, "Why has the Father Almighty forsaken His only begotten Son? For our sake. For no sin of His Son, but for our sins, the Father forsook Him."[364] Hindson says, "Certainly, God had forsaken the Lord Jesus in those moments on the cross, but the reason was that He had made Him who knew no sin to be sin for us (2 Corinthians 5:21). God turned His back on the sin He hated, not the Son He loved."[365]

Ironside said, "'My God, My God, why hast Thou forsaken Me?' Do you know the answer to that question? Well, I am the answer to it, and you are too. Why was He forsaken? In order that I might not be forsaken. In order that you might not be forsaken. It was because He was bearing our sins, taking our place, because He was made sin for us."[366]

Notably, in the Hebrew text (Psalm 22:31), Jesus' cry of abandonment ends with Jesus' cry of triumph, "It is finished!"[367] "They will tell people yet to be born about his righteousness—that he has finished it" (Psalm 22:31 GW). See John 19:30. What did Christ finish on the Cross? Salvation's redemptive plan (Romans 5:10).

"There was no cause in Him, why then was He deserted? Jesus is forsaken because our sins had separated between us and our God."[368]—C. H. Spurgeon.

## 93

### "Why Go Ye About to Kill Me?"

"Why go ye about to kill me?" (John 7:19). The crowd, seemingly unaware that their leaders sought to kill Jesus, counted the question absurd.[369] But they were wrong. Their leaders murdered Jesus at Calvary. "And when they were come to the place, which is called Calvary, there they crucified him" (Luke 23:33). What is the place called Calvary?

1. A planned place. Calvary was not "Plan B" of God to save the world. It was not an afterthought of God. It was precisely what was foreordained before the foundation of the world (1 Peter 1:19–21).

Since the Cross was divinely orchestrated, neither the power of man nor Hell could avert it.

2. A prophetic place. Multiple Old Testament passages prophesied the crucifixion of Christ with explicit details. Soldiers would pierce his hands and feet (Psalm 22:16; Zechariah 12:10), cast lots for his clothing (Psalm 22:18), and hurl insults at him (Psalm 22:17). None of His bones would be broken (Psalm 34:20); vinegar would be provided to Him to drink (Psalm 69:21); He would be crucified between two criminals (Isaiah 53:12); He would experience agony and suffering (Psalm 69:20–21). These and other prophecies of Messiah's death made hundreds of years in advance, were fulfilled in Christ at the Cross.

The scapegoat in the Old Testament foreshadowed the Lamb of God that would take away the world's sin. As it was driven outside the camp to atone for man's sin (Leviticus 16:21–22), the Messiah would be taken outside the city gates to be crucified to make possible man's forgiveness (Hebrews 13:12).

3. A painful place. Frederic Farrar describes the agony and torment of crucifixion. "Death by crucifixion seems to include all that pain and death can have of horrible and ghastly—dizziness, cramp, thirst, starvation, sleeplessness, traumatic fever, tetanus, publicity of shame, the long continuance of torment, horror of anticipation, mortification of untended wounds—all intensified just up to the point at which they can be endured at all, but all stopping just short of the point which would give the sufferer the relief of unconsciousness. The unnatural position made every movement painful; the lacerated veins and crushed tendons throbbed with incessant anguish; the wounds, inflamed by exposure, gradually gangrened; the arteries—especially of the head and stomach—became swollen and oppressed with surcharged blood; and while each variety of misery went on gradually increasing, there was added to them the intolerable pang of a burning and raging thirst. And all these physical complications caused an internal excitement and anxiety, which made the prospect of death itself—of death, the awful unknown enemy, at whose approach man usually shudders

most—bear the aspect of a delicious and exquisite release."[370] He concludes, "Such was the death to which Christ was doomed."[371]

4. A propitiatory place. Paul says, "God wiped out the charges that were against us for disobeying the Law of Moses. He took them away and nailed them to the cross" (Colossians 2:14 CEV). Man's eternal punishment for sin is inescapable in and of himself. But God did for man that which he could not do for himself. He put man's sin debt to Christ's account at Calvary, allowing Him, in man's place, to pay its penalty, satisfying His righteous wrath. John states, "He is the payment for our sins, and not only for our sins, but also for the sins of the whole world" (1 John 2:2 GW). Paul says, "For he hath made him to be sin for us, who knew no sin; that we might be made the righteousness of God in him" (2 Corinthians 5:21). Barclay asserts, "The sacrifice of Jesus was not only the paying of debt; it was the giving of a victory. What Jesus did puts a man right with God, and what He does enables a man to stay right with God."[372]

5. A permanent place. It is unrepeatable. "For Christ died for sins once and for all, a good man on behalf of sinners, in order to lead you to God" (1 Peter 3:18 GNT). MacArthur asserts, "Christ's one sacrifice for sins was of such perpetual validity that it was sufficient for all and would never need to be repeated."[373]

6. A procuring place. The thief at Christ's right hand on the cross found salvation (Luke 23:43). Calvary is the only place where salvation is available. Foolish it is to look to baptism, the church, morality, or good deeds to save. Charnock said, "Let us look upon a crucified Christ, the remedy of all our miseries. His cross hath procured a crown; His passion hath expiated our transgression. His death hath disarmed the law; His blood hath washed a believer's soul. This death is the destruction of our enemies, the spring of our happiness, and the eternal testimony of divine love."

"Come and see the victories of the cross. Christ's wounds are thy healings, His agonies thy repose, His conflicts thy conquests, His groans thy songs, His pains thine ease, His shame thy glory, His death thy life, His sufferings thy salvation."—Matthew Henry.

### 94

### "Why Are You So Afraid?" (Matthew 8:26)

"Why are you so afraid?" (Matthew 8:26 NIV). A dangerous storm suddenly developed at sea, jeopardizing the lives of the disciples (or so they thought). They awaken Jesus, saying, 'Lord, save us! We're going to drown!' He replied, 'You of little faith, why are you so afraid?' Then He got up and rebuked the winds and the waves, which was completely calm (Matthew 8:25–26). The question is our question when we, like the disciples, panic and become afraid in times of trouble.

"Why are you afraid?" Three arguments ought to assuage the saints' fear.

1. The power of God. God is omnipotent, without limit or restriction in His power or authority. His power surpasses every hardship and hurt, conflict and concern, challenge and crisis. The "immeasurable greatness of his power" (Ephesians 1:19 ESV) provides a firm foundation for the believer to rest secure despite the circumstances. A. W. Pink said, "Everything about God is great, vast, incomparable. He never forgets, fails, falters, or forfeits His word. To every declaration of promise or prophecy, the Lord has exactly adhered; every engagement of covenant or threatening He will make good."

Pompey boasted that with one stamp of his foot, he could marshal all of Italy to battle. But God, by one word, yea even a thought, can elicit all the powers of Heaven and earth to the aid of His children in distress. Tozer remarks, "With the goodness of God to desire our highest welfare, the wisdom of God to plan it, and the power of God to achieve it, what do we lack? Surely, we are the most favored of all creatures."

2. The past performances of God. The psalmist said, "I recall the many miracles he did for me so long ago" (Psalm 77:11 TLB). Newton says, "Assurance grows by repeated conflict, by our repeated experimental proof of the Lord's power and goodness to save; when we have been brought very low and helped, sorely wounded and healed, cast down and raised again, have given up all

hope and been suddenly snatched from danger and placed in safety; and when these things have been repeated to us and in us a thousand times over, we begin to learn to trust simply to the word and power of God, beyond and against appearances. And this trust, when habitual and strong, bears the name of assurance; for even assurance has degrees."

3. The promises of God. Spurgeon asserts, "There is no lie in God's word, and no sham in His works; in creation, providence, and revelation, unalloyed truth abounds."[374] "Don't be afraid. I am with you. Don't tremble with fear. I am your God. I will make you strong, as I protect you with my arm and give you victories" (Isaiah 41:10 CEV). A. W. Pink argues, "But why should we not place implicit confidence in God and rely upon His word of promise? Is anything too hard for the Lord? Has His word of promise ever failed? Then let us not entertain any unbelieving suspicions of His future care of us. Heaven and earth shall pass away, but not so His promises." God will do that which He said.

Ryle asserts, "Let us not doubt that every word of God about His people concerning things future shall as surely be fulfilled as every word about them has been fulfilled concerning things past. Their safety is secured by promise. The world, the flesh, and the Devil shall never prevail against any believers. Their acquittal on the last day is secured by promise. They shall not come into condemnation but be presented spotless before the Father's throne. Their final glory is secured by promise. Let us be persuaded of these promises. They will never fail us. God's word is never broken. He is not a man that He should lie." "Let us hold fast the confession of our hope without wavering, for he who promised is faithful" (Hebrews 10:23 ESV).

A storm overtook a ship, putting the ship's captain in a state of complete terror. Caesar, the conqueror, cried out, "Why do you fear for the ship? Do you not know that it carries Cæsar?" Don't be afraid. You are aboard the old ship of Zion in a troublesome world that carries the greatest of conquerors, Jesus.[375]

"God writes with a pen that never blots, speaks with a tongue that never slips, acts with a hand that never fails."[376]—C. H. Spurgeon.

## 95

### "How Much More Shall Your Heavenly Father Give the Holy Spirit to Them That Ask Him?"

"How much more shall your heavenly Father give the Holy Spirit to them that ask him?" (Luke 11:13). Jesus' response to a disciples' request for instruction about prayer includes the need to ask for the infilling of the Holy Spirit.

Watchman Nee asserts, "Just as the right relationship with Christ generates a Christian, so the proper relationship with the Holy Spirit breeds a spiritual man." The believer's infilling of the Holy Spirit (control of life to a more significant measure by Him) is necessary to live a victorious Christian life and succeed in ministry work. Oswald Smith said of this infilling, "It is not a question of us getting more of the Holy Spirit, but rather of the Holy Spirit getting more of us."

How is the believer infilled with the Holy Spirit?

1. It takes a thirsting. The Holy Spirit infills the person who has nothing less than an aching void for more of His fullness, control, and power.

2. It takes a cleansing. Sin must be confessed and renounced (1 John 1:9). The Holy Spirit will only infill and use a clean vessel.

3. It takes surrendering. The total self must be submitted to His fullest control (withholding nothing). In faith, claim the promise of the Holy Spirit's infilling (empowering, enabling, emboldening, quickening).

4. It takes asking. Jesus said, "If ye then, being evil, know how to give good gifts unto your children: how much more shall your heavenly Father give the Holy Spirit to them that ask him?" (Luke 11:13). Pray with Augustine, "O Holy Spirit, descend plentifully

into my heart. Enlighten the dark corners of this neglected dwelling and scatter there Thy cheerful beams." Based upon God's command to be infilled, walk in faith, believing the promise that all who meet the condition of the command are infilled (Luke 11:11–13).

A slow-witted farmer purchased a chainsaw after being told it was guaranteed to cut down forty trees daily. In a week, he returned the chainsaw to the store. The salesman inquired about the problem, and the farmer replied, "I have been working my head off, and I ain't able ta bring down more than five trees a day." Frowning, the salesman looked at the chainsaw and pulled its starter cord. As it roared to life, the farmer jumped back and exclaimed, "What's that noise?"

Sadly, far too many believers, when told about the liberating, illuminating, triumphing, enabling, equipping, and emboldening power of the Holy Spirit available to live the victorious Christian life and accomplish ministry undertakings, exclaim, "What's that?"

Such ignorance leads to a life of religious self-effort, which results in defeat, discouragement, and little fruit. Christians who are not walking under the control of the Holy Spirit are like slow-witted farmers; they are trying to cut down trees with chainsaws that are not powered on.

"The Spirit-filled life is not a special, deluxe edition of Christianity. It is part and parcel of the total plan of God for His people."—A. W. Tozer.

## 96

### "Is a Candle Brought to Be Put Under a Bushel, or Under a Bed? and Not to Be Set on a Candlestick?"

"Is a candle brought to be put under a bushel, or under a bed? And not to be set on a candlestick?" (Mark 4:21). In Matthew, Jesus gives the answer and application to the question, saying, "Let your light so shine before men, that they may see your good works, and glorify your Father which is in Heaven" (Matthew 5:16).

1. Why to shine? Shine to magnify Christ. The candle is to display Christ, not the Christian; the work and wonders, not the worker and wrappings. The light that calls attention to itself is arrogant and vain, depriving God of the glory due to His name. Shine to be winsome. Beecher said, "The success of the Gospel was made to depend not on preaching, but upon living men." Shining saints reveal Christ to the people in darkness, making the need for salvation and its way known.

2. How to shine? Shine through a life of "good works" and good examples. "Whoever is a believer in Christ is a new creation. The old way of living has disappeared. A new way of living has come into existence" (2 Corinthians 5:17 GW). God is glorified most when others witness His work of grace manifest in our lives.

3. Where to shine? We do not shine shut up in a monastery or church building but in the world "before men." To be lights to the world, we must mingle with the world. It's impossible to impact the world for Christ in a telephone booth of solitariness. Saints are to let their light shine at home before spouse and children, in the workplace and at the water fountain, at the school house and playground, at the restaurant, and in social activity.

4. When to shine? We are to shine all the time. "Let it shine till Jesus comes; I'm gonna let it shine."

Don't hamper your light from shining brightly. To the degree that a bushel basket covers a light, it causes the light's beam to wane and flicker, its luster and radiance to dampen, and its purpose to be impeded. That's what happens to the believers' light when their walk and talk is contrary to the Word of God. B. B. McKinney challenges

> While passing through this world of sin
>    And others your life shall view
> Be clean and pure without, within;
>    Let others see Jesus in you.

Note that there are times when secrecy in doing good works is profitable in order not "to be seen of [men]" (Matthew 6:1). The motivation for the good deed or work (exalting God or extolling self) is the determining factor.

**"Do not be as a dark lantern, burning with the shades down and illuminating nothing and nobody."**—Alexander Maclaren.

97

"Judas, Betrayest Thou the Son of Man with a Kiss?"

"Judas, betrayest thou the Son of man with a kiss?" (Luke 22:48). To be betrayed means "to disclose a secret or confidence treacherously; to break a promise, or be disloyal to a person's trust; to disappoint the expectations of" *(Collins Dictionary).* Betrayals originate as a rule by those close to us (Mark 13:12).

Jesus warned there would be "many...offended, and shall betray one another" (Matthew 24:10).

1. A betrayal by a friend. Judas wounded Jesus with his betrayal in the garden. "Yea, mine own familiar friend, in whom I trusted, which did eat of my bread, hath lifted up his heel against me" (Psalm 41:9). It is a crushing blow when a friend violates the trust placed in them or turns away in times of trouble or crisis. "A friend is forsaken," states C. H. Spurgeon, "by one upon whom he leaned, to whose very soul he was knit, so that their two hearts had grown into one, and he feels that his heart is broken, for the other half of himself is severed from him. When Ahithophel forsakes David, when the kind friend we have always told our sorrows betrays our confidence, the consequence may be a broken heart."[377] Job was betrayed by his closest friends (Job 19:19), as was the woman mentioned in Lamentations 1:2.

2. A betrayal by a lover. Delilah betrayed Samson to the Philistines (Judges 16:16–21).

3. A betrayal by a son. Absalom betrayed his father, King David, in an effort to steal the kingdom (2 Samuel 15:10–17).

4. A betrayal by a politician. Haman betrayed the King and God's people in an attempt to eradicate the Jews (Esther 3:8–11).

5. A betrayal by a preacher. Nehemiah was betrayed by Shemiah, one considered to be a "godly" man, a priest (Nehemiah 6:10–14).

6. A betrayal by an adulterer. David betrayed Uriah to conceal his sin (2 Samuel 11:14–15).

7. A betrayal by brothers. Joseph was sold into captivity by his brothers (Genesis 37:26–28).

8. A betrayal by an ally. Ahithophel, David's counselor, betrayed him by aiding Absalom in overthrowing his kingdom (2 Samuel 15:31). It was a betrayal by the wicked. The psalmist prayed for protection from the sharp tongues and cruel words of the ungodly who sought to undermine his walk and plans (Psalm 64:2–4).

9. A betrayal by a church member. Jeremiah's critics aroused opposition against him and his message (Jeremiah 18:18).

10. A betrayal by a military commander. As he embraced Amasa to kiss him with one arm, Joab slew him with a sword with the other (2 Samuel 20:9–10).

11. A betrayal by a disciple. Peter betrayed Jesus for fear of persecution (John 18:15–27).

Note:

1. Anticipate betrayal (Proverbs 26:24–26).

2. Betrayal inflicts deep pain and anguish. Upon being betrayed, Spurgeon wrote, "My heart has been ready to sink within me....Friends have forsaken me."[378]

3. Remember that there is a Jonathan who sticks closer than a brother for every Shemaiah or Absalom who betrays you.

4. Don't lock people who love you out.

5. The betrayal will not thwart God's plans for you or His kingdom (Philippians 1:6). Judas' betrayal of Jesus did not hinder God's sovereign purpose from being accomplished.

6. Forgive the betrayer and move on with your life. William Blake said, "It is easier to forgive an enemy than a friend."[379]

Solomon says, "He who covers and forgives an offense seeks love, but he who repeats or harps on a matter separates even close friends" (Proverbs 17:9 AMP).

7. Cling to the promise of God that He will never forsake you and is ever ready to heal your broken heart (Psalm 147:3).

"It is a terrible wounding when he who should have been your friend becomes your foe, and when, like your Lord, you also have your Judas Iscariot. This is an excruciating kind of wounded spirit."[380]—C. H. Spurgeon.

## 98
### "Where Are the Nine?"

"Where are the nine?" (Luke 17:17). Ten lepers (nine Jews, one Samaritan) were healed by Jesus, but only one returned to give Him gratitude. Ten prayed, but only one gave praise. Ten healed, but only one remembered the Healer. When asked why his friends didn't join him in expressing thankfulness, he did not reply. He could only answer for himself as to why he did.

What might explain the ingratitude of the nine?

1. They valued the gift above the giver.

2. They counted what they received owed them.

3. They wanted to wait to make sure they were healed instead of trusting Jesus' word that they were.

4. They were so enthralled with their healing that it eclipsed gratitude.

5. They were too eager to get the priest to pronounce them clean so they could rejoin society.

6. They were too hurried to tell their family and friends of their healing.

7. They didn't want to associate with a Samaritan in giving gratitude.

Whatever the reason for their ingratitude, it was inexcusable.

As David, the believer must say, "Soul…forget not all His benefits" (Psalm 103:2). We must guard against becoming like "the other nine" lepers. Let none of God's favors go unnoticed and unacknowledged with ingratitude. Horne comments, "Thanksgiving cannot be sincere and hearty unless a man bear impressed upon his mind, at the time, a quick sense of 'benefits' received; and 'benefits' we are most of us apt to 'forget'; those especially, which are conferred upon us by God."[381] In Psalm 103, David cites five benefits for which Christians should express heartfelt gratitude. Plumer states, "No man ever yet made a complete catalog of the benefits he had received. Here we have an excellent beginning."[382]

1. "Who forgiveth all thine iniquities." In recital of the divine benefits afforded to man, the first is the forgiveness of sins. To know that Christ forgives sin, to have experienced that pardon personally, is man's foundational reason to praise Him.

2. "Who healeth all thy diseases." Give praise to God for the physical and mental diseases that He heals. Scott said, "Sinful passions are the diseases of the soul."[383] Plumer wrote, "Did God's blessing stop at the forgiveness of sins and not go on to cure the madness in our hearts, we should be both vile and miserable forever."[384]

3. "Who redeemeth thy life from destruction." Render praise to the Lord for deliverance from temporal dangers and troubles, but most especially from an eternity in Hell.

4. "Who crowneth thee with lovingkindness and tender mercies." The meaning of "crowneth" is to "envelope or surround." The believer is ever enveloped in the loving-kindness (unfailing love, grace, faithfulness, goodness of God) and mercy (divine favor, pity; not receiving that which is justly deserved in the way of punishment for sin) of the Lord. Matthew Henry said, "What greater dignity is a poor soul capable of than to be advanced into the love and favor of God? This honor has all His saints. What is the crown of glory but God's favor?"[385]

5. "Who satisfieth thy mouth [soul] with good things." Praise God for supplying the good things that make life happy and satisfying. Matthew Henry states, "It is only the favor and grace of God that can give satisfaction to a soul, can suit its capacities, supply its needs, and answer to its desires."[386] Plumer comments, "The blessing spoken of in this clause goes beyond the satisfying of the sensitive appetite. It embraces all the good we receive for nourishment, sustentation, and comfort."[387]

Render gratitude promptly, humbly, and sincerely. "Bless the Lord, O my soul, and forget not all his benefits."

"**One of the saddest proofs of our fallen condition is our propensity to forget God's benefits, especially his unspeakable gift, Jesus Christ. Nothing but the basest ingratitude could chill our hearts or shut our lips.**"[388]—W. S. Plumer.

## 99

### "What Will a Woman Do if She Has Ten Silver Coins and Loses One of Them?"

"What will a woman do if she has ten silver coins and loses one of them? Won't she light a lamp, sweep the floor, and look carefully until she finds it?" (Luke 15:8 CEV). The coin pictures the lost soul. The woman pictures the loving Savior. The lamp pictures the glorious Gospel. The broom pictures the work of the Holy Spirit. The neighbors picture the host of Heaven celebrating a sinner's salvation. Note three spiritual contrasts.

1. Her possession of the nine coins didn't diminish the importance and value of the lost coin. Christ counts each soul of immeasurable value. "Just as one digit is valuable in the multiplication table and one letter in the alphabet, far more valuable is just one soul in God's sight."[389] Keble said, "The salvation of one soul is worth more than the framing of a Magna Charta of a thousand worlds." Christ misses one lost soul; as the woman, the coin; the shepherd, the sheep; and the father, the son. To Him, no man is of less importance than another to save.

Spurgeon asserts, "If there existed only one man or woman who did not love the Savior, and if that person lived amongst the wilds of Siberia, and if it were necessary that the millions of believers on the face of the earth should journey thither and every one of them plead with him to come to Jesus before he could be converted, it would be well worth all the zeal and labor and expense of all that effort. One soul would repay the travail in the birth of myriads of zealous Christians....We have not yet sufficiently learned the value of an immortal soul if we do not feel that we would be willing to live, say, seventy years, to be the means of saving one soul and be willing to compass the whole globe and preach in every city and town and village, if we might only be rewarded at last with just one convert."[390]

2. She did all that could be done to find the lost coin. With a lighted candle, she searched diligently for it, and with a broom, she swept every spot of the house for it. Christ did all that could be done to recover the lost sinner.

a. He came to Earth, making salvation possible through His atoning, death, and resurrection.

b. He sought out the lost and won them (Luke 19:10). His ministry commenced with the winning of Andrew (John 1:40) and ended with the winning of the penitent thief on the Cross (Luke 23:43). The New Testament records at least nineteen soulwinning encounters of our Lord.

c. He implemented a plan to save the world through His servants (Matthew 28:19–20).

d. He sent the Holy Spirit to enable the task (Acts 1:8).

e. He mandated the work of soulwinning to be "instant in season, out of season" (2 Timothy 4:2).

3. She rejoiced in finding the lost coin. When the woman finds the lost coin, she invites her neighbors to rejoice with her (Luke 15:9). Christ displays joy over recovering the lost soul. A soul is so precious and valuable to Jesus that He and the angels rejoice when that soul is found. "Could we know, as well as angels do, the

reality of a sinner's repentance, we should know better how to rejoice."³⁹¹

"Jesus was saying that God searches for lost sinners!"³⁹²— Warren Wiersbe.

### 100

### "Why Do You See the Speck That Is in Your Brother's Eye, but Do Not Notice the Log That Is in Your Own Eye?"

"Why do you see the speck that is in your brother's eye, but do not notice the log that is in your own eye?" (Matthew 7:3 ESV). On the heels of telling the disciples not to worry, Jesus tells them not to judge. Nolland says, "The rhetorical questioning and the grotesque imagery represent a shock tactic designed to get through to the self-deceived."³⁹³ Note, a "speck" is a tiny splinter of wood; a "log" is a plank or large piece of lumber.

The question suggests several lessons.

1. With a log in our eye, expunging a speck from a brother's eye is hypocritical.

2. We must be harsh on our sins but merciful toward the sins of others.³⁹⁴

3. Stand ready to help a brother to overcome a fault compassionately. Adrian Rogers asserts, "There are people who are hurting, in the church and out of the church. They don't need your condemnation; they need your mercy."³⁹⁵

Once, I had to have an embedded speck of metal removed from my eye. Though the injury was excruciating, the doctor removed it with tenderness and care. That's how the Christian is to care for the "speck" in a brother's eye.

4. Pride prompts the little faults of others to eclipse the big faults of our own.

5. Sin is seen in everyone but ourselves.

6. Shallow examination of self is deceiving. Close inspection is required (Psalm 139:23–24).

7. The man always hunting for faults in others is too busy to see them in himself. Solomon says, "A worthless person digs up evil" (Proverbs 16:27 NASB).

A colored glass window painting in an old English church illustrates this teaching of Christ. A man with a large plank of wood before his eyes is seen diligently trying to extract a mere speck from the eye of another man. The painting reminds preachers and people to examine themselves closely before trying to extract a fault from another's eye.[396]

"As God is exalted to the right place in our lives, a thousand problems are solved all at once."—A. W. Tozer

## Endnotes

[1] Needham, George C. *The Life and Labors of Charles H. Spurgeon.* (Boston: D. L. Guernsey, 1887), 7.

[2] Spurgeon, C. H. "Is Anything Too Hard for the Lord?" sermon delivered April 22, 1888, Metropolitan Tabernacle.

[3] Hancock, J. L. *All the Questions in the Bible* (1st ed.). (Logos Research Systems, Inc., 1998).

[4] Spurgeon, C. H. "Strengthening Medicine for God's Servants." Sermon delivered 1875, Metropolitan Tabernacle.

[5] Spurgeon, C. H. "God's First Words to the First Sinner." Sermon delivered October 6, 1861, Metropolitan Tabernacle.

[6] Spence-Jones, H. D. M. (Ed.). *Genesis.* (London; New York: Funk & Wagnalls Company, 1909), 68.

[7] Secker, William. *The Nonsuch Professor in His Meridian Splendour; Or, The Singular Actions of Sanctified Christians.* (London: Richard D. Dickinson, 1867), 139.

[8] Spurgeon, C. H. "Is Anything Too Hard for the Lord?" sermon delivered April 22, 1888, Metropolitan Tabernacle.

[9] Spurgeon, C. H. "God's Fire and Hammer." Sermon delivered March 26, 1886, Metropolitan Tabernacle.

[10] Spurgeon, C. H. "Is Anything Too Hard for the Lord?" sermon delivered April 22, 1888, Metropolitan Tabernacle.

[11] Exell, J. S. *The Biblical Illustrator: Romans,* Vol. 1. (New York; Chicago; Toronto; London; Edinburgh: Fleming H. Revell Company), 310.

[12] Spurgeon, C. H. "Is Anything Too Hard for the Lord?" sermon delivered April 22, 1888, Metropolitan Tabernacle.

[13] Henry, M. *Matthew Henry's Commentary on the Whole Bible: Complete and Unabridged in One Volume.* (Peabody: Hendrickson, 1994), 1293.

[14] Spurgeon, C. H. "Harvest Men Wanted." Sermon delivered August 17, 1873, Metropolitan Tabernacle.

[15] Lucado, M. and T. A. Gibbs. *Grace for the Moment: Inspirational Thoughts for Each Day of the Year.* (Nashville, Tenn.: J. Countryman, 2000), 218.

[16] Blackaby, Henry. *Experiencing God.* (B&H Publishers).

[17] Ibid.

[18] *Benson Commentary on the Old and New Testaments*, Jeremiah 18:1.

[19] Spurgeon, Charles. Entry for "Pride: in Dictating to God." *Spurgeon's Illustration Collection.* https://www.studylight.org/dictionaries/eng/fff/p/pride-in-dictating-to-god.html, 1870.

[20] Exell, J. S. *The Biblical Illustrator: Exodus.* (New York: Anson D. F. Randolph & Company, n.d.), 92.

[21] Exell, J. S. *The Biblical Illustrator: I Samuel.* (New York: Anson D. F. Randolph & Company, n.d.), 471.

[22] Exell, J. S. *The Biblical Illustrator: Exodus.* (New York: Anson D. F. Randolph & Company, n.d.), 94.

[23] Spurgeon, C. H. "The Two Talents." Sermon delivered January 31, 1858, New Park Street Pulpit.
[24] Exell, J. S. *The Biblical Illustrator: Exodus.* (New York: Anson D. F. Randolph & Company, n.d.), 90.
[25] Yates. *Preaching from the Prophets*, 30.
[26] Henry, M. *Matthew Henry's Commentary on the Whole Bible: Complete and Unabridged in One Volume.* (Peabody: Hendrickson, 1994), 1412
[27] Ibid.
[28] Spurgeon, C. H. "The Restoration and Conversion of the Jews." Sermon delivered June 16, 1864, Metropolitan Tabernacle.
[29] Simeon, C. *Horae Homileticae: Hosea to Malachi* (Vol. 10). (London: Holdsworth and Ball, 1832), 127.
[30] Ironside, H. A. *Notes on the Book of Proverbs.* (Neptune, NJ: Loizeaux Bros., 1908), 414–415.
[31] Henry, M. *Matthew Henry's Commentary on the Whole Bible: Complete and Unabridged in One Volume.* (Peabody: Hendrickson, 1994), 1487.
[32] Robertson, A. T. *Paul and the Intellectuals.* (Nashville: Broadman,1959), 98.
[33] Spurgeon, C. H. "Life Eternal." Sermon delivered in 1866, Metropolitan Tabernacle.
[34] Ibid.
[35] Exell, J. S. *The Biblical Illustrator: St. John* (Vol. 2). (New York: Anson D. F. Randolph & Company, n.d.), 222
[36] Packer, J. I. *Knowing God.* (Downers Grove, Ill: InterVarsity Press, 1973), 241–242.
[37] Spurgeon, C. H. *Morning and Evening.* (London: Passmore & Alabaster), May 31 (Evening).
[38] Henry, M. *Matthew Henry's Commentary on the Whole Bible: Complete and Unabridged in One Volume.* (Peabody: Hendrickson, 1994), 950.
[39] *Expositor's Greek Testament,* Mark 6:31.
[40] Spurgeon, *Lectures to My Students,* 158.
[41] Ibid., 157.
[42] Spurgeon, C. H. "Cheer up, My Comrades!" Sermon delivered January 1, 1880, Metropolitan Tabernacle.
[43] Spence-Jones, H. D. M. (Ed.). *1 Kings.* (London; New York: Funk & Wagnalls Company, 1909), 480.
[44] Spurgeon, C. H. *Morning and Evening.* (London: Passmore & Alabaster), July 13 (Morning).
[45] https://www.brainyquote.com/topics/anger, accessed January 28, 2018.
[46] http://www.christianity.com/christian-life/christian-living-faq/how-should-i-deal-with-my-anger-11555743.html, accessed March 5, 2016.
[47] Strong, Debbie. "7 Ways Anger Is Ruining Your Health." https://www.everydayhealth.com/news/ways-anger-ruining-your-health/, accessed December 5, 2023.

# Endnotes

[48] Stanley, Charles. "The Cost of Uncontrolled Anger," May 26, 2013 (devotional).
[49] Bridges, C. *An Exposition of the Book of Proverbs.* (New York: Robert Carter & Brothers, 1865), 168.
[50] Spurgeon, C. H. "The Eye and the Light." Sermon delivered October 13, 1889, Metropolitan Tabernacle.
[51] Spurgeon, C. H. "Soul-Satisfying Bread," Sermon delivered May 18, 1873, Metropolitan Tabernacle.
[52] Spurgeon, C. H. "A Free Salvation." Sermon delivered June 11, 1858, on the Grand Stand, Epsom Race-Course.
[53] Exell, J. S. *Isaiah* (Vol. 3). (New York; Chicago; Toronto; London; Edinburgh: Fleming H. Revell Company, n.d.), 207.
[54] Ibid., 206.
[55] Spurgeon, C. H. "Grace Abounding over Abounding Sin," (Sermon delivered March 4, 1888). https://www.spurgeon.org/resource-library/sermons/grace-abounding-over-abounding-sin/#flipbook/, August 23, 2021.
[56] Spurgeon, C. H. *The Treasury of David: Psalms 120–150* (Vol. 6). (London; Edinburgh; New York: Marshall Brothers, n.d.), 119.
[57] Henry, M. *Matthew Henry's Commentary on the Whole Bible: Complete and Unabridged in One Volume.* (Peabody: Hendrickson, 1994), 736.
[58] Wuest, K. S. *Wuest's Word Studies from the Greek New Testament: for the English Reader* (Vol. 2). (Grand Rapids: Eerdmans, 1997), 202–203.
[59] Ibid.
[60] MacArthur, J. F., Jr. *Romans* (Vol. 2). (Chicago: Moody Press, 1991), 135.
[61] Exell, J. S. *The Biblical Illustrator: Romans,* Vol. 2. (New York; Chicago; Toronto; London; Edinburgh: Fleming H. Revell Company), 431.
[62] Henry, M. *Matthew Henry's Commentary on the Whole Bible: Complete and Unabridged in One Volume.* (Peabody: Hendrickson, 1994), 2225.
[63] Ibid., 756.
[64] Spurgeon, C. H. "A Happy Christian," (sermon).
[65] Spence-Jones, H. D. M. (Ed.). *Romans.* (London; New York: Funk & Wagnalls Company, 1909), 341.
[66] "10 Quotes from Billy Graham on Truth," March 10, 2021. https://billygrahamlibrary.org/blog-10-quotes-from-billy-graham-on-truth/, accessed February 11, 202.
[67] Spurgeon, C. H. "The Eye and the Light." Sermon delivered October 13, 1889, Metropolitan Tabernacle.
[68] Ibid.
[69] Adapted from a radio talk by Hank Hanegraaff numerous years ago.
[70] Rogers, Adrian.Crossing God's Deadline. https://sermons.love/adrian-rogers/15367-adrian-rogers-crossing-gods-deadline.html, accessed December 15, 2023.
[71] Ibid

[72] Spurgeon, C. H. *The Treasury of David: Psalms 27–57* (Vol. 2). (London; Edinburgh; New York: Marshall Brothers, n.d.), 45.
[73] Henry, M. *Matthew Henry's Commentary on the Whole Bible: Complete and Unabridged in One Volume.* (Peabody: Hendrickson, 1994), 782.
[74] Waltke, Bruce. *The Book of Proverbs, Chapters 1–15.* (Grand Rapids: Eerdmans, 2004), 614.
[75] Henry, M. *Matthew Henry's Commentary on the Whole Bible: Complete and Unabridged in One Volume.* (Peabody: Hendrickson, 1994), 987.
[76] Ibid., 1275.
[77] Spurgeon, C. H. *The Treasury of David: Psalms 120–150* (Vol. 6). (London; Edinburgh; New York: Marshall Brothers, n.d.), 259.
[78] Simeon, C. *Horae Homileticae: Jeremiah to Daniel* (Vol. 9). (London: Holdsworth and Ball, 1832), 172.
[79] Spurgeon, C. H. "The Omnipresence of GOD."
[80] Spurgeon, C. H. "The Christian—a Debtor." Sermon delivered August 10, 1856, Exeter Hall, Strand.
[81] Spence-Jones, H. D. M. (Ed.). *Isaiah* (Vol. 2). (London; New York: Funk & Wagnalls Company, 1910), 122.
[82] Exell, J. S. *The Biblical Illustrator: Revelation.* (New York; Chicago; Toronto; London; Edinburgh: Fleming H. Revell Company), 255.
[83] Henry, M. *Matthew Henry's Commentary on the Whole Bible: Complete and Unabridged in One Volume.* (Peabody: Hendrickson, 1994), 1157.
[84] Janzen, W. *Exodus.* (Waterloo, ON; Scottdale, PA: Herald Press, 2000), 178.
[85] https://www.inspiringquotes.us/author/8177-f-b-meyer/about-prayer, accessed June 22, 2022.
[86] https://www.preceptaustin.org/prayer_quotes, accessed June 22, 2022.
[87] Cowman, *Streams in the Desert,* October 2.
[88] Thomas, W. H. G. *Life Abiding and Abounding: Bible Studies in Prayer and Meditation.* (Chicago: The Bible Institute Colportage Association, n.d.), 12.
[89] Spurgeon, C. H. *An All-Around Ministry,* Chapter One.
[90] Henry, M. *Matthew Henry's Commentary on the Whole Bible: Complete and Unabridged in One Volume.* (Peabody: Hendrickson, 1994), 302.
[91] Ibid.
[92] Ibid., 933.
[93] Spurgeon, C. H. *Morning and Evening.* (London: Passmore & Alabaster), October 7.
[94] https://www.christianquotes.info/quotes-by-topic/quotes-about-doubt/, accessed August 20, 2021.
[95] Henry, M. *Matthew Henry's Commentary on the Whole Bible: Complete and Unabridged in One Volume.* (Peabody: Hendrickson, 1994), 756.
[96] Ibid., 1245.
[97] Spurgeon, C. H. "Grace Abounding" (Sermon delivered May 23, 1863). https://www.studylight.org/commentary/hosea/14-4.html, accessed September 1, 2021.

# Endnotes

[98] Spurgeon, C. H. *The Treasury of David: Psalms 27–57* (Vol. 2). (London; Edinburgh; New York: Marshall Brothers, n.d.), 126.

[99] Henry, M. *Matthew Henry's Commentary on the Whole Bible: Complete and Unabridged in One Volume.* (Peabody: Hendrickson, 1994), 1245.

[100] Ibid.

[101] MacArthur, J. F., Jr. *James.* (Chicago: Moody Press, 1998), 35.

[102] Lawson, George., Proverbs 1:2.

[103] Henry, M. *Matthew Henry's Commentary on the Whole Bible: Complete and Unabridged in One Volume.* (Peabody: Hendrickson, 1994), 1009.

[104] Ironside, H. A. *Notes on the Book of Proverbs.* (Neptune, NJ: Loizeaux Bros., 1908), 331.

[105] Wardlaw, R. *Lectures on the Book of Proverbs.* (J. S. Wardlaw, Ed.) (Second Edition, Vol. 2). (Edinburgh; London; Dublin: A. Fullarton & Co, 1869), 93.

[106] Exell, J. S. *Proverbs.* (New York; Chicago; Toronto; London; Edinburgh: Fleming H. Revell Company, n.d.), 423.

[107] Aitken, K. T. *Proverbs.* (Louisville, KY: Westminster John Knox Press, 1986), 46.

[108] Spurgeon, C. H. *The Treasury of David: Psalms 88–110* (Vol. 4). (London; Edinburgh; New York: Marshall Brothers, n.d.), 195.

[109] Exell, J. S. *The Biblical Illustrator: The Psalms,* Vol. 4. (New York; Chicago; Toronto; London; Edinburgh: Fleming H. Revell Company, 1909), 186–187).

[110] Henry, Matthew. *Matthew Henry's Commentary on the Whole Bible,* Genesis 4:6.

[111] Spurgeon, C. H. *The Treasury of David: Psalms 56–87* (Vol. 3). (London; Edinburgh; New York: Marshall Brothers, n.d.), 329.

[112] Bridges, Jerry. *Trusting God.* (1988), 37.

[113] Plumer, W. S. *Studies in the Book of Psalms: Being a Critical and Expository Commentary, with Doctrinal and Practical Remarks on the Entire Psalter.* (Philadelphia; Edinburgh: J. B. Lippincott Company; A & C Black, 1872), 883.

[114] Henry, M. *Matthew Henry's Commentary on the Whole Bible: Complete and Unabridged in One Volume.* (Peabody: Hendrickson, 1994), 1077.

[115] Simeon, C. *Horae Homileticae: Proverbs to Isaiah XXVI* (Vol. 7). (London: Holdsworth and Ball, 1833), 465.

[116] Watts, J. D. W. *Isaiah 1–33* (Vol. 24). (Dallas: Word, Incorporated, 1985), 20.

[117] Henry, M. *Matthew Henry's Commentary on the Whole Bible: Complete and Unabridged in One Volume.* (Peabody: Hendrickson, 1994), 1077.

[118] Spurgeon, C. H. "Obedience Better Than Sacrifice." Sermon delivered in 1866, Metropolitan Tabernacle.

[119] Ibid.

[120] Vine, W. E. *Isaiah: Prophecies, Promises, Warnings,* 14.

[121] Murray, Andrew. *Humility: The Journey Toward Holiness.* (1896), 36. Quotation taken from its Ichthus Publication, 2014.

[122] Ibid., 42.
[123] Lewis, C. S. *Mere Christianity.* "The Great Sin," Chapter 8.
[124] Henry, M. *Matthew Henry's Commentary on the Whole Bible: Complete and Unabridged in One Volume.* (Peabody: Hendrickson, 1994), 991.
[125] Exell, J. S. *The Biblical Illustrator* (Vol. 7). (New York; Chicago; Toronto; London; Edinburgh: Fleming H. Revell Company), Proverbs 16:18.
[126] Spurgeon, C. H. *Morning and Evening.* (London: Passmore & Alabaster), April 5 (Evening).
[127] Spence-Jones, H. D. M. (Ed.). *Haggai.* (London; New York: Funk & Wagnalls Company, 1909), 7.
[128] Exell, J. S. *The Biblical Illustrator: The Minor Prophets* (Vol. 10). (New York: Anson D. F. Randolph & Company, n.d.), 10.
[129] Spurgeon, C. H. *Spurgeon's Devotional Bible.* (Grand Raids, MI: Baker, 1964), 460.
[130] Spence-Jones, H. D. M. (Ed.). *Isaiah* (Vol. 2). (London; New York: Funk & Wagnalls Company, 1910), 78.
[131] Horne, G. *A Commentary on the Book of Psalms.* (New York: Robert Carter & Brothers, 1856), 521.
[132] Exell, J. S. *The Biblical Illustrator: Exodus.* (New York: Anson D. F. Randolph & Company, n.d.), 545.
[133] Henry, M. *Matthew Henry's Commentary on the Whole Bible: Complete and Unabridged in One Volume.* (Peabody: Hendrickson, 1994), 13.
[134] Spurgeon, C. H. *The Treasury of David: Psalms 27–57* (Vol. 2). (London; Edinburgh; New York: Marshall Brothers, n.d.), 83.
[135] Spurgeon, C. H. "A Sermon to Little Children." Sermon delivered March 18, 1883, Metropolitan Tabernacle.
[136] Ibid.
[137] Simeon, C. *Horae Homileticae: Jeremiah to Daniel* (Vol. 9). (London: Holdsworth and Ball, 1832), 42.
[138] *Benson Commentary on the Old and New Testaments*, Psalm 141:9.
[139] Exell, J. S. *The Biblical Illustrator: Jeremiah* (Vol. 1). (New York: Anson D. F. Randolph & Company, 1905), 56.
[140] Exell, J. S. *Isaiah* (Vol. 1). (New York; Chicago; Toronto; London; Edinburgh: Fleming H. Revell Company, n.d.), 504.
[141] Packer, J. I. *Knowing God.* https://www.goodreads.com/work/quotes/276686-knowing-god?page=5, accessed May 15, 2021.
[142] https://gracequotes.org/quote/remember-that-if-you-are-a-child-of-god-you-wil, accessed October 19, 2017.
[143] https://ccel.org/ccel/bunyan/miscellaneous.v.html, accessed October 29, 2024.
[144] Spurgeon, C. H. "Interrogating Our Conduct."
[145] Henry, M. *Matthew Henry's Commentary on the Whole Bible: Complete and Unabridged in One Volume.* (Peabody: Hendrickson, 1994), 1240.

[146] Exell, J. S. *The Biblical Illustrator: Genesis* (Vol. 2). (New York: Anson D. F. Randolph & Company, n.d.), 301, adapted.

[147] Carson, D. A. "How Long, O Lord?: Reflections on Suffering and Evil." (Baker Academic, 2006), 170.

[148] Spurgeon, C. H. "Are You Prepared to Die?" Sermon delivered, 1865, Metropolitan Tabernacle.

[149] Fouse, Michael. *Baptist Press,* November 16, 2005. https://www.baptistpress.com/ resource-library/news/in-his-final-days-adrian-rogers-told-those-gathered-around-him-i-am-at-perfect-peace/, accessed October 22, 2020.

[150] Truett. *Quest for Souls,* 99.

[151] Spurgeon, C. H. "Are You Prepared to Die?" Sermon delivered, 1865, Metropolitan Tabernacle.

[152] Spurgeon, C. H. *Morning and Evening.* (London: Passmore & Alabaster), July 2 (Morning).

[153] Spence-Jones, H. D. M. (Ed.). *Job.* (London; New York: Funk & Wagnalls Company, 1909), 615.

[154] Criswell, W. A., P. Patterson, E. R. Clendenen, D. L. Akin, M. Chamberlin, D. K. Patterson & J. Pogue (Eds.). *Believer's Study Bible* (electronic ed.). (Nashville: Thomas Nelson, 1991), Job 38:4–6.

[155] Bridges, Charles, 35.

[156] Adapted. Source unknown.

[157] Exell, J. S. *The Biblical Illustrator: Job.* (New York: Anson D. F. Randolph & Company, n.d.), 602.

[158] Wenham, G. J. *Genesis 1–15* (Vol. 1). (Dallas: Word, Incorporated, 1987), 106.

[159] Henry, M. *Matthew Henry's Commentary on the Whole Bible: Complete and Unabridged in One Volume.* (Peabody: Hendrickson, 1994), 18.

[160] Exell, J. S. *The Biblical Illustrator: Genesis* (Vol. 1). (New York: Anson D. F. Randolph & Company, n.d.), 347.

[161] Spurgeon, C. H. "Am I My Brother's Keeper?," delivered at the Metropolitan Tabernacle.

[162] Ibid.

[163] Exell, J. S. *The Biblical Illustrator: Genesis* (Vol. 1). (New York: Anson D. F. Randolph & Company, n.d.), 251, adapted.

[164] Vaughan, Dean, cited in Exell, J. S. *The Biblical Illustrator: Genesis* (Vol. 1). (New York: Anson D. F. Randolph & Company, n.d.), 259.

[165] Henry, M. *Matthew Henry's Commentary on the Whole Bible: Complete and Unabridged in One Volume.* (Peabody: Hendrickson, 1994), 13.

[166] Wiersbe, W. W. *With the Word Bible Commentary.* (Nashville: Thomas Nelson, 1991), Gen. 3.

[167] Henry, M. *Matthew Henry's Commentary on the Whole Bible: Complete and Unabridged in One Volume.* (Peabody: Hendrickson, 1994), 13.

[168] Criswell, W. A., P. Patterson, E. R. Clendenen, D. L. Akin, M. Chamberlin, D. K. Patterson & J. Pogue (Eds.). *Believer's Study Bible* (electronic ed.). (Nashville: Thomas Nelson, 1991), Gen. 3:7.
[169] Spurgeon, C. H. "The Great Change—Conversion." *Autobiography.*
[170] Spurgeon, C. H. "The Ethiopian." Sermon delivered May 15, 1884, Metropolitan Tabernacle.
[171] Ibid.
[172] John MacArthur, Charles Simeon, Lightfoot, and W. A. Criswell ascribe to this view.
[173] Henry, M. *Matthew Henry's Commentary on the Whole Bible: Complete and Unabridged in One Volume.* (Peabody: Hendrickson, 1994), 330.
[174] Ibid.
[175] Spurgeon, C. H. "Bochim; or, The Weepers." Sermon delivered August 10, 1882, Metropolitan Tabernacle.
[176] Henry, M. *Matthew Henry's Commentary on the Whole Bible: Complete and Unabridged in One Volume.* (Peabody: Hendrickson, 1994), 330.
[177] Ibid.
[178] Simeon, C. *Horae Homileticae: Judges to 2 Kings* (Vol. 3). (London: Holdsworth and Ball, 1836), 8.
[179] Exell, J. S. *The Biblical Illustrator: Hebrews*, Vol. 2. (London: James Nisbet & Co.), 613.
[180] Spurgeon, C. H. *New Park Street Pulpit,* Vol. 4. "As Thy Days, So Shall Thy Strength Be" (Sermon No. 210, August 22, 1858).
[181] A.B. Mackay cited in Exell, J. S. *The Biblical Illustrator: Joshua, Judges, and Ruth* (Vol. 1). (New York: Anson D. F. Randolph & Company, n.d.), 18.
[182] Spurgeon, C. H. "Strengthening Medicine for God's Servants." Sermon delivered 1875, Metropolitan Tabernacle.
[183] Criswell, W. A., P. Patterson, E. R. Clendenen, D. L. Akin, M. Chamberlin, D. K. Patterson & J. Pogue (Eds.). *Believer's Study Bible* (electronic ed.). (Nashville: Thomas Nelson, 1991), Mal. 3:8–10.
[184] Smith, Ralph. *Word Biblical Commentary,* Vol 32.
[185] Exell, J. S. *The Biblical Illustrator: The Minor Prophets* (Vol. 12). (New York: Anson D. F. Randolph & Company, n.d.), 83.
[186] *King James Version Study Bible,* (electronic ed.). (Nashville: Thomas Nelson, 1997), Malachi 3:7.
[187] Henry, M. *Matthew Henry's Commentary on the Whole Bible: Complete and Unabridged in One Volume.* (Peabody: Hendrickson, 1994), 1603.
[188] Ibid., 1806.
[189] Criswell, W. A., P. Patterson, E. R. Clendenen, D. L. Akin, M. Chamberlin, D. K. Patterson & J. Pogue (Eds.). *Believer's Study Bible* (electronic ed.). (Nashville: Thomas Nelson, 1991), Mal. 3:8–10.
[190] *Daily Devotional:* "God Blesses Through the Tithe," October 12, 2017. https://www.lwf.org/daily-devotions/god-blesses-through-the-tithe, accessed January 28, 2024.

# Endnotes

[191] Spurgeon, C. H. "The Plumbline." Sermon delivered August 27, 1876, Metropolitan Tabernacle.

[192] Ibid.

[193] "10 Quotes from Billy Graham on Integrity," February 13, 2021. https://billygrahamlibrary.org/blog-10-quotes-from-billy-graham-on-integrity/, accessed February 16, 2024.

[194] Criswell, W. A., P. Patterson, E. R. Clendenen, D. L. Akin, M. Chamberlin, D. K. Patterson & J. Pogue (Eds.). *Believer's Study Bible* (electronic ed.). (Nashville: Thomas Nelson, 1991), Job 40:10–14.

[195] Henry, M. *Matthew Henry's Commentary on the Whole Bible: Complete and Unabridged in One Volume.* (Peabody: Hendrickson, 1994), 1293.

[196] Spurgeon, C. H. "The Mighty Arm." Sermon delivered September 17, 1876, Metropolitan Tabernacle.

[197] Parker, Joseph. *The People's Bible,* Psalm 20:7.

[198] Spurgeon, C. H. *The Treasury of David: Psalms 88–110* (Vol. 4). (London; Edinburgh; New York: Marshall Brothers, n.d.), 27.

[199] Exell, J. S. *The Biblical Illustrator: Exodus.* (New York: Anson D. F. Randolph & Company, n.d.), 100.

[200] Henry, M. *Matthew Henry's Commentary on the Whole Bible: Complete and Unabridged in One Volume.* (Peabody: Hendrickson, 1994), 101.

[201] Spurgeon, C. H. "Power with God." Sermon delivered in 1864, Metropolitan Tabernacle.

[202] Exell, J. S. *The Biblical Illustrator: Exodus.* (New York: Anson D. F. Randolph & Company, n.d.), 97.

[203] Simeon, C. *Horae Homileticae: Genesis to Leviticus* (Vol. 1). (London: Holdsworth and Ball, 1836), 333.

[204] Spurgeon, C. H. *Morning and Evening.* (London: Passmore & Alabaster), February 20 (Morning).

[205] Spurgeon, C. H. "The Glorious Right Hand of God." Sermon delivered February 24, 1861, Metropolitan Tabernacle.

[206] Henry, M. *Matthew Henry's Commentary on the Whole Bible: Complete and Unabridged in One Volume.* (Peabody: Hendrickson, 1994), 200.

[207] Bobgan, Martin and Deidre. *Psycho Heresy.* (Santa Barbara, CA: EastGate Publishers, 1987), 7.

[208] Ironside, H. A. *Notes on the Book of Proverbs.* (Neptune, NJ: Loizeaux Bros., 1908), 242.

[209] Graham, Billy. Peace with God. (Waco, TX: Word, 1953), 83.

[210] Spurgeon, C. H. "Thoughts on the Last Battle." (Sermon, May 13, 1855).

[211] Henry, M. *Matthew Henry's Commentary on the Whole Bible: Complete and Unabridged in One Volume.* (Peabody: Hendrickson, 1994), 2427.

[212] Spurgeon, C. H. "The Filling of Empty Vessels." Sermon delivered January 13, 1889, Metropolitan Tabernacle.

[213] *The Spurgeon Study Bible,* 776.

[214] From The Gospel Herald as cited at http://www.moreillustrations.com/Illustrations/sowing%20and%20reaping%201.html, accessed August 24, 2017.

[215] Exell, J. S. *The Biblical Illustrator: Galatians.* (New York; Chicago; Toronto; London; Edinburgh: Fleming H. Revell Company, n.d.), 489.

[216] Spurgeon, C. H. "Life Eternal." Sermon delivered in 1866, Metropolitan Tabernacle.

[217] Adrian Rogers. "Christian Warfare" (Sermon). https://sermons.love/adrian-rogers/17631-adrian-rogers-christian-warfare.html, accessed August 28, 2024.

[218] Adrian Rogers. "Overcoming the Evil One" (Sermon). https://www.oneplace.com/ministries/love-worth-finding/player/overcoming-the-evil-one-138032.html#now-playing, accessed August 28, 2024.

[219] Spurgeon, C. H. "Satan in a Rage." Sermon delivered November 2, 1879, Metropolitan Tabernacle.

[220] Henry, M. *Matthew Henry's Commentary on the Whole Bible: Complete and Unabridged in One Volume.* (Peabody: Hendrickson, 1994), 1579.

[221] Exell, J. S. *The Biblical Illustrator: Jeremiah* (Vol. 1). (New York: Anson D. F. Randolph & Company, 1905), 43.

[222] Henry, M. *Matthew Henry's Commentary on the Whole Bible: Complete and Unabridged in One Volume.* (Peabody: Hendrickson, 1994), 1224.

[223] This meditation is adapted from a sermon by T. De Witt Talmage (*The New Tabernacle Sermons*, 368–371).

[224] Ibid.

[225] Swanson, J. *Dictionary of Biblical Languages with Semantic Domains: Hebrew (Old Testament)* (electronic ed.). (Oak Harbor: Logos Research Systems, Inc., 1997).

[226] MacArthur, John. "Dealing with Sorrow." April 5, 2004. http://www.gty.org/resources/daily-devotion/DN462/Dealing-with-Sorrow, accessed March 29, 2005.

[227] Swindoll, Chuck. "Expressing Grief," November 29, 2011. http://www.insight.org/library/insight-for-today/expressing-grief.html, accessed March 31, 2011.

[228] Dunn, Ronald. *When Heaven is Silent: Trusting God When Life Hurts.* (Nashville: Thomas Nelson Publishers, 1994).

[229] https://hopeispossible.wordpress.com/tag/anne-graham-lotz/, accessed February 28, 2022.

[230] Stott, John W. *The Letters of John (An Introduction and Commentary.* (Tyndale New Testament Commentaries, 1988), 150.

[231] https://www.princeofpreachers.org/quotes/category/promises-of-god, accessed November 9, 2022.

[232] Spurgeon, C. H. *The Treasury of David.* (Grand Rapids, Michigan: Kregel Publications, 2004), Psalm 30:5.

[233] Exell, J. S. *The Biblical Illustrator: I Samuel.* (New York: Anson D. F. Randolph & Company, n.d.), 373.

# Endnotes

[234] Hannah, J. D. In J. F. Walvoord & R. B. Zuck (Eds.). *The Bible Knowledge Commentary: An Exposition of the Scriptures* (Vol. 1). (Wheaton, IL: Victor Books, 1985), 114.

[235] "How Can The Disabled Still Serve God?," accessed March 17, 2023.

[236] Exell, J. S. *The Biblical Illustrator: Jeremiah* (Vol. 1). (New York: Anson D. F. Randolph & Company, 1905), 13.

[237] Moody, D. L. *Pleasure & Profit in Bible Study.*

[238] MacArthur, John. "How to Treat False Teachers, Part 1." October 6, 1985. www.gty.org, accessed January 2, 2015.

[239] Henry, M. *Matthew Henry's Commentary on the Whole Bible: Complete and Unabridged in One Volume.* (Peabody: Hendrickson, 1994), 1646.

[240] Nolland, J. *The Gospel of Matthew: A Commentary on the Greek Text.* (Grand Rapids, MI; Carlisle: W. B. Eerdmans; Paternoster Press, 2005), 336.

[241] Spurgeon, C. H. *Morning and Evening.* (London: Passmore & Alabaster), November 7 (Morning).

[242] Spurgeon, C. H. "God's Memorial of His People." Sermon delivered at Metropolitan Tabernacle. Published on Thursday, January 14, 1915.

[243] Henry, M. *Matthew Henry's Commentary on the Whole Bible: Complete and Unabridged in One Volume.* (Peabody: Hendrickson, 1994), 1174.

[244] Packer, J. I. *Knowing God.* (Downers Grove, Ill: InterVarsity Press, 1973), 41–42.

[245] Henry, M., & T. Scott. *Matthew Henry's Concise Commentary.* (Oak Harbor, WA: Logos Research Systems, 1997), Isa. 49:13.

[246] Clarke, Adam. *Commentary on the Bible.* (1831), Ezekiel 18:23.

[247] Exell, J. S. *The Biblical Illustrator: Ezekiel.* (New York; Chicago; Toronto; London; Edinburgh: Fleming H. Revell Company, 1906), 348.

[248] Smith, B. K., & F. S. Page. *Amos, Obadiah, Jonah* (Vol. 19B). (Broadman & Holman Publishers, 1995), 160.

[249] Henry, M. *Matthew Henry's Commentary on the Whole Bible: Complete and Unabridged in One Volume.* (Peabody: Hendrickson, 1994), 1518.

[250] Ibid.

[251] Exell, J. S. *The Biblical Illustrator: The Minor Prophets* (Vol. 6). (New York: Anson D. F. Randolph & Company, n.d.), 15.

[252] Ibid.

[253] Ibid, 10.

[254] Ibid, 6.

[255] Spurgeon, C. H. "Is the Spirit of the Lord Straitened?" Sermon delivered February 26, 1891, Metropolitan Tabernacle.

[256] Spurgeon, C. H. "God's Firebrands." Sermon delivered at the Metropolitan Tabernacle on a Sunday Evening. Published January 19, 1911.

[257] Henry, M. *Matthew Henry's Commentary on the Whole Bible: Complete and Unabridged in One Volume.* (Peabody: Hendrickson, 1994), 1572.

[258] http://www.kjbbc.org/soulwinning-and-visitation.html, accessed November 15, 2013.

[259] Henry, M. *Matthew Henry's Commentary on the Whole Bible: Complete and Unabridged in One Volume.* (Peabody: Hendrickson, 1994), 1572.
[260] Spurgeon, C. H. "Mr. Facing Both-Ways."
[261] Charnock, Stephen. *A Puritan Golden Treasury.*
[262] Henry, M. *Matthew Henry's Commentary on the Whole Bible: Complete and Unabridged in One Volume.* (Peabody: Hendrickson, 1994), 1596.
[263] Exell, J. S. *The Biblical Illustrator: The Minor Prophets* (Vol. 12). (New York: Anson D. F. Randolph & Company, n.d.), 15.
[264] Spurgeon, C. H. *An All-Round Ministry.* (Carlisle, PA: Banner of Truth Trust, 1978), 76–77.
[265] Henry, M. *Matthew Henry's Commentary on the Whole Bible: Complete and Unabridged in One Volume.* (Peabody: Hendrickson, 1994), 1596.
[266] Spurgeon, C. H. "An All Important Question." Sermon delivered January 13, 1867, Metropolitan Tabernacle.
[267] Spence-Jones, H. D. M. (Ed.). *Malachi.* (London; New York: Funk & Wagnalls Company, 1909), 14.
[268] Ibid.
[269] Spurgeon, C. H. *The Sword and the Trowel,* January 1867, 20.
[270] http://www.spurgeongems.org, accessed November 16, 2013.
[271] Spurgeon, C. H. "Royal Proclamation" (sermon).
[272] MacArthur, J., Jr. (ed.). *The MacArthur Study Bible* (electronic ed.). (Word Pub, 1997), 1020.
[273] Spurgeon, C. H. "Royal Proclamation" (sermon).
[274] Henry, M. *Matthew Henry's Commentary on the Whole Bible: Complete and Unabridged in One Volume.* (Peabody: Hendrickson, 1994), 1158.
[275] Ibid.
[276] Ibid.
[277] McGee, J. V. *Thru the Bible Commentary* (electronic ed., Vol. 3). (Thomas Nelson, 1997), 292.
[278] Henry, M. *Matthew Henry's Commentary on the Whole Bible: Complete and Unabridged in One Volume.* (Peabody: Hendrickson, 1994), 733.
[279] Spurgeon, C. H. *Spurgeon's Faith's Checkbook.* "The Dew of Heaven." (September 13th).
[280] Spurgeon, C. H. *The Treasury of David: Psalms 120–150* (Vol. 6). (London; Edinburgh; New York: Marshall Brothers, n.d.), 168.
[281] Knight, G. A. F. *Psalms* (Vol. 2). (Westminster John Knox Press, 2001), 300.
[282] Craigie, P. C. *Twelve Prophets* (Vol. 1). (Westminster John Knox Press, 1984), 49.
[283] Exell, J. S. *The Biblical Illustrator: Job.* (New York: Anson D. F. Randolph & Company, n.d.), 611.
[284] Exell, J. S. *The Biblical Illustrator: The Minor Prophets* (Vol. 5). (New York: Anson D. F. Randolph & Company, n.d.), 78.
[285] McDuff, John Ross. *Sunsets on the Hebrew Mountains.* (New York: Robert Carter and Brothers, 1862), 201.

## Endnotes

[286] McGee, J. V. *Thru the Bible Commentary* (electronic ed., Vol. 3). (Thomas Nelson, 1997), 766.

[287] Spurgeon, C. H. "The Christian's Great Business." Sermon delivered September 7, 1873, Metropolitan Tabernacle.

[288] Criswell, W. A., P. Patterson, E. R. Clendenen, D. L. Akin, M. Chamberlin, D. K. Patterson & J. Pogue (Eds.). *Believer's Study Bible* (electronic ed.). (Nashville: Thomas Nelson, 1991), Job 40:8.

[289] MacArthur, J., Jr. (ed.). *The MacArthur Study Bible* (electronic ed.). (Word Pub, 1997), 737.

[290] *Pulpit Commentary,* Job 40:8.

[291] Henry, M. *Matthew Henry's Commentary on the Whole Bible: Complete and Unabridged in One Volume.* (Peabody: Hendrickson, 1994), 737.

[292] Spence-Jones, H. D. M. (Ed.). *Job.* (London; New York: Funk & Wagnalls Company, 1909), 614.

[293] This paragraph is a summation from Alexander Maclaren's sermon "Me, a Christian!"

[294] Alexander Maclaren. "Me, a Christian!" (Acts 26:28). https://www.ccel.org/ccel/maclaren/acts.iii.xlviii.html, accessed May 24, 2024.

[295] Ibid.

[296] Wiersbe, W. W. *Be Patient.* (Victor Books, 1996), 145.

[297] Alden, R. L. *Job* (Vol. 11). (Broadman & Holman Publishers, 1993), 369.

[298] Henry, M. *Matthew Henry's Commentary on the Whole Bible: Complete and Unabridged in One Volume.* (Peabody: Hendrickson, 1994), 220.

[299] Exell, J. S. *The Biblical Illustrator: Leviticus and Numbers* (Vol. 2). (New York; Chicago; Toronto; London; Edinburgh: Fleming H. Revell Company, n.d.), 238.

[300] Lawson, George. Proverbs 22:24.

[301] *Criswell Study Bible,* Job 41:1.

[302] Ibid.

[303] Barclay, W., (ed.). *The Gospel of Matthew* (Vol. 1). (The Westminster John Knox Press, 1976), 120.

[304] Henry, M. *Matthew Henry's Commentary on the Whole Bible: Complete and Unabridged in One Volume.* (Peabody: Hendrickson, 1994), 1630.

[305] Criswell, W. A., P. Patterson, E. R. Clendenen, D. L. Akin, M. Chamberlin, D. K. Patterson & J. Pogue (Eds.). *Believer's Study Bible* (electronic ed.). (Nashville: Thomas Nelson, 1991), Mt. 5:13–16.

[306] Henry, M. *Matthew Henry's Commentary on the Whole Bible: Complete and Unabridged in One Volume.* (Peabody: Hendrickson, 1994), 19556.

[307] Pink, A. W. *Exposition of the Gospel of John.* (Bible Truth Depot, 1923–1945), 361.

[308] Spurgeon, C. H. *Morning and Evening.* (London: Passmore & Alabaster), October 23 (Morning).

[309] Beasley-Murray, G. R. *John* (Vol. 36). (Word, Incorporated, 1999), 405

[310] Henry, M. *Matthew Henry's Commentary on the Whole Bible: Complete and Unabridged in One Volume.* (Peabody: Hendrickson, 1994), 2058.
[311] Spurgeon, C. H. "Lovest Thou Me?" Sermon delivered February 27, 1876, Metropolitan Tabernacle.
[312] Ibid.
[313] Ibid.
[314] Ibid.
[315] Ibid.
[316] Exell, J. S. *The Biblical Illustrator: St. Luke* (Vol. 3). (New York; Chicago; Toronto; London; Edinburgh: Fleming H. Revell Company, n.d.), 385.
[317] Spence-Jones, H. D. M. (Ed.). *St. Luke* (Vol. 2). (London; New York: Funk & Wagnalls Company, 1909), 131.
[318] Henry, M. *Matthew Henry's Commentary on the Whole Bible: Complete and Unabridged in One Volume.* (Peabody: Hendrickson, 1994), 1892.
[319] MacArthur, J. *Mark 1–8.* (Moody Publishers, 2015), 411–412.
[320] Gill, John. *Exposition of the Entire Bible.* (1746–63), Mark 8:28–29.
[321] Vines, Jerry. *Exploring the Gospels: Mark,* 163.
[322] Spence-Jones, H. D. M. (Ed.). *St. John* (Vol. 2). (London; New York: Funk & Wagnalls Company, 1909), 161.
[323] Criswell, W. A. *The Criswell Study Bible,* Isaiah 7: 14.
[324] As cited in "Must We Believe in the Virgin Birth." http://www.albertmohler.com/2011/12/14/must-we-believe-in-the-virgin-birth, accessed December 27, 2013.
[325] Piper, John. "What Passages in Scripture Say That Jesus Never Sinned?" (April 22, 2009). https://www.desiringgod.org/interviews/what-passages-in-Scripture-say-that-jesus-never-sinned, accessed July 2, 2024.
[326] Did Jesus live a sinless life? https://www.lwf.org/questions-and-answers/did-jesus-live-a-sinless-life, accessed July 3, 2024.
[327] Ryle, J. C. "What Think Ye of Christ?" (Christmas Sermon).
[328] Spurgeon, C. H. "Questions of the Day and the Question of the Day." Sermon delivered January 26, 1873, Metropolitan Tabernacle.
[329] Ibid.
[330] The Always Be Ready Apologetics Blog: "New Discovery in Megiddo Mentions Jesus," December 22, 2005.
[331] Josephus, Flavius. *Antiquities*, xviii, 33. http://en.wikipedia.org/wiki/Josephus_on_Jesus, accessed May 31, 2011.
[332] Habermas, Gary R. "Was Jesus Real?" InterVarsity.org, August 8, 2008, http://www.intervarsity.org/studentsoul/item/was-jesus-real.
[333] Plumer, W. S. *Studies in the Book of Psalms: Being a Critical and Expository Commentary, with Doctrinal and Practical Remarks on the Entire Psalter.* (Philadelphia; Edinburgh: J. B. Lippincott Company; A & C Black, 1872).
[334] Gill, John. *Exposition of the Entire Bible*, Psalm 34:8.
[335] Exell, J. S. *Isaiah* (Vol. 1). (New York; Chicago; Toronto; London; Edinburgh: Fleming H. Revell Company, n.d.), 396.

# Endnotes

[336] Barnes, Albert. *Notes on the Bible.* (1834), Matthew 20:22.
[337] Clarke, Adam. *Commentary on the Bible.* (1831), Matthew 20:22.
[338] Henry, M. *Matthew Henry's Commentary on the Whole Bible: Complete and Unabridged in One Volume.* (Peabody: Hendrickson, 1994), 1717.
[339] Cowman, L. B. *Streams in the Desert.* (Grand Rapids: Zondervan, 1997), October 7.
[340] Spurgeon, C. H. "Good Cheer for the New Year." (Sermon # 728). Delivered January 6, 1867, at the Metropolitan Tabernacle, Newington.
[341] www.brainyquote.com/quotes/keywords/anxiety.html, accessed September 4, 2017.
[342] Graham, Billy. *The Billy Graham Christian Worker's Handbook.* (Charlotte, NC: BGEA, 1984), 49.
[343] https://www.scrapbook.com/quotes/doc/26631.html, accessed July 2, 2020.
[344] Knight, Walter B. *Knight's Illustrations for Today.* (Chicago: Moody Press, 1975), 352.
[345] Rogers, Adrian. "Two Days That Will Steal Your Joy" (devotional). http://www.lwf.org, accessed July 25, 2014.
[346] Exell, J. S. *The Biblical Illustrator: Matthew.* (New York; Chicago; Toronto; London; Edinburgh: Fleming H. Revell Company, 1952), 111.
[347] Cowman, L. B. *Streams in the Desert.* (Grand Rapids: Zondervan, 1997), October 7.
[348] Exell, J. S. *The Biblical Illustrator: Matthew.* (New York; Chicago; Toronto; London; Edinburgh: Fleming H. Revell Company, 1952), 111.
[349] Ibid.
[350] Ibid.
[351] Cowman, L. B. *Streams in the Desert.* (Grand Rapids: Zondervan, 1997), October 7.
[352] Weber, Frederick Parkes. *Aspects of Death and Correlated Aspects of Life in Art, Epigram, and Poetry.* (New York: Paul B. Hoeber, 1918), 357.
[353] Henry, M. *Matthew Henry's Commentary on the Whole Bible: Complete and Unabridged in One Volume.* (Peabody: Hendrickson, 1994), 1699.
[354] Exell, J. S. *The Biblical Illustrator: Matthew.* (New York; Chicago; Toronto; London; Edinburgh: Fleming H. Revell Company, 1952), 358.
[355] Ibid., 363.
[356] Spurgeon, C. H. "The Parable of the Lost Sheep." Sermon delivered September 28, 1884, Metropolitan Tabernacle.
[357] Spurgeon, C. H. *The Soul Winner,* "The Cost of Being a Soul-Winner."
[358] Ibid.
[359] Exell, J. S. *The Biblical Illustrator: St. Luke* (Vol. 3). (New York; Chicago; Toronto; London; Edinburgh: Fleming H. Revell Company, 1904), 82.
[360] Ellsworth, R. *Opening Up Psalms.* (Leominster: Day One Publications, 2006), 197.

[361] Plumer, W. S. *Studies in the Book of Psalms: Being a Critical and Expository Commentary, with Doctrinal and Practical Remarks on the Entire Psalter.* (Philadelphia; Edinburgh: J. B. Lippincott Company; A & C Black, 1872), 302.
[362] Spurgeon, C. H. *Morning and Evening.* (London: Passmore & Alabaster), April 15 (Morning).
[363] Kidner, D. *Psalms 1–72: An Introduction and Commentary* (Vol. 15). (InterVarsity Press, 1973), 123.
[364] *The Biblical Illustrator,* Psalm 22:1.
[365] Hindson, E. E. & W. M. Kroll (eds.). *KJV Bible Commentary.* (Thomas Nelson, 1994), 1007–1008.
[366] Ironside, H. A. *Studies on Book One of the Psalms.* (Loizeaux Brothers, 1952), 141.
[367] Ibid., 139.
[368] Spurgeon, C. H. *The Treasury of David: Psalms 1–26* (Vol. 1). (London; Edinburgh; New York: Marshall Brothers, n.d.), 325.
[369] Beasley-Murray, G. R. *John* (Vol. 36). (Word, Incorporated, 1999), 109.
[370] Frederic W. Farrar, The Life of Christ (1964), 641.
[371] Ibid.
[372] Barclay, W. (Ed.) *The Letter to the Hebrews, The Daily Study Bible Series,* (Rev. ed.). (Philadelphia: The Westminster Press, 2000), 104.
[373] MacArthur, J., Jr. (ed.). *The MacArthur Study Bible* (electronic ed.). (Word Pub, 1997), 1945.
[374] Spurgeon, C. H. *The Treasury of David: Psalms 27–57* (Vol. 2). (London; Edinburgh; New York: Marshall Brothers, n.d.), 105.
[375] Exell, J. S. *The Biblical Illustrator: Matthew.* (New York; Chicago; Toronto; London; Edinburgh: Fleming H. Revell Company, 1952), 150.
[376] Spurgeon, C. H. *The Treasury of David: Psalms 27–57* (Vol. 2). (London; Edinburgh; New York: Marshall Brothers, n.d.), 105.
[377] Spurgeon, C. H. "Healing for the Wounded." November 11, 1855. http://www.spurgeon.org, accessed June 28, 2014.
[378] Letter, *An Exposition of Matthew,* 274.
[379] http://www.goodreads.com/quotes/tag/betrayal, accessed July 6, 2014.
[380] C. H. Spurgeon. The Cause and Cure of a Wounded Spirit, April 16th, 1885. http://www.ccel.org, accessed December 8, 2013.
[381] Horne, G. *A Commentary on the Book of Psalms.* (New York: Robert Carter & Brothers, 1856), 363.
[382] Plumer, W. S. *Studies in the Book of Psalms: Being a Critical and Expository Commentary, with Doctrinal and Practical Remarks on the Entire Psalter.* (Philadelphia; Edinburgh: J. B. Lippincott Company; A & C Black, 1872), 914.
[383] Ibid.
[384] Ibid.
[385] Henry, M. *Matthew Henry's Commentary on the Whole Bible: Complete and Unabridged in One Volume.* (Peabody: Hendrickson, 1994), 890.
[386] Ibid.

# Endnotes

[387] Plumer, W. S. *Studies in the Book of Psalms: Being a Critical and Expository Commentary, with Doctrinal and Practical Remarks on the Entire Psalter.* (Philadelphia; Edinburgh: J. B. Lippincott Company; A & C Black, 1872), 914–915.

[388] Plumer, W. S. *Studies in the Book of Psalms: Being a Critical and Expository Commentary, with Doctrinal and Practical Remarks on the Entire Psalter.* (Philadelphia; Edinburgh: J. B. Lippincott Company; A & C Black, 1872), 917.

[389] Knight, Walter B. *Knights Master Book of New Illustrations.* (Grand Rapids: Wm B. Eerdmans, 1956), 644.

[390] Allen, Kerry James. *Exploring the Mind & Heart of the Prince of Preachers.* (Oswego, Illinois: Fox River Press, 2004), 453.

[391] Spence-Jones, H. D. M. (Ed.). *St. Luke* (Vol. 2). (London; New York: Funk & Wagnalls Company, 1909), 58.

[392] Wiersbe, W. W. *The Bible Exposition Commentary* (Vol. 1). (Victor Books, 1996), 234.

[393] Nolland, J. *The Gospel of Matthew: A Commentary on the Greek Text.* (W. B. Eerdmans; Paternoster Press, 2005), 319.

[394] Rogers, Adrian. "Tolerance: The Good, the Bad and the Ugly," June 7, 2022.

[395] Ibid.

[396] Exell, J. S. *The Biblical Illustrator: Matthew.* (New York; Chicago; Toronto; London; Edinburgh: Fleming H. Revell Company, 1952), 119.

www.ingramcontent.com/pod-product-compliance
Lightning Source LLC
Chambersburg PA
CBHW061301110426
42742CB00012BA/2010